RENEWALS 458-4574
DATE DUE

WITHDRAWN
UTSA LIBRARIES

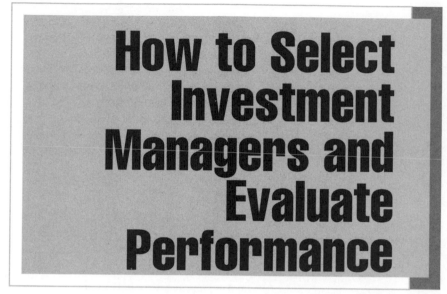

How to Select Investment Managers and Evaluate Performance

A Guide for Pension Funds,
Endowments, Foundations,
and Trusts

G. TIMOTHY HAIGHT
STEPHEN MORRELL
GLENN E. ROSS

BICENTENNIAL
1807
WILEY
2007
BICENTENNIAL

John Wiley & Sons, Inc.

Copyright © 2007 by John Wiley & Sons, Inc. All rights reserved.

Published by John Wiley & Sons, Inc., Hoboken, New Jersey.
Published simultaneously in Canada.

Wiley Bicentennial Logo: Richard J. Pacifico

No part of this publication may be reproduced, stored in a retrieval system, or transmitted in any form or by any means, electronic, mechanical, photocopying, recording, scan-
ning, or otherwise, except as permitted under Section 107 or 108 of the 1976 United States
Copyright Act, without either the prior written permission of the Publisher, or authorization
through payment of the appropriate per-copy fee to the Copyright Clearance Center, Inc., 222
Rosewood Drive, Danvers, MA 01923, (978) 750-8400, fax (978) 646-8600, or on the web
at www.copyright.com. Requests to the Publisher for permission should be addressed to the
Permissions Department, John Wiley & Sons, Inc., 111 River Street, Hoboken, NJ 07030,
(201) 748-6011, fax (201) 748-6008, or online at www.wiley.com/go/permissions.

Limit of Liability/Disclaimer of Warranty: While the publisher and author have used their
best efforts in preparing this book, they make no representations or warranties with respect
to the accuracy or completeness of the contents of this book and specifically disclaim any
implied warranties of merchantability or fitness for a particular purpose. No warranty may
be created or extended by sales representatives or written sales materials. The advice and
strategies contained herein may not be suitable for your situation. You should consult with a
professional where appropriate. Neither the publisher nor author shall be liable for any loss
of profit or any other commercial damages, including but not limited to special, incidental,
consequential, or other damages.

For general information on our other products and services or for technical support, please
contact our Customer Care Department within the United States at (800) 762-2974, outside
the United States at (317) 572-3993, or fax (317) 572-4002.

Wiley also publishes its books in a variety of electronic formats. Some content that appears in
print may not be available in electronic books. For more information about Wiley products,
visit our web site at www.wiley.com.

ISBN: 978-0-470-04255-7

Printed in the United States of America.

10 9 8 7 6 5 4 3 2 1

Library
University of Texas
at San Antonio

G. Timothy Haight
This book is dedicated to my wife, Ann, for her love and
support during my career.

Stephen Morrell
Dedicated to Kelley for all the joy she has brought me,
to Linda for all the years she has given me,
and to Lennie for his brotherly love.

Glenn Ross
Dedicated to Debbie for her remarkable proofreading talents
and to Matthew and Bradley for having unwavering patience
while this book was written.

Contents

Preface

Investment professionals manage the vast majority of institutional and individual financial assets. They employ an ever-widening range of research tools, analytical methods, trading techniques, and investment strategies intended to effectively manage their clients' portfolios. To be sure, the array of investment choices and opportunities has expanded markedly during the past decade. Investment mangers have responded with improved knowledge, skills, technologies, and methods to better serve their clients' needs.

The key to successful investment management is to select investment professionals who can best meet clients' investment goals, objectives, and needs. *How to Select Investment Managers and Evaluate Performance* is intended to equip the reader with the essential knowledge and skill set required to properly select investment managers, and to then evaluate their performance in a systematic manner. Our purpose is to improve the effectiveness of those individuals who are entrusted with the oftentimes daunting responsibility of selecting, overseeing, managing, and evaluating investment professionals.

The passage of the Sarbanes-Oxley Act of 2002 combined with explosive growth in the number and types of financial instruments has raised the bar on what is required for those entrusted with oversight responsibilities. Individuals who serve on investment committees of retirement funds, endowments funds, mutual funds, trusts, and similar entities have a fiduciary duty to ensure that the funds are managed properly. This requires individuals who are in such roles to be well versed on the techniques used to evaluate the effectiveness of investment professionals.

How to Select Investment Managers and Evaluate Performance was written for this purpose. Readers will be exposed to cutting-edge techniques that are used to evaluate the performance of investment funds and their managers. The book provides valuable insight as to the roles and responsibilities of those charged with this oversight. Topics covered include establishing investment policy statements, alternative investments, investment approaches and styles, return-risk measurements, and how to conduct a search for investment managers.

This book explains how overall portfolio performance is evaluated as well as its individual equity, fixed income, cash equivalent and alternative investment components. Evaluation techniques using benchmarks such as indexes and universes are presented in a clear and understandable fashion.

ACKNOWLEDGMENTS

How to Select Investment Managers and Evaluate Their Performance was inspired by the authors' decades of working with investment managers. We are grateful for the assistance of many individuals. We would like to thank Alex Fisher at Archstone Portfolio Solutions, Richard Berkeley, Richard Johnston, and Catharine Burkett at Camden Partners, Kevin Campbell at Montagu Newhall Associates, and Members of the Independent Consultants Cooperative. Martin Villavicencio provided excellent research assistance throughout the writing of the book.

C. H. Walker-Black served as a truly valuable source of advice and encouragement. Steve Claiborne of the Frank Russell Company was instrumental in providing data and charts on fixed income universes. Teri Geske of Interactive Data Fixed Income Analytics was most helpful with the Bond-Edge system. Richard Murphy of Capital and Credit Holdings, Inc. provided useful insights throughout the writing of the book. Marshall Geller, Senior Manager of St. Cloud Capital Partners, LP has been an inspiration to us all.

We would be remiss not to give a special thanks to Mr. Gil Hammer of Wilshire Associates who has assisted us on many occasions during the past 10 years. We are indeed grateful for his continuous support. We would like to single out Mr. Robert Waid of Wilshire Associates who was instrumental in preparing the tables and charts attributed to Wilshire Associates.

About the Authors

G. Timothy Haight

G. Timothy Haight, DBA is the President of Menlo College located in Silicon Valley, California. Dr. Haight is Chairman of the Board of Commonwealth Business Bank. He also serves as a member of Southern California Edison's Nuclear Power Decommissioning Fund Committee. Dr. Haight is a member of the Board of Advisors of St. Cloud Capital Partners, LLC, a Beverly Hills firm that provides mezzanine financing for high technology firms seeking funding for growth. Dr. Haight earned a Doctorate in Business Administration (DBA) with a major in Business Finance and Investments from George Washington University. He received his MBA and BS degrees from the University of Dayton.

Stephen O. Morrell

Dr. Morrell is Professor of Economics and Finance in the Andreas School of Business of Barry University in Miami Shores, Florida where he teaches and conducts research in financial institution strategy, financial markets analysis, and portfolio theory. He has been a visiting professor at the Monterey Institute of Technology (state of Mexico campus) and the Georg-Simon-Ohm University in Nuremberg, Germany. Dr. Morrell also serves as a consultant specializing in portfolio strategies for endowment funds. His professional experiences include service as Senior Vice President and Chief Economist for Southeast Banking Corporation; as a Financial Economist for the Federal Reserve System; and as Chairman of the Board of Directors of First State Bank of Ft. Lauderdale, Florida.

His research has been published in scholarly and professional journals such as *Derivatives Risk Management*, *The Journal of Economics and Business*, and *Economic Inquiry*. He is the coauthor of *The Analysis of Portfolio Management Performance* (Irwin/McGraw-Hill), which was translated into Japanese.

Dr. Morrell received his BS degree from Virginia Commonwealth University, and his MA and PhD degrees in economics from Virginia Polytechnic Institute.

Glenn E. Ross

Mr. Ross is a managing director and cofounder of Archstone Portfolio Solutions, a full-service Investment Consultant located in Baltimore, Maryland. His career spans nearly 30 years in the field of investments and consulting with extensive background in asset allocation modeling, development of investment policies, portfolio, and manager evaluations for endowments, foundations, retirement plans, and high-net-worth individuals. Mr. Ross has also served as a quantitative portfolio manager and director of quantitative research for a regional bank trust company.

He serves as a member of Towson University's College of Business and Economics Board, Alumni Board and he has been an Adjunct Professor in Towson University's Finance Department. He is also a member of the Society of Quantitative Analysts. Mr. Ross is President of the Board of Directors of the Albert P. Close Foundation and is a member of the Board of Directors of the Upper Chesapeake Health System Foundation. Mr. Ross earned his undergraduate degree from Towson University and his MBA at Loyola College in Baltimore. Mr. Ross is a Registered Investment Advisor Representative with the SEC.

Mr. Ross resides in Maryland with his wife Deborah and two sons, Matthew and Bradley.

Investment Sponsors

Individuals, households, businesses, governments, and nonprofit organizations have a number of motives for designing, developing and implementing saving and investment programs. Essentially, the savings component of these programs involves reducing current expenditures in order to set aside a portion of such things as current income, earnings, tax receipts, and contributions, while the investment component involves allocating these savings among seemingly ever-growing varieties and combinations of asset classes, investment vehicles and securities.

Individuals and households establish saving and investment programs, among other reasons, to provide retirement income security in order to maintain a desired standard of living during the portion of their lives when income is no longer being derived from work. Businesses and governments may be motivated to organize saving and investment programs as incentive devices to boost employee productivity, reduce worker turnover and take advantage of tax shelters in the case of businesses. Non-pofit organizations arrange saving and investment programs to support current operations, finance capital expenditures, and strengthen the financial basis of the organization. Clearly, there are numerous reasons for establishing saving and investment programs. These motives combined with the investment goals and processes of the investing entities in conjunction with the universe of investment alternatives determine the investment choices and investment portfolios of the saving and investing entities.

Regardless of the entity establishing it, assessing, analyzing and evaluating the performance of an investment program is a critical element in its success. Thorough, timely and accurate investment performance evaluation is a vital step in determining if the objectives of a saving and investment program are being attained, and in taking subsequent actions. Performance evaluation must be undertaken regardless of the decision to either manage the investment program internally or to employ outside investment professionals to manage all or parts of it.

While many entities have established their own saving and investment programs, for example roughly 4.6 million individuals have established their own retirement based saving and investment programs with assets totaling approximately $3.7 trillion, there are several reasons why certain organizations and individuals may be more effective and efficient in establishing programs for others, particularly those programs with long anticipated lives.[1] Individuals considering establishing retirement programs on their own as well as those who seek to contribute on their own to the viability and longevity of organizations such as universities, museums, hospitals and foundations confront difficult planning challenges and potentially high expenses. Specialized knowledge and skills, and substantial information in addition to initial and ongoing administrative costs are required. Moreover, sustained discipline is often necessary to implement such programs.

In contrast, some organizations and individuals may already possess the specialized knowledge and skills and be able to acquire information more easily. They may also enjoy the advantage of declining costs per participant in the development, maintenance, record keeping, compliance and the like for saving and investment programs. Besides economies of scale related to an existing knowledge base, information acquisition, and administrative costs, these organizations and individuals may have strong economic incentives, such as greater employee and contributor loyalty, for arranging saving and investment programs. They may also obtain for themselves and be able to offer tax benefits to participants in saving and investing programs.[2]

Investment sponsors is the term used to refer to organizations and individuals who undertake the responsibility for establishing, designing, developing, implementing, monitoring, and evaluating saving and investment programs on behalf of, and for the benefit of, other persons and groups. The number and variety of sponsored programs have soared over the last several decades. As illustrated in Table 1.1, the most recently available data show there are approximately 1.1 million tax exempt organization–sponsored investment programs with more than 100 million participants and total investments of roughly $12.1 trillion; more than 1.1 million taxable personal trusts with total assets of $1.0 trillion; and, as noted above, about 4.6 million IRA and Keough programs with investments of close to $3.5 trillion.

---

[1] The data are for the number and dollar amounts of assets in IRA and Keough accounts at year end 2004. See "Notes," *Employee Benefit Research Institute* 27, no. 1 (January 2006).

[2] The advantages possessed by some organizations and individuals allowing them to be more effective investment sponsors is discussed in greater depth in Zvi Bodie. "Pensions as Retirement Income," *Journal of Economic Literature* 28 (March 1990), pp. 28–49.

TABLE 1.1 The Variety of Investment Sponsors

Type of Plan Sponsor	Number of Plans	Number of Participants	Investment Assets (billions of $)
Retirement[a]	716,336[b]	109.1 million[c]	$10,927
Defined Benefit	30,336	44.1 million	$5,823[d]
Defined Contribution	686,000	65.0 million	$5,104
Charitable Organization[e]	365,000	NA	$1,212
501(c)(3)	212,000		$654
Foundations[f]	76,348	NA	$515
Trust[g]	1,100,000	NA	$1,000
IRA & Keogh	41,000,000	4.6 million	$3,667

[a] Includes private trusteed, federal government and state and local government plans.
[b] Includes only the number of private trusteed plans.
[c] Includes only participants in private trusteed plans.
[d] Assets of private defined benefit, federal government and state and local government retirement plans.
[e] Includes all 501(c)(3) through 501(c)(9) charitable organizations not classified as foundations by the Internal Revenue Service.
[f] Includes operating and nonoperating foundations.
[g] Includes only trusts at FDIC insured financial institutions.
Sources: Employee Benefits Research Institute, *Pension Investment Report: Fourth Quarter, 2005*; Board of Governors of the Federal Reserve, *Flow of Funds Accounts of the U.S., First Quarter, 2006*; Pension Benefit Guarantee Corporation, *Pension Insurance Data Book 2005*; U.S. Department of Labor, *Employee Benefits Security Administration: Private Pension Plan Bulletin*, July, 2006; U.S. Department of the Treasury, *Internal Revenue Service: Statistics of Income*; The Foundation Center: *Foundation Center Yearbook, 2006*; Federal Deposit Insurance Corporation, *Statistics of Depository Institutions*; and Investment Company Institute, *ICI Fundamentals 15*, no. 5.

The explosive growth in the number of sponsored investment plans indicates that the market for saving and investment programs has become significantly broader and deeper. Several factors appear to account for this robust growth. In terms of provision or supply, ongoing technological progress in communications and information processing combined with a wide range of product, investment management, market structure, institutional and regulatory innovations and changes in the financial sector have likely lowered the costs of establishing and maintaining saving and investment plans. Far reaching changes in the U.S. tax code and persistent, heightened competition for qualified employees have also enabled and motivated tens of thousands of midsized to smaller organizations to sponsor saving and investment programs. Sponsored programs are no longer the sole purview of organizations with large numbers of participants and large dollar portfolios—organizations that may experience economies of scale in operating such programs.

With regard to demand, healthy and sustained long-term growth in the U.S. economy has led to continuous increases in incomes and rising wealth, providing the necessary savings and net worth to fund such programs. Demographic trends, perhaps most notably the aging of the baby-boom generation, have spurred the desire to participate in retirement plans and stimulated the willingness for sizable increases in bequests, contributions, gifts and grants to charitable organizations, foundations and trusts.

THE INVESTMENT COMMITTEE

Organizations establishing saving and investment programs have ultimate fiduciary responsibility for the plans they sponsor. These substantial fiduciary responsibilities are vested in the governing body, such as the Board of Directors of a corporate sponsored pension plan and the Board of Trustees of a university endowment fund, of the organization sponsoring the saving and investment program. Governing bodies in turn frequently establish investment committees and delegate and entrust to them the responsibilities for fulfilling the investment mandates set forth by the sponsoring organization. These responsibilities may vary widely, ranging from placing a few thousand dollars of excess cash in a money market mutual fund to overseeing the investment of billions of dollars apportioned among a number of investment managers across several asset classes.

Committee Composition

The investment committee is chaired by a member of the organization's governing body, that is, a member of the Board of Directors or Board of Trustees, as it is a committee of the governing body. In those infrequent instances when a Board member does not chair the investment committee, at least one Board representative will nonetheless sit as a voting member of the committee. In addition the President, Chief Financial Officer and Chief Investment Officer—if one exists—of the organization will sit as *ex oficio* members of the investment committee.

The size of the investment committee is ultimately a decision of the organization's governing body. Factors such as the complexity of the investment mandate, the number of participants in the plan, the dollar amounts to be invested, and legal and regulatory compliance requirements appear to determine the size of the investment committee. For example, the California Public Employees Retirement System (CALPERS), the nation's largest public pension plan with roughly $210 billion in invested assets, has a 13 member Board of Administration and a 13-member investment committee comprised solely of Board members.[3] In contrast, the John D. and Catherine T. MacArthur Foundation, one of the largest philanthropic foundations in the country with about $5.5 billion in invested assets also has a 13-member Board of Trustees, but a seven-member investment committee comprised of four trustee and three nontrustee members.[4]

Trade-offs obviously exist in setting the size of the investment committee. Large committees may suffer from a diffusion of responsibilities, communications challenges, and tendencies to "group" decision making. Smaller committees may face responsibilities simply too daunting to adequately address. In recent years a trend towards reducing investment committee size from 10 to 15 members to five to seven members appears to have emerged.

While the size of the investment committee is important to its success, the qualifications and dedication of committee members are considerably more important. Individuals invited to serve on the investment committee should be selected based on their education, knowledge, experiences and background in a range of investment management and plan administration issues. Indeed, investment committee members of pension plans coming under the jurisdiction of the Employee Retirement Income Security Act (ERISA) are required to not just act in accordance with the "prudent man" rule but to act per the "prudent expert" rule; that is with the prudence someone familiar with investment management matters would exercise.

Prospective investment committee members should be clearly informed about their requirements, duties, responsibilities and expectations prior to joining the committee. Policies regarding potential conflicts of interest and disclosures should be fully addressed at this time. Orientation seminars for new members and ongoing education programs for all members will serve to keep the committee informed and current about important new developments.

Committee Responsibilities

The overarching responsibility of the investment committee is to design, develop and implement investment strategies and policies in order to achieve the investment goals of the saving and investment program. Effective committees focus on broad issues of strategy and policy rather than the micromanagement of the investment process.

[3] www.calpers.ca.org, accessed June 23, 2006.
[4] www.macfound.org, accessed June 23, 2006.

There are nine primary strategic and policy issues under the investment committee's purview:

1. *Determining investment goals.* Investment goals include specifying return objectives for the monies being invested; setting the risk tolerance(s) about the return objectives; and defining any constraints or limitations on the investment process.

2. *Identifying and monitoring asset classes and investment vehicles.* Determining investment goals will help direct the committee in selecting asset classes whose returns and risks are likely to be most consistent with its investment goals. As the number of asset classes and the variety of instruments for investing continue to rapidly expand the committee must also monitor the growing universe of asset classes and investment vehicles.

3. *Internal versus external investment management.* The committee must decide whether the day-to-day investment of the funds will be delegated to an in-house group of investment professionals and support staff under the direction of a Chief Investment Officer, or if external investment management professionals will be given this responsibility. If the decision is to build in-house capacity for investment management then the investment committee may have strategic and policy responsibilities for such things as its structure and organization. If the committee decides to employ outside investment professionals then procedures for hiring, monitoring, evaluating as well as terminating such firms must be established.

4. *Passive versus active investment strategies.* The committee must determine if monies should be invested such that returns and risks closely track those of relevant benchmarks—a so-called passive investment strategy or, instead, if monies should be invested to earn returns adjusted for risks and costs that consistently exceed relevant benchmarks—a so-called active strategy. Previous decisions regarding investment goals as well as anticipated results, expenses, and evaluation and monitoring costs play important roles here.

5. *Asset allocation guidelines.* The committee should specify permissible ranges for allocating funds among the identified asset classes. These ranges will be influenced by the committee's decisions on investment objectives, asset classes, and a passive versus active investment strategy.

6. *Establishing performance criteria.* In order to properly measure, assess and analyze success in achieving its investment objectives the committee must establish criteria and benchmarks against which actual performance results will be judged. The number and types of criteria have increased substantially in recent years in conjunction with the growth

in the number and variety of asset classes and investment vehicles. Consistency and appropriateness with investment goals, permissible asset classes, and investment strategy and portfolio composition are important in this regard.

7. *Performance evaluation.* The committee must decide how frequently actual investment performance results will be evaluated, the most useful methodologies for evaluating performance, and the parties responsible for undertaking the performance evaluation. The committee must be skilled in assessing and analyzing the performance evaluation data and information presented to it.

8. *Changes to the process.* A host of factors may cause the investment committee to reexamine the strategies and policies in items 1 through 7 above. For example, the tolerance for risk may diminish on a long-term basis; new constraints may emerge; new asset classes may be available for investments; the costs of maintaining an in-house investment department may be considerably increasing; fiduciary responsibilities may become more stringent; or the performance of outside investment professionals may be disappointing. The committee must decide when incremental changes as opposed to more fundamental changes to its strategies and policies need to be made.

9. *Communications and reporting to governing body.* As a committee of the Board the investment committee is responsible for periodically and regularly informing the Board on its progress in successfully implementing the mandates it received from the Board. Key reporting requirements include information on strategy and policy issues noted above; investment performance results and performance evaluations; and recommendations for substantial changes to investment strategy and policy which require Board approval.

Written Investment Policy Statements are the preferred and probably best device for the investment committee to communicate its investment strategy and policy to the Board, participants in the saving and investment programs and any regulatory officials. Investment Policy Statements are the subject of our next chapter.

THE VARIETY OF INVESTMENT SPONSORS

Taxable Status

The two primary types of investment sponsors are tax-exempt sponsors and taxable ones. Over the years the U.S. Congress has enacted, amended, and overhauled an array of laws under which organizations and individuals may sponsor saving and investment programs and qualify for either exemption or deferral from federal taxation. Qualified organization and individual sponsored retirement plans, public charities, and private foundations are the most prominent tax exempt—tax-deferred investment sponsors with trillions of dollars of invested assets. In contrast, individuals—except for their qualified retirement plans—corporations, partnerships and most trusts are taxable investment sponsors.

Qualified versus Nonqualified Retirement Plans

Qualified retirement plans meet certain requirements contained in the Internal Revenue Code to ensure they do not discriminate in favor of highly compensated employees. Sponsors of plans meeting these requirements receive tax benefits in that plan contributions are tax deductible and the investment returns on contributions are tax exempt. Depending on the type of qualified plan, participants' contributions—if any—as well as investment returns on participants' contributions are tax exempt until they are withdrawn by the beneficiary. Nonqualified retirement plans are generally targeted at highly compensated employees. These plans are not subject to the same Internal Revenue Code requirements as qualified plans. However, the broad types of nonqualified plans are similar to the qualified ones discussed below.

A wide variety of qualified retirement plans are offered by private sector, public sector, and nonprofit organizations. Table 1.2 reports the total dollar amounts of retirement plan assets in the U.S. from 1985–2005 by broadly defined plan sponsors. Retirement plan assets totaled almost $14.6 trillion dollars at yearend 2005, compared to about $2.4 trillion in 1985. This represents a compound annual growth rate of approximately 9%. Adjusted for inflation, retirement plan assets have expanded at a compound annual growth rate of close to 6%, roughly twice the pace of expansion of the U.S. economy.

Figure 1.1 illustrates the changing composition of retirement plan assets by broadly defined plan sponsor from 1985 to 2005. Four notable changes are apparent:

1. The share of retirement plan assets accounted for by private trusteed plans, that is private plans managed by a trustee, has fallen from 51% of the total in 1985 to just 34% in 2005.
2. The drop in private trusteed plans share has been exclusively in defined benefit plans, which have plunged from 34% to 14% of the total. Defined contributions plans share, in contrast, has inched up from 17% to 20% of the total.

TABLE 1.2 Total Retirement Plan Assets in the U.S.: 1985–2005 ($ in billions)

| | Total | Private Trusteed | | Private Insured | Federal Government Retirement | State and Local Governments | IRA & Keough |
		Defined Benefit	Defined Contribution				
1985	$2,395	$814	$417	$355	$172	$402	$235
1986	2,778	885	478	418	202	477	319
1987	3,028	833	523	467	233	532	390
1988	3,272	883	549	525	267.5	597	451
1989	3,746	942	672	582	304	700	546
1990	3,928	896	676	649	340	730	637
1991	4,577	1,048	829	691	382	852	776
1992	4,878	1,043	892	706	426	937	873
1993	5,237	1,170	1,014	750	468	1,042	993
1994	5,722	1,193	1,076	794	512	1,092	1,056
1995	n/a	1,444	1,312	n/a	541	1,327	1,288
1996	7,524	1,542	1,520	880	606	1,509	1,467
1997	9,106	1,783	1,853	1,288	659	1,795	1,728
1998	10,365	1,945	2,105	1,418	716	2,031	2,150
1999	11,640	2,085	2,272	1,532	774	2,326	2,651
2000	11,531	1,945	2,295	1,571	797	2,293	2,629
2001	10,842	1,707	2,118	1,331	860	2,207	2,619
2002	9,928	1,404	1,820	1,310	894	1,931	2,533
2003	11,918	1,715	2,246	1,574	959	2,344	3,080
2004	13,259	1,869	2,554	1,765	1,024	2,572	3,475
2005	14,594	2,056	2,907	2,197	1,075	2,692	3,667

Sources: Employee Benefit Research Institute, *Pension Investment Report,* Fourth Quarter 2005; and Board of Governors of the Federal Reserve, *Flow of Funds Accounts of the U.S.*, Second Quarter, 2006.

3. IRA and Keough plans proportion of total retirement plan assets has advanced strongly, rising from only 10% of the total in 1985 to 25% by 2005.
4. The proportions of retirement plan assets represented by private-insured plans, federal government plans, and state and local government plans have remained roughly constant from 1985 to 2005.

FIGURE 1.1

Panel A: Sponsor Shares of Retirement Plan Assets: 1985 (Total Assets: $2.395 trillion)

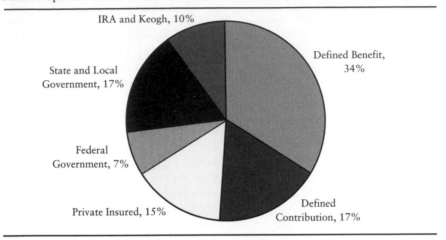

Panel B: Sponsor Share of Retirement Plan Assets: 2005 (Total Assets: $14.594 trillion)

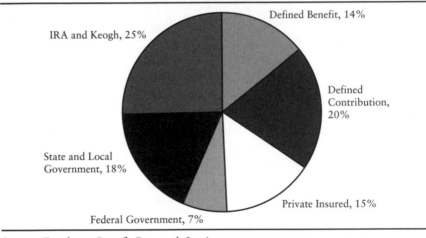

Source: Employee Benefit Research Institute.

Private Sector Retirement Plans

Plans designed to provide income during retirement fall into one of two basic categories: defined benefit plans and defined contribution plans. Fundamentally, these two basic types of plans differ in how they are funded; how benefits are determined; how investment risks are borne; whether or not the invested funds are pooled; and regulatory and compliance requirements.

Defined Benefit Plans

Defined benefit plans are designed to provide participants' retirement incomes that are reasonably certain as the benefits are based on identifiable, specific, predetermined criteria. Most frequently these criteria include length of service to the sponsoring organization; a measure of the participant's wages and salary during a particular time period; and known minimum and maximum annual benefits. These criteria are embedded in a variety of formulas so that participants can estimate and understand the retirement benefits they are likely to receive.

Sponsoring organizations are responsible for funding defined benefit plans. Defined benefit plans require the sponsor to make annual contributions to the plan. Funding requirements are therefore a liability of the sponsoring entity. At the same time, annual contributions made to defined benefit plans by profit-seeking enterprises are a business expense and, like other business expenses, reduce the corporation's taxable income and tax liabilities. The present value of the ongoing decrease in tax liabilities provides incremental value to the enterprise's shareholders in the form of a so-called "tax shield."

Annual contributions made by sponsors should be invested according to the plan's investment policy statement. These invested, accumulated annual contributions combined with the cumulative investment returns on them represent the plan's assets. The plan's assets, in turn, are the source of payment to its retirees. Ensuring that annual contributions and the returns on these invested monies are sufficient to meet the predetermined, promised benefits to retirees is the obligation of plan sponsors. Investment risks of defined benefit plans are thus borne by the entity sponsoring the plan.

The value of a defined benefit plan's assets is generally measured as the fair market value of all the plan's invested securities at a point in time. This fair market value is generally considered to be the same as the liquidation value of the portfolio of assets on the valuation date. Alternatively, the Pension Benefit Guarantee Corporation, the federal government agency that insures participants' pension benefits, allows plan sponsors to calculate asset market values using a maximum five-year average of market values as long as the smoothed market value is not less than 80% or more than 120% of the current market value of assets.

The value of a defined benefit plan's liabilities is the present value of the lifetime stream of future benefits promised to participants and, in some cases, to their surviving beneficiaries. Measuring the value of this liability hinges on a host of assumptions. Assumptions are required for contingencies such as employee turnover rates; retirement ages and the mortality rates of participants; whether benefits are considered to be those accrued to date, projected, or actually vested; and interest rates used to calculate present values.

A defined benefit plan's funding status is based on a comparison of the market value of the plan's assets to the present value of its liabilities. Plans with a positive net asset value are said to be either over funded or fully funded, while those with a negative net asset value are considered under funded. The Pension Benefit Guarantee Corporation reports that for fiscal year 2005 the total assets of all pension plans whose participants it insures were approximately $57.6 billion while total liabilities were about $80.7 billion, representing a system-wide under funding of roughly $23 billion. About 73% of all plans were under funded in fiscal year 2005, with the bulk of the under funding concentrated in single-employer plans.[5]

The landmark Employee Retirement Income Security Act (ERISA) of 1974 and its several amendments—the most comprehensive being the Pension Protection Act of 2006—provides the regulatory and compliance framework for retirement plans in general and defined benefit plans in particular. For purposes of investment performance evaluation the key existing features of ERISA are:

1. The stipulation that sponsors operate plans solely in the interest of participants and beneficiaries and for the exclusive purpose of providing benefits and paying plan expenses.
2. The extension of fiduciary responsibilities, that is, the highest standards of care, to plan trustees, plan administrators, and plan investment committee members.
3. The exercise of fiduciary responsibilities by acting in accordance with the prudent expert rule; diversifying the plan's asset portfolio; developing and following a written investment policy statement; and avoiding conflicts of interest.
4. Disclosure to plan participants of the plan's rules, usually embedded in the Summary Plan Description; disclosure of information on the plan's management, operations, financial status and financial performance; and the provision of an Annual Report.
5. The establishment of the Pension Benefit Guarantee Corporation to ensure that participants in defined benefit programs receive pensions even if their plans terminate without adequate assets to pay promised benefits.[6]

---

[5] The data are from page 2 and Tables S-1, S-20, M-1, and M-5 of the *Pension Insurance Data Book 2005*, Pension Benefit Guarantee Corporation, Washington, D.C. (Summer 2006).

[6] The PBGC pays pension benefits according to plan provisions up to specified maximum amounts. For 2006 the maximum is $48,000 per beneficiary, with the annual maximum tied to the national increase in wages.

The wide-ranging Pension Protection Act of 2006 was designed, among other things, to better ensure that defined benefit plans are adequately funded and to improve the Pension Benefit Guarantee Corporation's insurance reserve. Noteworthy provisions of the Act include:

- A revamping of funding rules for single employer plans beginning in 2008 pertaining to minimum funding requirements, funding requirements for severely under funded plans as well as increased limits on maximum contributions.
- Changes to the interest rate assumptions plans may use to determine the present value of liabilities. These changes will be phased in over two years starting in 2008. Different interest rates will be applied to different groups of benefits based upon when the benefits will be received.
- The time period for averaging plan asset values will be shortened beginning in 2008 to 24 months and the range for averaging will be reduced to no less than 90% and no more than 110% of current market value.
- Mortality assumptions used in calculating the present value of liabilities will be prescribed by the U.S. Treasury.
- Additional changes to the rules for Pension Benefit Guarantee Corporation insurance premia will be instituted, and limits on its exposure to plan benefit increases put in place just before an under funded plan is terminated will be implemented.

Notwithstanding the intent of the Pension Protection Act of 2006, the long-term decline in private sector defined benefit plans is likely to continue unabated. Table 1.3 contains data on the number of Single Employer and Multi-Employer (collective bargaining) defined benefit plans insured by the Pension Benefit Guarantee Corporation as well as the number of participants in these plans from 1985 to 2005. As can be seen in the table the total number of plans has plunged from more than 114,000 in 1985 to slightly more than 30,000 in 2005. Continuous declines have been registered in the numbers of both single- and multi-employer plans, but the fall-off has been most severe in the number of single-employer plans.

The long-term downtrend in the number of single employer plans had been concentrated in smaller plans, that is, plans with less than 100 participants. However, the Pension Benefit Guarantee Corporation reports that the number of larger plans (those with more than 5,000 participants) has also started to decline in recent years.[7] High administrative and operating costs, the concentrations of funding and investment risk with plan sponsors, and the relative attractiveness of defined contribution plans likely account for the downward spiral in the number of private-sector-defined benefit plans.

---

[7] *Pension Insurance Data Book, 2005.*

TABLE 1.3 Private Defined Benefit Pension Plans: Number of Plans and Participants, 1985–2005

	Number of Plans (PBGC Insured)			Number of Participants (in thousands)		
	Single Employer	Multi-Employer	Total	Single Employer	Multi-Employer	Total
1985	112,208	2,118	114,398	29,809	8,209	38,018
1986	111,944	2,153	114,097	30,043	8,154	38,197
1987	111,351	2,098	113,449	31,200	8,256	39,456
1988	108,279	2,081	110,360	31,461	8,294	39,755
1989	101,724	2,060	103,784	31,574	8,426	40,000
1990	91,899	1,983	93,882	31,633	8,534	40,167
1991	82,717	1,926	84,643	31,851	8,710	40,561
1992	71,589	1,936	73,525	32,056	8,780	40,836
1993	63,778	1,900	65,678	32,271	8,657	40,928
1994	57,010	1,880	58,890	32,372	8,559	40,931
1995	53,589	1,879	55,468	32,634	8,632	41,266
1996	48,748	1,876	50,624	32,724	8,649	41,373
1997	43,902	1,846	45,748	33,214	8,740	41,954
1998	41,462	1,817	43,279	33,545	8,876	42,421
1999	37,538	1,800	39,336	33,804	8,991	42,795
2000	35,373	1,744	37,117	34,108	9,132	43,240
2001	32,954	1,707	34,661	34,342	9,423	43,765
2002	31,229	1,671	32,900	34,248	9,630	43,878
2003	30,611	1,612	32,223	34,407	9,699	44,106
2004	29,651	1,587	31,238	34,617	9,826	44,443
2005	28,769	1,567	30,336	34,200	9,900	44,100

Source: Pension Benefit Guaranty Corporation, *Pension Insurance Data Book*, 2005.

And, although the number of plans has plummeted, the number of participants continues to modestly advance—rising from about 38 million in 1985
to 44 million in 2005 or at a pace of less than 1% per year.

Assets of defined benefit plans, as presented in Table 1.2, have also
experienced only modest growth since 1985. In current dollar terms defined
benefit plan assets have risen about 4.50% per year. Adjusted for inflation
the growth in assets has only been at a 1.40% annual rate. Assets per participant have doubled from $21,000 in 1985 to $42,000 in 2005, but adjusted
for inflation have moved up by only 16% or at roughly the same annual
growth rate as the number of participants.

FIGURE 1.2 Defined Benefit Plans Asset Allocations, 1985–2005

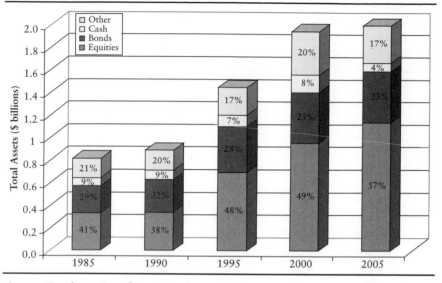

Source: Employee Benefits Research Institute.

The declining numbers of defined benefit plans in concert with sluggish increases in the number of participants and assets as well as the serious under funding challenges may be influencing the asset allocation choices of the investment professionals charged with implementing investment strategy and policy. Figure 1.2 depicts the broad asset allocations among equities, bonds, cash equivalents and other assets of defined benefit plans at five-year intervals from 1985 to 2005. A clear and pronounced shift of assets to equities and from the other asset classes has occurred. The asset allocation to equities has moved from about 40% of all assets in the 1985–1990 time periods to roughly 50% by the 1995–2000 timeframes to approximately 57% by 2005. Allocations to bonds, cash equivalents and other assets have trended downward during this period.

Defined Contribution Plans

In contrast to defined benefit plans, defined contribution plans are not structured to provide specific, predetermined retirement incomes to participants. Instead, the amount contributed by the plan sponsor for each participant is defined at either the discretion of the sponsor or via a fixed formula. Participants may augment the sponsors' contributions in certain types of plans. Retirement incomes for plan participants will be based on accumulated contributions, the length of time these contributions are invested and returns on the invested funds.

Since defined contribution plans do not guarantee benefits to retired workers investment risks are shifted to plan participants. Nonetheless, sponsors of defined benefit plans are not necessarily exempt from all liability, especially in the case of 401(k) plans. In addition to the prudent expert rule, ERISA requires plan sponsors to choose appropriate asset classes and investment vehicles for plan participants; to regularly evaluate the investment performance of the selected investment alternatives; and to provide participants sufficient information so that they can make informed investment decisions and thus assume responsibility for investment outcomes.[8] Moreover, the Pension Protection Act of 2006 contains provisions pertaining to defined contribution plans. Beginning in 2010 small employers, those with at least two but not more than 500 employees, can establish combined defined contribution and defined benefit plans. Temporary changes enacted in 2001 regarding increased contributions and portability of plans have been made permanent.

Unlike the pronounced two-decade downtrend in defined benefit plans, the number of defined contribution plans, participants, and plan assets have experienced strong, sustained advances. Between 1985 and 2002 the number of defined contribution plans surged from approximately 346,000 to 686,000 while the number of plan participants accelerated from approximately 11.2 million to in excess of 65 million.[9] The overwhelming majority of plans, about 74%, had less than 100 participants. And, as illustrated in Table 1.2, assets of defined contribution plans have soared from roughly $420 billion in 1985 to approximately $2.9 trillion in 2005. In inflation adjusted terms defined contribution plan assets have expanded at a solid annual rate of 6.67 % during this period. However, a different perspective emerges when the assets of defined contribution plans are looked at on a per participant basis. Assets per participant stood at $37,500 in 1985 and increased to almost $45,000 by 2005—an annual growth pace of roughly 1%. This rate of expansion fell short of the average inflation rate of approximately 3%, implying that inflation-adjusted assets per participant contracted by about 2% per year.

Table 1.4 presents a summary of the primary types of defined contribution plans for 2002, the latest year for which such data are available. A brief description of each plan type is presented together with the number of spon-

---

[8] The responsibilities of 401(k) sponsors are more fully described by Jay G. Sanders, "401(k) Plans and Liability Exposure for Plan Sponsors," *The CPA Journal* 75, no. 12 (December 2005), pp. 37–42.

[9] The data are from Chapter 11 of the *EBRI Databook on Employee Benefits*, Employee Benefit Research Institute, Washington, D.C. (May 2005).

sors for each plan type, the number of participants in each plan and the total assets of each plan. Internal Revenue Code 401(k) plans, first established in 1978, have come to dominate all other types of defined contribution plans. They now account for approximately 75% of all defined contribution plans; 82% of all plan participants; and 81% of all plan assets.

In a similar fashion as Figure 1.2, the asset allocations of defined contribution plans at five-year intervals from 1985 to 2005 are shown in Figure 1.3. At first glance the striking differences between the asset allocations of defined benefit and defined contribution plans are the sharp uptrend and concentrated allocation of defined contribution plan assets to the "Other Assets" class of investment vehicles. "Other Assets" have come to represent more than 50% of all defined contribution plan assets in recent years compared to about 30% in the 1985–1990 timeframes. Closer inspection, however, indicates roughly 75% of these "Other Assets" are mutual fund

TABLE 1.4   Primary Types of Defined Contribution Plans

Plan Type	Description	Number of Plans	Number of Participants	Assets (billions)
Profit sharing	Employer determined contributions to participants accounts.	193,238	5,200,000	$181
Money purchase	Like (1), but contributions fixed percentage.	77,444	4,115,000	$111
Stock bonus	Employer determined contribution of company stock.	2,875	1,559,000	$50
Target benefit	Contributions target a specific benefit.	2,519	79,000	$37
Cash benefit/ 401(K)	Matched employer— employee contributions.	388,204	53,300,000	$1,570
Cash benefit/ 403(B)	401(K) plan for employees of tax-exempt organizations.	16,309	137,000	$1,200
Cash benefit/457	Supplemental plan for state and local government employees.	NA	NA	$143
Other		4,966	924,000	$32
Totals		685,943	65,275,000	$3,324

Source: Employee Benefit Research Institute, *EBRI Databook.*

FIGURE 1.3   Defined Contribution Plans Asset Allocations, 1985–2005

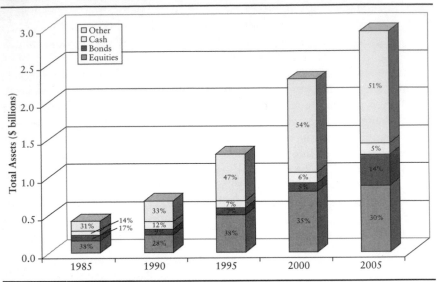

Source: Employee Benefit Research Institute.

shares—reducing the allocation to alternative investments closer to 13%.[10] Moreover, 2004 data for 401(k) plans reveals about 70% of their assets were held as mutual fund shares with roughly 46% held as equity mutual fund shares; 10% each held in balanced and bond mutual fund shares; and 4% in money market mutual fund shares.[11] When these factors are accounted for, it appears the 2005 asset allocation of defined contribution plans was roughly 59% to equities; 17% to bonds; 6% to cash equivalents; and 18% to other assets. Overall, the asset allocation of defined contribution plans is reasonably close to that of defined benefit plans.

Individual Retirement Plans

Self-employed persons can establish their own tax-deferred, saving-investment programs for retirement, as can individuals regardless of whether they are participating in a sponsored defined benefit or defined contribution plan. Several such individual retirement programs exist, with the Individual Retirement Account by far being the most popular. Traditional IRAs were es-

---

[10] These data are from the *Flow of Funds Accounts of the United States, Table L118. c*, Board of Governors of the Federal Reserve, Washington, D.C., first quarter 2006.
[11] The data are from Chapter 13 of the *EBRI Databook on Employee Benefits*, Employee Benefit Research Institute, Washington, D.C. (May 2005).

tablished by the ERISA legislation of 1974 and followed by Roth IRAs in 1997.

Individual Retirement Accounts

Employees establish these accounts with financial institutions and they are generally funded with payroll deductions. Contributions to IRAs are capped, with the maximum contribution to Traditional IRAs for 2006–2007 being $4,000 to $5,000 depending upon the individual's age.[12] Contributions to Traditional IRAs may be tax deductible in whole or in part, depending upon the individual's tax filing status and adjusted gross income. Investment returns on Traditional IRAs are tax exempt until they are distributed.

Roth IRAs are a variation on the Traditional IRA. The most notable differences are that contributions to Roth IRAs are not tax deductible, and distributions are not taxed. While the maximum allowable contributions to Roth IRAs are the same as for Traditional IRAs, the employee's tax filing status and adjusted gross income may further constrain the maximum allowable contribution to Roth IRAs. Like Traditional IRAs, the investment returns on Roth IRAs are not taxed. Finally, Keogh plans are IRAs for self-employed persons. In all of these three types of individual retirement plans the individual account holder bears the full investment risk.

As shown in Table 1.2, the approximately $3.7 trillion of total assets in IRA and Keogh accounts as of 2005 are by a sizable margin the largest of all the types of retirement plan assets. IRA and Keogh assets have expanded at a roughly 14% compound annual rate since 1985. Adjusted for inflation the growth rate has been roughly 10% per year. Growth has been especially rapid since 1997.

The median asset value of IRA and Keogh accounts stood at $40,000 in 2005 versus $20,000 in 1992. It is estimated that slightly more than 40% of all households representing about 41 million people owned either an IRA or Keogh account in 2005 compared to 26% in 1992, with Traditional IRA accounts comprising 80% of the total.[13] At the same time the total number of IRA account holders seems to have flattened out after declining throughout the 1990s, while the number of Keogh accounts has been rising. The Employee Benefits Research Institute reports that individual IRA accounts shrank to about 3.4 million in 2003 from roughly 5.2 million in 1990, and the number of Keogh accounts stood at approximately 1.2

---

[12] The Pension Protection Act of 2006 provides for allowable contributions to increase to $5,000 to $6,000 beginning in 2008.

[13] Sandra West and Victoria Leonard-Chambers, "The Role of IRAs in Americans' Retirement Preparedness," *ICI Fundamentals* 15, no. 1, pp. 1–12. Copyright 2006 by the Investment Company Institute (www.ici.org). Cited with permission.

million in 2003 compared to 825,000 in 1990.[14] Self-employed individuals with Keogh accounts may be the driving force behind the total asset growth in these types of retirement plans.

Sharp shifts in the allocation of IRA and Keogh assets among financial institutions may also lie behind their rapid asset growth. In 1985, Commercial Banks and Thrifts held 60% of all IRA and Keogh assets, with the remainder roughly equally apportioned among mutual funds, life insurance companies, and security broker-dealers. By 2005, the market shares of IRA and Keogh assets had dramatically shifted. Mutual funds and security broker–dealers now hold 45% and 38%, respectively, of all IRA and Keogh assets, with commercial banks and life insurance companies holding roughly 7% and 9% each.[15]

While Traditional and Roth IRAs have come to dominate tax advantaged individual retirement accounts, there are several additional individual retirement plans worth noting. These include the Simplified Employee Pension Plan, SEP for short, where the employer makes contributions to their own IRA account as well as employees' IRAs. Contributions to employees IRAs are made at the employer's discretion. Simple IRAs are like SEPs in that employers make contributions to employee's IRA accounts and employees also make contributions to their IRA accounts. These plans are thought to be less expensive to administer than most defined benefit and defined contribution plans, allowing the extension of retirement saving and investment programs to smaller organizations.

Qualified Tuition Programs

Qualified tuition programs, also known as IRC Section 529 plans, allow individuals to contribute to state-sponsored prepaid tuition and college saving programs for eligible institutions of higher education. Contributions to such programs are not capped, but are also not tax deductible for federal income tax purposes. In about 25 states, however, contributions are deductible for state income tax purposes (in states with individual income taxes) if the contributor is a resident of the state sponsoring the program. If the contributor is not a resident of the state sponsoring the program, the contributor may nonetheless qualify for a tax credit in their state of residence.

Earnings on the contributions to qualified tuition programs are exempt from federal income taxes. Additionally, distributions to the designated ben-

---

[14] Craig Copeland, "IRA and Keogh Assets and Contributions," *EBRI Notes* 27, no. 1 (January 2006), pp. 2–9.
[15] Peter Brady and Sarah Holden, "The U.S. Retirement Market in 2005," *ICI Fundamentals* 15, no. 5, pp. 1–12. Copyright 2006 by the Investment Company Institute (www.ici.org). Cited with permission.

eficiary of qualified tuition programs, as long as such distributions are for normal and reasonable higher education expenses, are tax exempt.

Public Sector Retirement Plans

Federal, state, and local governments provide qualified retirement plans to their employees. These plans are primarily defined benefit plans although the federal government through the Thrift Saving Plan and state and local governments via IRC 457 plans also provide supplemental defined contribution plans for qualified employees. Assets of these supplemental defined contribution plans still remain relatively small proportions of total retirement plan assets. They account for about 6% of all federal government retirement plan assets and represent roughly 6% of all state and local government plan assets.

Assets of federal, state, and local government retirement programs totaled more than $3.7 trillion in 2005, with the federal government share accounting for roughly 29% and the state and local share being about 71% the total, respectively, as depicted in Table 1.2. Federal government retirement program assets have been advancing at close to a 9% compound annual rate since 1985 (6% adjusted for inflation) while assets of state and local government retirement programs have been rising at a hefty 9.5% annual pace (6.5% adjusted for inflation).

Assets of the federal government retirement program are almost exclusively invested in nonmarketable U.S. government securities. Between 2000 and 2005 the allocation to this asset class averaged 86% of all assets. After peaking at 89% of all retirement assets in 2001, the allocation to nonmarketable U.S. government securities has diminished steadily and stood at 82% in 2005. Equities represented 11% of retirement plan assets and bonds—primarily U.S. Treasury securities—accounted for 7% of all federal government retirement plan assets.[16]

State and local government retirement plan assets are allocated across the same broad assets classes as are defined benefit and defined contribution plan assets. However, there are some notable differences in the investment mix for state and local government retirement assets. Figure 1.4 shows the asset allocations for state and local government retirement plans at five-year intervals from 1985 to 2005. The rising share of assets invested in equities and the declining share allocated to bonds are the most notable changes over the 21 year time period. Equity investments have steadily trended upwards and now account for 64% of all assets compared to only 30% in 1985. State and local governments now invest considerably more in equities, as a per-

---

[16] *Flow of Funds Accounts of the United States, Table L.120,* Board of Governors of the Federal Reserve, Washington, D.C., second quarter, 2006.

FIGURE 1.4   State and Local Government Retirement Plans Asset Allocations, 1985–2005

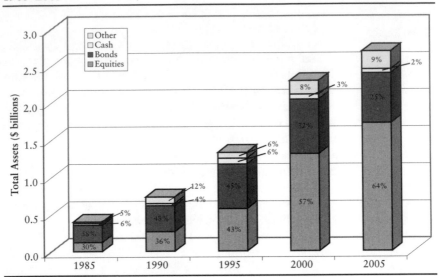

Source: Employee Benefit Research Institute.

cent of their total assets, than do either defined benefit or defined contribution plans. At the same time state and local government allocations to bonds have continuously slid from close to 60% in 1985 to just 25% in 2005.

Public Charities and Private Foundations

Sections 501(c)(3) through 501(c)(27) of the Internal Revenue Code specify the types of organizations that may be exempt from federal income taxation and the criteria that must be met to obtain and maintain federal tax exempt status. The types of organizations run the gamut from Civic Leagues to Charities to Chambers of Commerce to Cemetery Companies to Credit Unions Chartered by States to Cooperative Organizations to Finance Crop Operations. According to the Internal Revenue Service in 2003 there were more than 365,000 organizations of the 501(c)(3) to 501(c)(9) types, and their combined security investments totaled almost $1.2 trillion.[17]

By far, 501(c)(3) organizations, commonly referred to as charitable organizations, are the largest of all the types of tax-exempt organizations. In 2003, there were 288,206 such organizations, with investments in securities of roughly $998 billion, comprising close to 80% of the total number

[17] www.irs.gov/taxstats/charitablestats, accessed June 29, 2006. The data include private foundations but exclude most religious organizations.

of tax exempt organizations and almost 83% of all their security invest-ments.[18] Organizations are eligible for exemption from federal taxation and to receive tax deductible contributions from donors as 501(c)(3) entities if they are established and operated solely for one of the following purposes: charitable, religious, educational, scientific, literary, testing for public safety, fostering national or international amateur sports competition, and the pre-vention of cruelty to children or animals. Furthermore, the organization must be a corporation, community chest, fund or foundation.

All 501(c)(3) organizations are further categorized by the IRS under Internal Revenue Code section 509, with perhaps the most important dis-tinction being between public charities and private foundations. In order to be classified as a public charity the purposes and operations of the organiza-tion must be for the benefit of the public interest. Moreover, the organiza-tion must receive a substantial part of its income from the general public or government, and this public support must be broad-based and not limited to a few individuals or families. Public charities account for some 74% of the number and about 70% of total security investments, respectively, of all 501(c)(3) organizations. Both the number of public charities and their assets invested in securities have grown rapidly in recent years. The number of public charities has risen from about 124,000 in 1988 to almost 212,000 in 2003. Security investments accelerated from approximately $175 billion to roughly $654 billion between 1988 and 2003, representing a compound growth rate of close to 9% per year (7% adjusted for inflation).

501(c)(3) organizations that do not qualify as public charities are clas-sified as private foundations. A narrower base of control and financial sup-port are two characteristics of private foundations. In order for an organiza-tion to qualify as a private foundation, receive exempt status from federal income taxation, and be eligible to receive tax deductible contributions the IRS imposes several restrictions and requirements. These include:

1. Restrictions on self-dealing between the private foundation and its sub-stantial contributors.
2. Requirements that the foundation annually distribute income for chari-table purposes.
3. Limits on the foundation's holdings in private businesses.
4. Provisions that investments must not jeopardize the carrying out of the foundation's exempt purpose.
5. Provisions to ensure that the foundation's expenditures further its exempt purpose.

---

[18] www.irs.gov/taxstats/charitablestats, accessed June 29, 2006. The data include public charities and private foundations but exclude most religious organizations.

In addition, an excise tax is imposed on the net investment income of most domestic private foundations.[19]

The total number of private foundations exceeded 76,000 in 2003 and the market value of their security investments was slightly more than $344 billion. Like public charities, the number and security investments of private foundations have soared in recent years. For example, in 1991 only 41,348 private foundations existed and their security investments totaled about $139 billion. The value of security investments rose at a compound annual growth rate of close to 8% from 1991 to 2003 (almost 7% adjusted for inflation). Typically, private foundations have allocated a substantial portion of their security investments to corporate equities. Between 1991 and 2003 equities averaged 73% of the total security investments of private foundations, with government and corporate bonds holdings representing the balance.[20]

Private foundations, in turn, are additionally subclassified as either private operating or private nonoperating foundations. The former expend their incomes, including returns from investments, on the operations of the foundation. Libraries and museums are often organized as private operating foundations. In contrast, private nonoperating foundations allocate their incomes and earnings from investments to make grants to other organizations and individuals. Private nonoperating foundations also face a federal requirement that each year they must payout an amount equal to 5% of the value of their investments in the previous year adjusted for total givings in that year and operating, administrative and investment expenses.[21] Private nonoperating foundations account for about 90% of the total number of private foundations and roughly the same share of total security investments.

The IRS also classifies charitable trusts as private foundations. These organizations are usually supported and controlled by either an individual or family. However, they are not exempt from federal income tax. In 2003 there were 3,125 charitable trusts holding security investments with a fair market value of approximately $3.9 billion.

TAXABLE INVESTMENT SPONSORS

Saving and investment programs sponsored by trusts, corporations, partnerships and individuals are subject to federal income taxation. Federal tax policies may affect a range of investment choices made by these sponsors such as the choice of assets classes, portfolio composition, and the timing of

---

[19] www.irs.ustreas.gov/charities, accessed June 29, 2006.
[20] www.irs.gov/taxstats/charitablestats, accessed June 29, 2006.
[21] *Foundation Yearbook: 2006*. The Foundation Center, New York, N.Y.

security sales and purchases. In addition, tax considerations are an element in evaluating the performance of their investment portfolios.

Trusts

A trust is a legal agreement under which assets are held and managed by one entity for the benefit of another. The entity creating the trusts and providing the assets goes by several legal names including trustor, grantor, and settlor. The individual(s) or organization that holds legal title to the trust assets and has fiduciary responsibilities for administering the trust agreement and managing the trust's assets is known as the trustee. The beneficiary is the person or organization who receives the benefits (such as income) of a trust.

Trusts are established for a variety of reasons. The most prevalent reasons for establishing a trust include:

- Providing financial support for others.
- Postponing or reducing taxes.
- Controlling assets.
- Achieving social goals.

There are a variety of types of trusts, varying according to their purpose, how they are created, the nature of the assets included in the trusts, and their duration. Each type of trust offers varying degrees of flexibility and control. Most commonly, trusts are classified as either living trusts (*inter vivos*) or testamentary trusts.

Living trusts are established during the trustor's lifetime. In most states the assets held in a living trust are not subject to probate and therefore need not be disclosed in court records. This confidentiality may be an important motivation for creating living trusts. Moreover, the beneficiaries receiving income from a living trust may be in lower tax bracket than the trustor, resulting in tax savings for the trustor.

Living trusts may be "revocable" or "irrevocable." With the former, the trustor may change the terms of the trust or even cancel it altogether. Revocable Living Trusts thus provide flexibility to the trustor. Irrevocable Living Trusts, in contrast, can not be altered or canceled by the trustor once they have been established. However, they offer the advantages that the income earned on the trust assets may not be taxable to the trustor, and the trust assets may not be subject to death taxes in the trustor's estate.

Testamentary trusts, the second common type of trusts, are established as part of a will and become effective upon the death of the person making the will. These types of trusts give trustors substantial control over the distribution of the assets in their estates. Since a will may be altered or even canceled prior to death a testamentary trust can be changed or canceled up to the time of the trustor's death.

At yearend 2005 FDIC insured financial institutions held slightly more than $1.0 trillion of assets in almost 1.1 million personal trust accounts. Approximately 74% of the total number of personal trust accounts comprising 74% of total trust assets were managed, fiduciary accounts by financial institutions, with the balances being non-managed accounts. At yearend 1996, by contrast, FDIC insured financial institutions held about $858 billion in some 904,000 personal trust accounts. About 92% of all personal trust accounts and 80% of assets in these accounts were managed, fiduciary accounts by financial institutions.[22]

For tax purposes, trusts are treated by the IRS as separate, taxable entities. Income distributed to beneficiaries, unless the beneficiary is tax exempt, is taxed at the beneficiary's individual or organization tax rate. Income earned on trust assets that is not distributed to beneficiaries may result in a tax liability for the trust. For 2006, the tax rates range from a low of 15% on undistributed income up to $2,050 to a maximum tax rate of 35% on undistributed income of $10,500 and above.

The IRS also provides special tax treatment for what are known as split-interest trusts. In these types of trusts, trustors designate as beneficiaries both charitable organizations and noncharitable individuals or groups. The trustor receives tax benefits from establishing the trust. There are four primary types of split-interest trust, differing by the methods and timing of payments to beneficiaries, with the charitable remainder unit trusts being, by a substantial margin, the most prevalent type.

When a trustor establishes a charitable remainder unit trust, the trustor obtains a tax deduction for the assets provided to the trust. The trustee makes payments to non-charitable, taxable beneficiaries per the terms of the trust for a specified length of time. IRS rules stipulate that these annual payments can not be less than 5% of the net fair market value of the trust assets. When the defined period of time expires the remaining assets are transferred to a charitable organization. In 2004, charitable remainder unit Trust accounted for 73% of the 123,204 split-interest trust and 73% of the $65.3 billion of assets held in split-interest trusts.[23]

Corporations

While corporations are the primary issuers of marketable debt and equity securities, they also invest in financial assets. For example, in 2005, U.S.

[22] "Total Fiduciary and Related Assets of All Financial Institutions," *Statistics of Depository Institutions,* Federal Deposit Insurance Corporation, Washington, D.C. www2.fdic.gov/SDI, accessed June 30, 2006.

[23] www.irs.gov/taxstats/charitablestats, accessed June 30, 2006.

nonfinancial corporations held approximately $83 billion of longer-term maturity debt instruments issued by other corporations, state and local governments, and the U.S. government. The tax rates corporations face on income and capital gains from investments in financial assets are not the same across assets classes, and these different tax rates may affect their investment choices; the compositions of their financial asset portfolios; and the net performance of their investments.

Corporations face the same capital gains tax rates on investments in stocks and bonds. These tax rates are the corporation's marginal tax rates, which are depicted in Table 1.5. As illustrated in Table 1.5, corporate tax rates vary with a corporation's taxable income from a low of 15% on taxable income up to $50,000 to a high of 39% on taxable income between $100,000 and $335,000. Deductions are allowed for capital losses, to the extent they offset capital gains, and can be carried back three years or carried forward five years to apply against prior or future capital gains. Although individual tax rates on capital gains have been reduced to 15% for most individual tax payers, they have not been lowered for corporations.

Interest income corporations receive from investments in fixed income securities is also taxed at the corporate marginal tax rate. However, dividends corporations receive from equity investments are taxed differently. Corporations investing in equities are entitled to deduct at least 70% of the dividend income that they receive. Moreover, if the corporation owns at least 20% of another domestic corporation's stock then the deduction increases to 80% of the dividend income received from the corporation. In those cases where a corporation owns at least 80% of another corporation's equity, then the deduction is 100% of the dividends received from the corporation. The differential taxation of capital gains and interest income on bonds on the one hand versus dividend income from equity ownership on

TABLE 1.5 Corporate Marginal Tax Rates, 2006

Taxable Income Range	Tax Rate (%)
$0–$50,000	15
$50,001–$75,000	25
$75,001–$100,000	34
$100,001–$335,000	39
$335,001–$10,000,000	34
$10,000,001–$15,000,000	35
$15,000,001–$18,333,333	38
$18,333,334 and above	35

the other may be a powerful incentive shaping corporate investment decisions in financial assets.

Individuals and Partnerships

In addition to tax-deferred retirement based and trust-type saving and investment programs, individuals may establish taxable saving and investment programs for a host of reasons. Diversifying income and wealth from a job or occupation and from a small number of assets in order to smooth consumption expenditures may be one motive. Accumulating wealth to finance future expenditures may be another. Regardless of the motive, individual taxable saving and investment programs are substantial. In 2005, individuals directly owned (not in retirement programs) some $5.5 trillion in equity securities.[24] However, the individuals' investment goals and objectives along with their choices of asset classes, investment vehicles, investment strategies and tax considerations will shape their investment decisions, portfolios, and the performance of their investments.

Individual tax rates on financial asset investments are often based on complex and, at times, baffling aspects of federal and state tax laws. Tax rates on interest income from investments in interest yielding, short-term maturity debt instruments (often referred to as *cash equivalents*) as well as corporate and U.S. Treasury and agency bonds are the same as the individual's marginal income tax rate. These tax rates currently vary from 10% to 35%, excluding the alternative minimum tax, with the income they apply to depending on the individual's tax filing status. Tax rates on qualified dividends from investments in equity securities, in contrast, currently stand at 15%. There is already research indicating the 2003 tax rate reduction on dividends has influenced investor's decisions.[25]

Capital gains on investments in debt and equity securities also currently stand at 15%. Moreover, capital losses can be used to offset capital gains. Deductions for capital losses up to a maximum of $3,000 per year, if losses exceed gains, are currently allowed.

Partnerships, noncorporate businesses of at least two individuals established for the purpose of conducting business to make a profit, also may invest in financial assets. For tax purposes, partnerships are treated like individuals. In general partnerships there is only one class of partner and each partner has liability for the debts and obligations of the partnership. Limited

---

[24] *Flow of Funds Accounts of the United States, Table B.100.c.*, Board of Governors of the Federal Reserve, Washington, D.C., second quarter, 2006.

[25] Jennifer L. Blouin, Jana Smith Raedy, and Douglas A. Shackleford, The Initial Impact of the 2003 Reduction in the Dividend Tax Rate, working paper (October 2004). Available at SSRN: http://ssrn.com/abstract = 4462542.

partnerships have two classes of partners; general and limited. General partners carry out the business of the partnership and often are the motivating force behind establishing it. General partners usually face unlimited liability. Limited partners often provide the equity capital for the partnership. They are not usually involved in the day-to-day activities of the partnership. Their liability is usually limited to their investment in the partnership.

SUMMARY

Large numbers of organizations and individuals sponsor saving and investment programs for significant numbers of participants for a wide range of purposes. These organizations include businesses, governments, and nonprofit entities. The saving and investment programs they sponsor run the gamut from retirement support to profit sharing to assisting charitable organizations and foundations to providing income to others. Many sponsors obtain tax deferral and tax exempt status for the saving and investment programs they establish, while others are not eligible for tax deferral or tax-exempt status.

Investments of sponsored saving and investment programs totaled more than $20 trillion in 2005. The market value of investments, adjusted for inflation, has been growing faster than the U.S. economy's growth rate for the last 20 years. These investments reflect not only the contributions made to sponsored programs—the savings part of saving and investment programs—but countless investment decisions made by investment committees, trustees, professional investment managers, and private individuals—the investment part of saving and investment programs. These investment decisions and the resulting portfolios of securities reflect the investment goals, objectives and investment processes established by investment committees. As well, ongoing innovations and changes in the national and global financial sectors are shaping portfolio choices.

Regardless of the sponsor of the saving and investment program and the sponsor's goals the performance of the investment portfolio must be regularly and properly evaluated. Portfolio performance evaluation, however, must be carried out within the context of the goals and objectives of the saving and investment program.

CHAPTER 2

Investment Policy Statement

Investment policy statements specify the overall objectives of portfolios and the guidelines to be followed in reaching these goals. These statements should articulate the fund's investment philosophy, investment goals, return objectives, and the acceptable risk levels consistent with these goals and objectives. Additionally, they should explicitly disclose any constraints to be placed upon the investment manager, identify asset classes that are acceptable investments, and establish guidelines for asset allocation within these classes. Furthermore, investment policy statements should identify the investment strategy and/or strategies to be used in achieving the portfolio's goals and objectives. Finally, these policy statements should spell out the methods to be used in the evaluation of investment managers, and the frequency that the portfolio and its managers will be evaluated.

A well-written investment policy statement can be used as a blueprint to provide guidance for those with oversight responsibility as well as investment managers and beneficiaries. It should promote better communication between the parties and therefore minimize misunderstanding. The policy statement specifies what is to be accomplished, the strategies to be employed, and the basis for assessment. In short, the investment policy statement is an important tool in carrying out the fiduciary responsibility for those monitoring and managing the fund.

INVESTMENT PHILOSOPHY AND GOALS

The investment philosophy determines the overall portfolio goals. Specifically, the investment philosophy explicitly identifies the reasons for investing. These may include: providing for a secure future, funding scholarships, providing a steady source of income for a particular cause, as well as many other purposes. After the reasons for investing have been identified, then investment goals are set to be consistent with the portfolio's investment philosophy.

It is important that the policy statement explicitly state the portfolio's philosophy and identify the specific goals that will accomplish its purpose. Investment goals may be stated in terms of growth, income, or preservation of principal. An individual who desires to save for retirement would normally identify growth as a goal. In contrast, a retired worker would more likely desire high current yield from his investment portfolio, and would choose income as a goal.

INVESTMENT RETURN OBJECTIVES

Once the investment goals have been determined, they are then translated into investment return objectives. These return objectives should be quantifiable and time-specific, and must be consistent with the investment goals and philosophy of the portfolio. The return objectives can be stated in absolute and/or relative terms. For example, a growth-oriented equity portfolio may set a return objective of 12% per year. It may also set as an objective an annual rate of return of 2% over an index such as the Standard & Poor's 500.

The actual target return must be set after proper consideration of the portfolio's goals, its permissible holdings, and the range and quality of the investments permitted by the fund. The investment objectives of the fund should be clearly stated so that the portfolio managers as well as those monitoring the fund have a thorough understanding of its goal.

Foundations provide a special challenge as they are often required to have a set distribution policy. Often endowments also set a distribution policy. This distribution policy will help define the required return for the overall portfolio. For example, if the distribution policy has been set to equal 5% of the market value per year and inflation equals 3%, the investment committee will already have a base threshold of required return equal to 8% (5% distribution + 3% inflation assumed). With current projections of returns of asset classes, this automatically necessitates an aggressive asset allocation. Therefore a 100% invested in U.S. bonds just will not allow the fund to reach its goals. The acceptable tolerance level can often be determined through a query of committee members. If the tolerance level is too low, then managers may be unable to reach the fund's objectives. In such cases, the committee may consider reexamining the fund's objectives and/or tolerance level.

RISK TOLERANCES

A crucial responsibility of the investment committee is to establish an acceptable level of risk for the investments they are charged with overseeing.

Risk refers to the likelihood or probability that the actual investment out-comes will be different than the desired or expected ones. In particular, risk is the probability that the specified return objectives will not be met.

For most investors risk is undesirable, implying that higher risks should only be accepted if it is accompanied by the expectation of higher returns. Therefore, there must be reasonable consistency between the return objec-tives and the level of risk tolerance. Specifically, if the investment committee deems that a low tolerance for risk is appropriate, then they cannot also seek unreasonably high returns. The investment policy statement should specify as clearly as possible the degree of risk the investment sponsors are willing to assume for the investment portfolio in total and for each component.

CONSTRAINTS

The policy document should state explicitly any requirements which might af-fect the management of the portfolio. For example, if the fund is required to make disbursements on a periodic basis, this constraint must be reflected in the performance objectives. Furthermore, the portfolio must be structured in such a way that these disbursements do not hinder the investment performance. This document should deal with the issue of whether investment managers have full discretionary authority over the purchase and sale of securities.

Derivatives refer to any financial instrument whose value is based on or is derived from an underlying asset, index, or commodity. Based on this defini-tion, such instruments as mortgage backed securities are considered deriva-tives. Other types of derivatives include options, future and forward contracts, as well as equity, fixed income, and currency swaps. To be sure, derivatives can play an important role in determining investment performance.

The policy statement must carefully define the conditions and extent of the use of derivatives. The investment policy statement should set guidelines regarding the use of derivatives in achieving the portfolio's goals. Derivative instruments can be used either for speculative or hedging motives. While spec-ulation using derivatives may enhance the portfolio's returns, it may also lead to substantial losses. In contrast, the proper use of derivatives may reduce the portfolio's exposure to financial risk. In many instances, these instruments can provide a more efficient means of rebalancing a portfolio. (The use of deriva-tives in portfolio management is examined in Chapter 4.)

INVESTMENT STRATEGY

The investment strategy is the plan(s) and methods that will be employed to realize the investment return goals. Strategies can either be active, passive or a combination of the two. Active strategies seek to achieve returns that exceed those of the relevant market indexes and/or benchmarks. Using the first approach, the portfolio managers would be actively involved in decisions regarding both asset allocation and security selection with the objective of achieving a portfolio return that outperforms the relevant market indexes. Various investment styles might be utilized in order to generate acceptable returns. Among the approaches which could be used are: value investing, market timing, or perhaps contrarian investing.

In contrast, a passive strategy would involve designing a portfolio that seeks to match the returns of a predetermined index or group of indexes. For example, the investment committee may decide to structure the portfolio in such a way that it tracks the performance of the S&P 500. Under this approach the committee would periodically rebalance the portfolio so that it replicates the targeted index. Each of these approaches is examined in later chapters.

IN-HOUSE OR OUTSIDE MANAGER

One of the most elementary issues to be addressed by the investment policy statement is who is responsible for managing the portfolio. Broadly speaking, the portfolio can be managed either by the investment committee or by an outside investment manager. There are several questions to ask prior to making this decision. First and foremost, is the level of expertise sufficient within the committee? If the expertise is there, are the members willing to put in the time necessary to properly manage the investment portfolio? What are the relative costs of inside versus outside management? Are there any conflicts of interest? Who will evaluate the investment performance? The investment policy statement should specifically deal with the sensitive issue of using in-house versus outside investment managers.

INVESTMENT POLICY

The policy statement should specify the types of securities to be held and the acceptable risk level in terms of the individual holdings, as well as the overall diversification level required, and guidelines for asset allocation. These considerations should be addressed for equities, fixed income securities, cash and equivalents, and other financial and nonfinancial assets that are permissible investments in the portfolio as well.

SECURITIES TYPES AND RISK CHARACTERISTICS

Equities

Equities are ownership claims in a corporation. The ownership claims or shares originate when the corporation is formed, and additional claims or shares may be created or issued during the life of the corporation. The shares give their owners the right to vote on issues of corporate control and governance. Generally, each of these shares provides the owner with one vote. Some corporations, however, might issue several different classes of common stock, and each class might have different voting rights.

The equity claims in a corporation are residual in nature. That is, the shareholders' claims on the corporation's earnings and assets come last, after the claims of all other parties have been satisfied. In essence, an ongoing corporation must first pay all of its contractually obligated expenses (such as interest on debt, taxes, wages and salaries) before earnings can be distributed to shareholders. If the corporation is in liquidation, then all liabilities must first be satisfied before the distribution of any remaining assets is made to shareholders.

A shareholder's legal liability for the corporation's obligation is limited to the shareholder's initial investment. Limited liability protects the personal assets of shareholders from claims made on the corporation.

Equity securities can be classified along a number of dimensions, including the market capitalization of the company (i.e., the number of shares of stock outstanding multiplied by the current market value per share,) the corporation's industry classification, the market in which the shares are traded, and the financial characteristics of the company. A number of financial characteristics have been developed to help classify stocks. Earnings growth rates, the percentage of earnings paid out as dividends, the ratio of price to earnings, and a host of other financial ratios are commonly used as a classification tool. These financial characteristics can be used by the investment committee to set investment policy guidelines for permissible stock holdings.

As stated earlier, the investment policy statement should contain explicit guidelines as to the permissible levels of risk exposure within the equity portfolio. Along these lines, the statement should require that equities are well diversified. It should specify a maximum investment amount permitted in any individual equity issue. The limit can be on the basis of market value and/or cost. For example, a policy statement may limit the amount of funds concentrated in a single investment to 5% (cost basis) or 8% (market value). Avoiding stock concentration is a necessary diversification strategy, although it may not solve the diversification problem entirely. Additional constraints may be needed. For example, a portfolio may have a concentration in one or a few industries or sectors, such as a portfolio with 4% interests in Citibank, Bank of America, Wells Fargo, and BBT. The investment performance of a portfolio with a large concentration in these banks could be adversely affected by some unanticipated economic event. It is for this reason that the equity portion of the portfolio should be diversified among many unrelated industries. The policy statement should state this explicitly. Since many investment opportunities are appearing in foreign markets, the policy statement should address the extent to which diversification globally is appropriate. Guidelines in terms of foreign investment should include the overall level of investments, as well as the degree of concentration within each market.

The investment policy statement guidelines should identify which equity investments, if any, are prohibited. These guidelines may specify that managers only hold equities above a minimum capitalization amount. Investment in initial public offerings may not be suitable for certain portfolios. Likewise, an investment policy statement may prohibit owning securities which are not traded on the major exchanges or NASDAQ. These constraints are often used to safeguard against investing in stocks with too little liquidity. The investment policy statement can also address various characteristics of equities. A portfolio with an income objective may prohibit investing in equities which do not pay cash dividends. Additionally, the policy statement can require equities to possess a certain price/earnings ratio and/or dividend yield. Other measures, such as the ratio of market value to book value, may be addressed by the investment policy statement.

The investment policy guidelines are sometimes used to address social issues. Prior to the elimination of apartheid, it was common for policy statements to prohibit investments in those firms which conducted a significant part of their business with South Africa. In addition, policy statements may prohibit the investing in tobacco, liquor, and any number of other such industries.

The portfolio's exposure to market risk is another issue which should be addressed in the policy statement. The level of market risk is typically measured by the portfolio's beta. The beta indicates the responsiveness of the portfolio to movement in the overall equity market. Portfolios can be designed to assume more risk than the market (i.e., beta > 1), the same risk (beta = 1), or less than market risk (beta < 1). The portfolio's desired exposure to market risk will depend upon its return objectives. If the objective is to match the market, then a portfolio with a beta of 1 would be appropriate. By establishing a beta of 1, the portfolio is assuming a risk level equivalent to the market. Likewise, if the portfolio's objective is to outperform the market, then a portfolio's beta value greater than one would be appropriate.

This strategy would increase both the expected return and risk of the port-folio. Additionally, if the portfolio's objective is to assume less than market risk, then it would be appropriate to design a portfolio having a low beta. In this instance, both the expected return and risk would be below market levels. The investment policy statement should establish ranges for beta consistent with the portfolio's overall return/risk objectives.

Fixed Income Securities

The investment policy statement sets guidelines as to the types and characteristics of the fixed income securities. Fixed income securities or bonds are notes of indebtedness. Issuers include U.S. Treasury notes and bonds, government agency bonds, mortgage backed securities, Eurobonds, foreign bonds, corporate bonds, and municipal bonds. Bonds are now issued with an ever-growing array of features, but the typical bond possesses the following:

1. *Stated maturity.* The length of time until principal is repaid.
2. *Principal or par value.* The amount the bondholder receives at maturity.
3. *Coupon payment.* The periodic interest received by the bondholder, computed by multiplying the coupon rate of interest by the principal value.

The suitability of each type of fixed income security must be evaluated in terms of the portfolio's goals.

One important consideration which must be addressed in the policy statement is the amount of risk to be assumed within the fixed income component of the portfolio. Specifically, the money manager should have guidelines as to the level of credit (default) risk and interest rate (market fluctuations) risk that should be present in the fund. In making this determination, the investment committee must weigh carefully the trade-off between return and risk.

Default or credit risk refers to the ability of the borrower to make timely interest payments and principal repayments. The proper assessment of default risk requires a careful evaluation of the borrower's financial strength as well as his leverage position. Default risk can be eliminated by investing solely in U.S. Treasury and other U.S. government agency securities. However, such an investment strategy can reduce the overall return available to the portfolio. In order to increase investment returns, a portfolio manager may decide to purchase nongovernment securities. In these instances, the additional returns are accompanied by some level of default risk and event risk.

The investment policy guidelines should specify the minimum acceptable rating for fixed income securities to be suitable for the portfolio. In addition to default risk, the investment policy statement should provide guidelines concerning the appropriate level of interest rate risk within the fixed income securities component of the portfolio. (This guideline can be specified in terms of average maturity levels and/or durations, which are discussed in Chapter 9.)

In addition to default risk and interest rate risk, the policy statement should develop guidelines limiting marketability risk. Marketability risk refers to the ability of an investor to sell a security at or near its true value. It is prudent to avoid entering into transactions where the market is thin. Marketability is also influenced by the size of the issue. As a general rule, the larger the issue, the more marketable the securities tend to be. Other risks that are associated with fixed income securities are examined in Chapter 9.

Cash and Equivalents

The cash and equivalents component of the portfolio is typically used to provide income, add liquidity and stability to the portfolio, and to provide a reserve for purchasing equities and fixed income securities at attractive prices. It is characterized by short-term, high-quality instruments. Typically, U.S. Treasury Bills, commercial paper, certificates of deposit, and various other money market instruments are categorized as cash and equivalents. Ratings for cash and equivalents are presented in Table 2.1.

The investment policy statement should also specify the acceptable risk level for cash equivalents. For example, the investment policy guidelines may prohibit investing in cash and equivalents with a rating less than A1 by Standard & Poor's or P1 by Moody's. Higher rates of returns are generally

TABLE 2.1   Reserve Ratings

Standard & Poor's	Moody's	Interpretation
A-1+	—	Extremely Strong
A-1	P-1	Very Strong
A-2	P-2	Strong
A-3	P-3	Satisfactory
NP	Not Prime	
B	—	Adequate
C	—	Doubtful
D	—	Close to Default

associated with a greater degree of risk. The fund objectives and risk tolerance levels should be taken into account when determining the appropriate cash and equivalent mix for the portfolio.

ASSET ALLOCATION GUIDELINES

The single most important determinant of a portfolio's performance is the asset allocation decision. The investment policy statement must explicitly spell out the portfolio's acceptable asset allocation range. Asset allocation refers to the distribution of the fund's investments among permissible investments such as between equities, fixed income securities, and cash and equivalents. The asset allocation guidelines specify the maximum and minimum percentages that may be invested in each of these categories. Rather than a precise percentage, these guidelines specify a range which each asset type must fall within.

Table 2.2 presents a hypothetical asset allocation guideline for Fund XYZ, a balanced portfolio. The asset allocation guidelines found in the table specify the acceptable range for each investment category. For example, the guidelines specify the amount that is invested in cash and equivalents to be between zero and 25% of the total portfolio value. Likewise, investment in equities can range from 40% to 70% of the funds. Finally, fixed income securities are required to represent between 15% and 50% of the portfolio's market value.

The selection of specific ranges for each asset type will depend upon the portfolio's investment objectives. For example, portfolios with a growth emphasis and no annual distribution requirement would have a higher upper limit on investment in equities and a lower range for fixed income securities. This type of portfolio would have an asset allocation range similar to that shown in Table 2.3.

A portfolio whose objective is growth would be heavily invested in equities. As Table 2.3 illustrates, under these circumstances the investment portfolio would be made up primarily of equity securities (i.e., 70% to 100%) with considerably less invested in fixed income securities. This reflects the likelihood that equities are expected to appreciate over time.

TABLE 2.2 Fund XYZ (Balanced Portfolio) Asset Allocation Guidelines

Investment Type	Range
Cash and equivalents	0–25%
Equity securities	40–70%
Fixed income securities	15–50%

TABLE 2.3   XYZ Portfolio (**Growth Objective**) Asset Allocation Guidelines

Investment Type	Range
Cash and equivalents	0–20%
Equity securities	70–100%
Fixed income securities	0–10%

TABLE 2.4   XYZ Portfolio (Current Income Objective) Asset Allocation Guidelines

Investment Type	Range
Cash and equivalents	0–20%
Equity securities	0–25%
Fixed income securities	50–80%

The asset allocation for an investment portfolio whose objective is to produce current income would be heavily weighted toward fixed income securities. Table 2.4 depicts the asset allocation guidelines for such a portfolio. As shown in the table, the current income needs would be met by investing primarily in fixed income securities. In this illustration, the investment range in fixed income securities would be between 50% and 80%, while the range for equities would be considerably less. Furthermore, the equity component would likely be invested in high dividend yield common and preferred stocks. Nevertheless, the predictability associated with the payment of a debt obligation's coupon rate along with its higher current yield relative to equities is reflected in fixed income securities higher allocation percentage.

Thus the asset allocation decision is not arbitrary. The actual mix between equities, fixed income securities, and cash and equivalents will be influenced by the overall objectives of the portfolio. The proper asset allocation ranges cannot be determined without considering the portfolio's investment objectives. Although the upper and lower limits are set by the fund's policy, the individual portfolio manager has the responsibility to determine the actual mix at any given point in time. Many managers use fixed income securities to add stability to the fund while using the equities component to generate high returns. It is well recognized that over time, equities will outperform fixed income securities. However, it is also accepted that this higher return comes with higher risk as well. The total fund's performance will be the result of the asset allocation within the measurement period as well as the individual securities held during this time. Once the decision is made regarding the appropriate range for each of the asset categories, criteria must be established as to the appropriate investment holdings in each of these groups.

EVALUATION OF PERFORMANCE

The investment policy statement should specifically identify the benchmarks that evaluate performance results. This is accomplished by designating an index, a composite index, and/or a universe to serve as the comparison reference. Under this approach, the investment policy guidelines would require that the portfolio maintain a return relative to an index, or achieve specific ranking within that universe. These investment performance measurement tools are presented next.

Using Indexes as an Evaluation Tool

If the investment committee decides to employ indexes, then the investment policy statement should specifically identify the index and/or indexes which will be utilized for comparison purposes. Indexes can be used to evaluate a fund's equity, fixed income, cash and equivalent holdings, real estate, collectibles, municipals, commodities, as well as various other asset types. The selection of a particular index is a function of the investment goals, objectives, and fund constraints.

Since these indexes are used to provide the investment committee with a benchmark of the portfolio's performance, extreme care should be used in identifying the most appropriate index among those available. It is important that the index's construction is consistent with the assets being measured.

Most indexes are constructed using either a *price-weighted* or *value weighted* method. With a price-weighted index, the price of each stock in the index is added up and then divided by the number of separate stocks in the index. For example, if the index included 10 stocks, then at the end of each trading day the prices of the 10 stocks would be added together, and the total would then be divided by 10. This average of prices would be reported as the numerical value of the index. To simplify the measurement and evaluation, the starting value of the index is assigned a numerical value of 100. Additionally, the divisor of the index is adjusted to account for stock splits or additions to or deletions from the number of stocks in the index. The Dow Jones Industrials Average (DJIA), which measures the stock prices of 30 large U.S.-based corporations, and the Nikkei 225 average of large Japanese company stocks are examples of price-weighted indexes. One shortcoming of price-weighted indexes is that higher-priced securities are, using the method that constructs the index, assigned more weight or importance than lower-priced securities. In contrast, several indexes such as the S&P 500 are constructed using the value-weighted approach. This method determines the relative influence of each security on the index based on its market capitalization. In addition to price and value considerations, other factors such as time weighting influence the suitability of one index relative to another.

Equity Indexes

There are numerous equity indexes available for evaluating portfolio performance. These indexes can be categorized according to several dimensions such as geographic territories (domestic, global, country) or investment style. Equity funds which primarily invest within the United States may be evaluated using indexes such as the S&P 500, S&P 100, DJIA, Russell 2000, Value Line, and the Wilshire 5000. These indexes are intended to be representative of the U.S. equity markets and are presented in Table 2.5.

Over the last several years there has been a great deal of interest in global investing. Portfolio managers are increasingly taking advantage of foreign equity securities. In fact, the percentage of equity foreign holdings by investment sponsors has increased steadily over the last decade. The index used to evaluate these portfolios should be representative of the markets in which these investments are found. Indexes are available for evaluating funds with a global, regional and/or country orientation(s). Table 2.6 presents a sample of these global equity indexes. The global and regional markets reported in the table can be used to evaluate global and/or regional equity funds.

The globalization of markets has provided new opportunities for investment managers to increase returns and provide additional diversification to its sponsors. These new opportunities can be evaluated by employing

TABLE 2.5   Sample U.S. Equity Market Indexes

Amex Major Market Index	NASDAQ 100
Dow Jones Industrial Average	NASDAQ Composite Index
Dow Jones Wilshire 4500	Russell 3000 Index
Dow Jones Wilshire 5000	S&P 500 Index
MSCI–US Broad Market Index	Value Line Arithmetic
NYSE Composite Index	

Source: Wilshire Associates.

TABLE 2.6   Sample Equity Indexes Global and Regional Indexes

FTSE All-World
Dow Jones Wilshire Global Total Market Index
MSCI–All Country World Index
MSCI–EAFE Index
S&P/Citigroup Global Markets–BMI World
S&P/IFC Emerging Market Index

Source: Wilshire Associates.

indexes that reflect the market in a specific country. Table 2.7 provides a list of indexes that can be used to evaluate performance results of funds' investing within a given country. For example, the performance of a manager who invests in Japan could be evaluated using either the Nikkei 225 Stock Index or Tokyo Stock Exchange Index. Here, the evaluator can compare the returns of the individual fund with those achieved using the specific country's index.

TABLE 2.7 Country Indexes

Argentina Merval Index	China: Shanghai Se B Share Index
Argentina Burcap Index	China: Shenzhen Se A Share Index
M.Ar. Merval Argentina Index	China: Shenzhen Se B Share Index
Argentina Indices Bolsa General	China: Shanghai Se Composite Ix
Australia: S&P/ASX 200 Index	China: Shenzhen Se Composite Ix
Australia: S&P/ASX 300 Index	China: Shanghai Se 180 A Shr Ix
Australia: All Ordinaries Index	China: Shanghai G-Shares
Austrian Traded Atx Index	China: Shenzhen G-Shares
Austrian Vienna Stock Ex	Colombia IGBC General Index
Austrian Atx Prime Index	BCT Corp Costa Rica Index
Bahrain: BHSE All Share Index	Croatia Zagreb Crobex
Bahrain: BHSE Esterad Index	Czech Republic: Prague Stock Exchange Index
Bangladesh: Dhaka Stock Exchange Index	Denmark: OMX Copenhagen 20 Index
Belgian 20 Index	Denmark: OMX Copenhagen Index
Belgian Stock Market Ret Index	Egypt: Hermes Index
Belgian Vlam-21 Index In	Egypt: CSE Case 30 Index
Bermuda Stock Exchange	Estonia: OMX Tallinn Index
Botswana Stock Market Do	DJ Euro Stock 50 € Pr
Brazil Bovespa Stock Index	DJ Stock 50 € Pr
Brazil IBX-50 Index	DJ Euro Stock € Pr
Brazil IBX Index	DJ Stock 600 € Pr
Brazil Electric.Enrgy Index	DJ Stock Euro Enlarged 15
Brazil Telecom Index	DJ Stoxx Euro Enlarged Tmi
Brazil Corp Gov Index	FTSE Eurotop 100 Index
Brazil Val/Bov 2 Tier Index	FTSEurofirst 300 Index
Bulgaria: SofIndex Index	MSCI Euro
Canada: S&P/TSX Composite Index	MSCI Pan-Euro
Canada: S&P/TSX Equity Index	S&P Europe 350 Index
Canada: S&P/TSX 60 Index	S&P Euro Index
Canada: S&P/TSX Venture Comp Index	Euronext Top 100 Index
Chile Stock Market Select	Euronext Top 150 Index
Chile Stock Market General	FTSEurofirst 80 Index
Chile Inter-10 Index	FTSEurofirst 100 Index
China: Shse-Szse300 Index	New Europe Blue Chip Index
China: Shanghai Se A Share Index	Finland: OMX Helsinki Index

TABLE 2.7   (Continued)

Finland: OMX Helsinki 25 Index	India: Bombay Stock Ex 500 Index
Finland: OMXhcap	Indonesia: Jakarta Composite Index
Finland: Hextech Index	Indonesia: Jakarta Lq-45 Index
France: CAC 40 Index	Irish Overall Index
France: CAC Next 20 Index	Israel: Tel Aviv 25 Index
France: CAC Mid 100 Index	Israel: Tel Aviv 100 Index
France: NextCAC 70 Index	Italy: Milan MIB 30 Index
France: CAC Mid & Small 190 Index	Italy: Milan MIB Telematico
France: CAC Small90 Index	Italy: Milan Mid-Cap Index
France: CAC Allshares Index	Italy: All Stars Index
France: SBF 250 Index	Italy: Techstar Index
Germany: DAX Index	Italy: Star Index
Germany CDAX Performance	Italy: S&P/MIB Index
Germany: HDAX Index	DJ Italy Titans 30 €
Germany: DDAX Mid-Cap Index	Jamaica Stock Exchange Market Index
Germany: TecDAX Performance Index	Japan: TOPIX Index (Tokyo)
Germany: Prime All Share Perf Index	Japan: TOPIX Core 30 Index (TSE)
Germany: Midcap Market Perf Index	Japan: TOPIX Large 70 Index (TSE)
Germany: Technology All Share Perf Index	Japan: TOPIX 500 Index (TSE)
Germany: Classic All Share Perf Index	Japan: TOPIX Small Index (TSE)
Greece: ASE General Index	Japan: TOPIX Mid 400 Index (TSE)
Greece: FTSE/ASE 20 Index	Japan: TOPIX 100 Index (TSE)
Greece: FTSE/ASE Midcap 40 Index	Japan: TSE2 TOPIX 2nd Sect Index
Greece: FTSE/ASE Small Cap 80 Index	Japan: Nikkei 225
Hong Kong: Hang Seng Index	Japan: Nikkei 300 Index
Hong Kong: Hang Seng Composite Index	Japan: Nikkei 500
Hong Kong: Hang Seng Freefloat Comp Index	Japan: Jasdaq: Stock Index
Hong Kong: Hang Seng Hk Freeflt Ix	Japan: Nikkei Jasdaq
Hong Kong: Hang Seng China Ent Index	Japan: TSE REIT Index
Hong Kong: Hang Seng China Aff.Crp	Japan: TSE Mothers Index
Hong Kong: Hang Seng Mainland Freefloat Ix	Japan: Osaka Se Hercules Index
Hong Kong: Hang Seng 50 Index	Jordan: Amman Se General Index
Hong Kong: Hang Seng Hk 25 Index	Kenya Stock Exchange Ns
Hong Kong: Hang Seng Mainland 25 Ix	Korea: Krx 100 Index
Hong Kong: S&P/Hkex Largecap Index	Korea: Kospi Index
Hong Kong: S&P/Hkex Gem Index	Korea: Kospi 200 Index
Hungary: Budapest Stock Exch Index	Korea Kospi 100 Index
Hungarian Traded Index	Korea Kospi 50 Index
Iceland: Icex 15	Korea Kospi Info/Tech Ix
Iceland: Icex Main	Korea: Kosdaq Index
India: NSE S&P CNX Nifty Index	Korea: Kosdaq Star Index
India: Bombay Stock Ex Sensex 30 Index	Kuwait Global General Index
India: Bombay Stock Ex 100 Index	Kuwait Stock Exchange
India: Bombay Stock Ex 200 Index	Latvia: OMX Riga Index

TABLE 2.7 (Continued)

Lithuania Nsel 30 Ns	Russian Rts Index $
Lithuania: OMX Vilnius Index	Russia: Rts-2 Index
Luxembourg Luxx Index	Russian Traded Index
Luxembourg Luxx Return	Russia: Micex 10 Index
Malaysia: Kuala Lumpur Comp Index	Russia: Asp General, Rb
Malaysia: Kuala Lumpur 2nd Board	Russia: Asp Mt Index, Rb
FTSE Malaysia EMAS Index	Saudi Arabia: Tadawul All Share Index
Malta Stock Exchange Ind	Serbia & Montenegro: Belex15 Index
Mauritius Stock Exchange	Serbia & Montenegro: Belgrade Free Market Compos
Mexico Bolsa Index	
Mexico Inmex Index	Singapore: Straits Times Index
Mexico Imc30 Index	Singapore All Index
MSE Total Return Index	Slovakia: Slovak Share Index
Morocco Cfg 25 Index Cf	Slovenian Total Market
Morocco: Casablanca New All Share Index	Slovenian Blue Chip Index
Morocco Most Actives Index	South Africa: FTSE/JSE Africa Top40 Index
Namibia Stock Exchange Ov	South Africa: FTSE/JSE Africa All Share
Netherlands: Amsterdam Exchanges Index	South Africa: FTSE/JSE Africa Ind25 Index
Netherlands: Amsterdam Midkap Index	Spain: Ibex 35 Index
New Zealand 50 Ff Gross Index	Spain Ma Madrid Index
New Zealand Top 10 Index	DJ Spain Titans 30 €
New Zealand 15 Gross Index	Sri Lanka Colombo All Share
New Zealand All Index	Sweden: OMX Stockholm 30 Index
Nigeria Stock Indices In	Sweden: OMX Stockholm Benchmark
Norway: OBX Stock Index	Sweden: OMX Stockholm Index
Norway: OBX Price Index	DJ Sweden Titans 30 Sek
Norway: OSE All Share Index	Swiss Market Index
Norway: OSE Benchmark Index	Spi Swiss Performance Index
Norway: OSE Mutual Fund Index	DJ Swiss Titans 30 Sf
Norway: OSE Small Cap Index	Swiss: Spi Extra Price Return
Oman: Msm30 Index	Swiss: Smim Price Index
Pakistan Karachi 100 Index	Taiwan Taiex Index
Peru Lima General Index	Taiwan Gre Tai Exchange
Peru Lima Selective Index	Tsec Taiwan 50 Index
Peru 15 Selective Index	Stock Exch of Thai Index
PSEI–Philippine SE Index	Thai SET 50 Index
Poland: WSE Wig Index	Tunisia Stock Market Index
Poland: WSE Wig 20 Index	Turkey: ISE National 100 Index
Poland: WSE Techwig Index	Turkey: ISE National 30
Poland: WSE Midwig Index	DJ Turkey Titans 20
Portugal PSI General Index	United Arab Emirates: Dubai Financial Market Index
Portugal PSI-20 Index	
Qatar: DSM 20 Index	United Arab Emirates: Abu Dhabi Sec Market Index
Romania: Bucharest Bet Index	

TABLE 2.7   (Continued)

UK: FTSE 100 Index	UK: FTSE Aim Index
UK: FTSE 250 Index	Ukraine: Pfts Index
UK: FTSE 350 Index	Ukraine Kac-20 Index We
UK: FTSE Smallcap Index	Venezuela Stock Market Index
UK: FTSE All-Share Index	Vietnam: Ho Chi Minh Stock Index
UK: FTSE Techmark 100 Index	

Source: Wilshire Associates.

There are additional equity indexes which can be used to evaluate the performance of professionals who employ varying management specialties. The evaluator would choose one of these indexes, if the investment professional was charged with investing in certain types of equity securities. Recently, there has been renewed interest in real estate as an investment instrument. The more common indexes which can be used to evaluate the investment results of these managers are listed in Table 2.8.

TABLE 2.8   Specialties Equity and Real Estate Indexes

Specialties Indexes

  CSFB—Leveraged Index
  CSFB/Tremont—Credit Suisse/Tremont Hedge Fund Index
  Dow Jones—AIG Commodity Index
  Froley Revy—Convertible Index
  Goldman Sachs—Commodities Total Index
  Goldman Sachs—Convertible 100 Index
  Inter@Ctive Week Internet
  Merrill Lynch—All Convertibles, E.M.—All Quality
  Phil Gold & Silver Index
  Phil Semiconductor Index
  Phil KBW Banks Index
  Phil Utility Index

U.S. Real Estate Indexes

  Dow Jones Wilshire—REIT Index
  Dow Jones Wilshire—Real Estate Securities Index
  MSCI—US REIT Index
  Nareit All Index
  Nareit Equity Index
  S&P REIT Composite Index

Source: Wilshire Associates.

Fixed Income Indexes

Indexes are also used to evaluate the fixed income component of portfolios. The fixed income index chosen should be representative of the portfolio's guidelines relating to credit risk, liquidity, interest rate risk, and maturity required. For example, if the policy statement prohibits investing in nongovernment securities, then an index using corporate securities may be inappropriate. Furthermore, if the investment policy statement prohibits investing in long-term bonds, an index should be chosen to reflect this constraint.

Table 2.9 lists corporate fixed income indexes that are available for performance comparison purposes. The bond indexes in this table vary according to maturity and risk. The choice of an index should be based on the return/risk guidelines within the investment policy statement. The investment guidelines should be matched carefully with the characteristics of the index to be used for comparison purposes.

Table 2.10 presents the most common U.S. Government Bond indexes used to evaluate government bond fund managers. Since these financial assets possess virtually no default risk, the main consideration when deciding on the appropriate comparison index is its maturity, duration, and convexity characteristics. Thus the evaluator should select an index based on

TABLE 2.9 U.S. Market-Corporate Bond Indexes

Citigroup Global Markets–3–7 Corporate Index	Lehman–Corporate Intermediate Index
Citigroup Global Markets–3–7 Year Corporate A Index	Lehman–Corporate Long Index Lehman–Credit Index
Citigroup Global Markets–Corporate Index	Lehman–Credit Intermediate Index
Lehman–Long Credit A or Better Index	Lehman–Credit Long-Term Index
Lehman–A+ US Credit Index	Lehman–US Corporate Investment Grade Index
Lehman–A Corporate Index	Lehman–Yankee Index
Lehman–A Intermediate Corporate Index	Merrill Lynch–1–3 Yr Corporates Index
Lehman–A Long-Term Corporate Index	Merrill Lynch–1–3 Yr Med Qual Corp BBB–A Rated Index
Lehman–AA Corporate Index	
Lehman–AA Intermediate Corporate Index	Merrill Lynch–1–5 Yr Corporates Index
Lehman–AA+ US Credit Index	Merrill Lynch–10+ Yr Corporate Index
Lehman–AAA Corporate Index	Merrill Lynch–3–5 Yr Corporates Index
Lehman–AAA Long-Term Corporate Index	Merrill Lynch–Corporates Master Index
Lehman–Aa Long-Term Corporate Index	Merrill Lynch–Real Estate Corporate Bond Index
Lehman–Aaa Intermediate Corporate Index	
Lehman–BAA Corporate Index	Merrill Lynch–U.S. Corporates A-AAA Rated 1–10 Index
Lehman–Baa Long-Term Corporate Index	
Lehman–Baa Intermediate Corporate Index	Merrill Lynch–U.S. Corporates A-AAA Rated 10+ Index
Lehman–Corporate BB Intermediate Index ($)	

Source: Wilshire Associates.

TABLE 2.10   U.S. Government Indexes

Citigroup Global Markets–1–10 Treasury/ Agency Index	Lehman–Long-Term Government Index
	Lehman–Long-Term Treasury Index
Citigroup Global Markets–Long Treasury Index (10+ yrs)	Lehman–Mutual Funds: (5–10) U.S. Gov Index
Citigroup Global Markets–Treas/Agency Index	Lehman–Mutual Funds: (5–10) U.S. Treasury Index
Lehman–20+ Yr Treasury Index	Lehman–Treasury Index
Lehman–4–10 Treasury Index	Lehman–Treasury Index (Coupon Return)
Lehman–Agencies Long Index	Lehman–Treasury Index (PRICE RETURN)
Lehman–Agency Index	Merrill Lynch–1–10 Yr Treasuries Index
Lehman–GNMA Index	Merrill Lynch–15+ Yr Treasuries Index
Lehman–Government Index	Merrill Lynch–Treasuries, 5–7 Yrs
Lehman–Government/Mortgage Index	Merrill Lynch–Treasury Bill 0–3 months Index
Lehman–Intermediate Government Index	
Lehman–Intermediate Treasury Index	Payden & Rygel–10 Yr Treasury Note Index

Source: Wilshire Associates.

the fund's return/risk objectives. Here again, the investment policy guidelines should be used to determine which index is the most appropriate.

Fixed income portfolio managers may also invest in mortgage-backed and/or convertible securities. Mortgage-backed securities provide generally returns higher than those paid by U.S. Treasuries. Furthermore, they have distinguishing characteristics, such as prepayment considerations, which differ from the call feature associated with straight debt instruments. For example if interest rates fall, home owners refinance their existing mortgages. This results in the mortgaged-backed securities holders experiencing early principal repayments. Table 2.11 presents a sample list of indexes appropriate for these types of funds.

For taxable fund managers, the state and local municipal bonds may be an attractive portfolio choice. In these instances the manager not only must evaluate the credit aspects of the underlying issue but the desirability of varying maturities. Table 2.12 presents some of the more common indexes available for evaluating taxable investment funds.

TABLE 2.11   Mortgage Indexes

Citigroup Global Markets–Mortgage Index
Citigroup Global Markets–Treasury/Govt Mortgage Index
Lehman–MBS Fixed Rate Index (Coupon Return)
Lehman–MBS Fixed Rate Index (PRICE RETURN)
Lehman–Mortgage Index
Merrill Lynch–Mortgage 30 Year Index

Source: Wilshire Associates.

TABLE 2.12   Sample U.S. Municipal Bond Indexes

Lehman–1 Yr Municipal Bond Index
Lehman–1–10 Yr Blend-Municipal
Lehman–10 Yr Municipal Bond Index
Lehman–3 Yr Municipal Bond Index
Lehman–5 Yr Municipal Bond Index
Lehman–7 Yr Municipal Bond Index
Lehman–California Municipal Bond Index
Lehman–Municipal Bond Index
Merrill Lynch–California Municipal Bond Index

Source: Wilshire Associates.

In some instances, fixed income managers may be permitted to invest in non-traditional fixed income instruments. There are a wide variety of investment choices for these managers. Table 2.13 provides a guide to indexes that pertain to these investment choices.

Finally, many professional managers invest in fixed income securities of nondomestic entities. Foreign investing can often provide the investor with diversification benefits and attractive returns. For these types of investments, the investor's returns are not only tied to the issuing country's interest rates, but also to changes in the currency exchange rate. Therefore, it is important to select an index that reflects the characteristics of these securities as well. Table 2.14 presents a list of foreign fixed income indexes to conduct such an evaluation.

TABLE 2.13   Sample U.S. Specialty Bond Indexes

CSFB–Distressed Loan Index
CSFB/Tremont–Fixed Income Arbitrage Index
Citigroup Global Markets–Brady Bond Index
Lehman–6 Month Swap Index
Lehman–20 Year Swap Index
Lehman–B 2% Issuer Cap Index
Lehman–CMBS Aaa Index
Lehman–CMBS Index
Lehman–Credit Default Swaps Composite Equal Weighted Index
Lehman–Credit Default Swaps Composite Mkt Weighted Index
Lehman–U.S. Tips 1–10
Lehman–U.S. Tips 10+
Lehman–U.S. Tips Index
Lehman–U.S. TIPS 5+ Year Index
Merrill Lynch–Preferred Stock Hybrid Index

Source: Wilshire Associates.

TABLE 2.14   Global Fixed Income Indexes

Barclays Capital–Global Inflation Linked Bond Index
Citigroup Global Markets–European Composite Index ($)
Citigroup Global Markets–Non-U.S. Govt Bond Index ($)
Citigroup Global Markets–Non-U.S. Government Non-Yen Index
Citigroup Global Markets–World Government Hedged Index
Citigroup Global Markets–World Government Bond Index ($)
Citigroup Global Markets–World Government Bond, 1–3 Years ($)
Citigroup Global Markets–World Government Bond, 3–5 Years ($)
J.P. Morgan–EMBI Global ($)
J.P. Morgan–Emerging Markets-Latin America ($)
J.P. Morgan–European Bond Index ($)
J.P. Morgan–Global Index ($)
J.P. Morgan–Latin Euro Bond Index ($)
J.P. Morgan–Non-U.S. Index ($)
Lehman–Emerging Markets Ex-Aggregate Index
Lehman–Emerging Markets Index
Lehman–Global Aggregate Bond Index
Lehman–Global Inflation Linked Index
Merrill Lynch–1–3 Yr Global Government Bond Index
Merrill Lynch–EMU Direct Government 1–10 Years
Merrill Lynch–EMU Direct Government 1–5 Years
Merrill Lynch–Euro High Yield Constrained Index
Merrill Lynch–Global High Yield BB–B Constrained
Merrill Lynch–Global High Yield BB–B Index

Source: Wilshire Associates.

Cash and Equivalents

The cash and equivalent component of a portfolio can also be evaluated in terms of an index. U.S. Treasury Bills and other short-term money market indexes are readily available for performance evaluation purposes. Again, the index chosen must be consistent with the goals and objectives of the portfolio's cash and equivalent component. Several indexes used for performance comparisons for these portfolios are listed in Table 2.15.

TABLE 2.15   Cash and Equivalent Indexes

Commercial Paper Index
Payden & Rygel Treasury Note (One year)
Salomon Brothers Certificate of Deposit Index (Three months)
Salomon Brothers Treasury Bill Index (Three months)
Salomon Brothers Treasury Bill Index (Six months)
Salomon Brothers US Dollar Euro-Certificate of Deposit (Three months)
ScotiaMcLeod 30-Day Treasury Bill Index

BENCHMARK PORTFOLIOS

Customized benchmarks indexes may be appropriate for some funds. These indexes may be designed and developed by the fund managers, in consultation with the investment committee. They appear best suited for portfolios that have highly specific return and risk requirements that are not closely tracked by existing indexes. For example, an endowment fund may have very near term income requirements as well as very long-term planned withdrawal goals for its fixed income portfolio. A customized benchmark may better reflect whether or not this goal is being achieved than a weighting of standardized ones.

A type of customized benchmark that has received increasing attention is recent years is the so-called "normal" portfolio. These normal portfolios contain all of the securities from which a manager normally chooses, weighted as a manager would weight them in a portfolio. Normal portfolios appear to have the benefit of reflecting the style of the investment manager, allowing the investment committee to evaluate results independent of the manager's style. Universe comparisons can be made more readily. At the same time, the construction and maintenance of these indexes is an added expense.

Composite Indexes

The indexes identified earlier are employed when the funds being evaluated are comprised exclusively of equities, fixed income securities, or cash and equivalents. Unfortunately, funds which comprise all of these financial assets cannot be properly evaluated using only one of these indexes. For example, it would be inappropriate to evaluate the performance of a balanced fund using the S&P 500 or a similar index. It is important that the benchmark tool have similar characteristics to the fund which is to be evaluated.

This problem can be overcome by using a composite index approach. Under these circumstances, each component is "matched" with an index possessing the desired attributes as specified by the investment guidelines. These indexes are then used to develop a composite, which represents the weighted average of the individual component's returns. For example, if the portfolio consists of 60% equities, 25% in fixed income securities, and 15% in cash equivalent, then the composite return would be found by multiplying each component's return by its proportionate weight within the portfolio. In turn, these results would then be summed up, to arrive at a composite return.

This procedure may be used to create a strategic target index which is locked with the allocation of the indexes comprising the target. This index when compared to the portfolio measures the manager's ability to asset allocate and add value versus the set allocation of asset classes. Conversely an index that allows the weight to float to match the manager's allocation would measure the manager's ability to pick securities that add value within their asset class.

Using Universes as an Evaluation Tool

The use of indexes for comparison purposes provides the evaluator with many advantages. Indexes are readily available to the evaluators of investment managers, for example, and performance results can be updated rather easily. There are some drawbacks, however. Comparisons of investment performance to that of an index may put the fund manager at a disadvantage, or an advantage. Specifically, index performance is not affected by transaction costs and cash holdings, while the manager's performance results are affected by these factors. Furthermore, the indexes do not reflect the effect of fees charged by investment professionals. Finally, other investment constraints faced by the investment professional, such as required cash distributions, are not reflected in these indexes.

The utilization of investment universes can overcome many of the problems associated with using indexes as a means of evaluating investment performance. An investment universe is a grouping of portfolios with investment characteristics similar to the fund being evaluated.

Several services are available which rank a portfolio's performance relative to other portfolios with similar goals and objectives. This allows for a comparison of the portfolio's performance with portfolios managed by other investment professionals. Thus, the evaluator can tailor the universe to fit the requirements of the fund manager. The investment policy guidelines should state how fund performance is to be evaluated. Typically, the investment policy statement might set as an objective that the portfolio returns rank within the given quartile of the universe chosen over a given period of time.

PERIODIC REVIEW

The investment policy statement should specify how and when the performance of the portfolio will be evaluated. Performing a periodic review is an essential part of a committee member's fiduciary responsibilities. The performance of an investment portfolio can be monitored on a monthly, quarterly, or annual basis. At a minimum, the investment policy statement should require annual meetings with the portfolio's money managers. Chapter 12 presents an overview of the areas to be addressed during these reviews. The importance of conducting periodic reviews cannot be overstated.

SUMMARY

The investment policy statement provides guidelines to assist managers in achieving the investment goals and objectives of the portfolio. The document specifies the return objective as well as the risk level to be assumed. It provides guidance regarding the type of securities to be held, their risk attributes, and the level of diversification to be achieved. In short, the policy statement should provide all parties with the information necessary to carry out their fiduciary responsibilities.

The policy statement should identify what standard is to be used for evaluation purposes. The evaluator can choose from a single index, a composite index, and/or a universe. The selection of the appropriate index and/or universe can only be made after the investment goals, objectives, and risk considerations are determined. The policy statement should also state how and when performance will be measured and evaluated.

CHAPTER 3

Investment Overview

Providing oversight is the single most important duty of an investment committee. The committee's charge ensures that professional managers carry out goals and objectives contained in the investment policy statement while adhering to specific parameters. Proper oversight requires that the committee fully understand this document and that managers are acting within the scope of the policies, procedures and constraints. After all, the policy statement specifies the process for evaluating both investment and management performance.

Professional investment managers actually implement a sponsor's investment plan. Their job is to ensure that the investment sponsor's investment return objectives are met, while operating within the risk tolerance limits, time frame, tax status, and other constraints specified in the investment policy statement. Ultimately, it is the investment committee's job to make sure that the professional money managers do their job!

In light of the wide spectrum of investment sponsors, and the even wider variety of investment goals and objectives sponsors seek to achieve, professional investment managers can be assigned a considerable range of responsibilities. At one extreme, professional managers may be charged with a complete scope of duties—from helping to draft the investment policy statement, to making the asset allocation decisions, to the actual selection of securities in each asset class for a multibillion dollar fund. At the other extreme, professional investment managers may be responsible for security selection only within a relatively small subsector of the overall portfolio. For example, and individual investment manager may be selected to focus on a specialized area such as foreign equities, technologies, or real estate.

CAPITAL APPRECIATION VERSUS CURRENT INCOME

Broadly speaking, investors can be classified as desiring growth, current income, and/or a combination of these two objectives. In both cases, these objectives are balanced by the degree of risk desired. The investor's objectives are stated in the investment policy statement and consequently, reflected in the investment characteristics of the portfolio. For example, a trust that is required to make a predetermined payment at a specified future date might engage a professional investment manager to invest in a portfolio consisting of equity securities that are expected to appreciate over the investment period. Since the trust may have little need for immediate funds, capital appreciation might be more desirable than current income.

Most retired individuals, in contrast, prefer current income to the prospect of future capital appreciation. In fact, they may rely on dividend and interest income to supplement their other retirement income. In these instances, investing in a portfolio which provides high current income may be the most sensible course of action. These portfolios are characterized by investing in fixed income securities and high-dividend-yield preferred and common stocks. The managers of these portfolios would be charged to look for stocks with above-average growth in dividends, a high dividend yield, and a consistent record of dividend payments. Furthermore, companies that pay out a significant portion of their earnings in the form of dividends are frequently emphasized. Often the high dividend payout is possible since these companies' growth prospects are insignificant. This lack of growth contributes to lower price/earnings multiples than growth stocks and thus much higher dividend yields. Investors that desire high current income, while minimizing their exposure to taxes, would seek out portfolios consisting of municipal bonds and other tax-exempt instruments.

Many investment sponsors fall in between these two categories. For example, a pension plan generally requires current income in order to provide retirement benefits to qualified recipients as well as growth in the fund's value in order to meet future obligations to retirees. Balanced portfolios that provide both capital appreciation and current income are available to these sponsors. These portfolios consist of both equities and fixed income securities. The investment professional will manage the portfolio within a predetermined asset mix range. Typically, the portfolio manager is required to maintain a minimum percentage of assets invested in a fixed income category. For example, the portfolio guidelines may specify that the fixed income component is at least 25% of the total investment portfolio size.

Given the fact that our life expectancy has increased remarkably during the past half century, more and more investment experts are recommending that retirees maintain a significant portion of their investment assets in equity. As Table 3.1 suggests, for those individuals 65 years or older, approximately 20% of their income is derived from asset income. Therefore, if you are either planning on retiring or are already retired, the performance of your investment portfolio plays an important role during these years.

TABLE 3.1 Income Sources (65 years and older)

Category	
Social Security	37.6%
Earnings	20.7
Asset income	19.9
Employer benefits	18.7
Other	03.1
Total	100.0%

Source: Bureau of Labor Statistics.

ACTIVE VERSUS PASSIVE INVESTMENT APPROACHES

Investment professionals can take either an active or passive approach in investing their clients' monies. An active approach requires the managers to identify investment classes and securities within these classes which are expected to achieve superior performance relative to a market benchmark index over a given investment horizon. On the other hand, a passive investment approach calls for the identification of a performance benchmark and the construction of a synthetic portfolio which will mirror the performance of that benchmark.

Often an index, such as the S&P 500 is chosen as the appropriate benchmark to be used to evaluate investment performance. In short, performance is based on the ability of the portfolio to achieve the investment results of that index. The investment objective would be to earn a return equal to this index. Obviously, a passive manager would not knowingly select securities that he or she believes will out perform the index. Rather, the manager is charged with achieving the same results.

Unlike passive investing, the active approach requires investment professionals to use their expertise in terms of the asset allocation and security selection decisions. To be sure, the performance of active managers has been under close scrutiny. Each quarter their performance is judged against a host of indexes and universes. Thus these managers are not only expected to "beat the market" but their peers as well.

INVESTMENT STYLES-EQUITY MANAGERS

Investment managers who pursue active strategies have followed a variety of investment strategies and approaches. These approaches not only reflect how these managers invest, but where. Portfolios are categorized according to investment managers "style." While the classification of investment approaches often varies, they generally fall within the following categories:

- Capitalization
- Growth
- Value
- Cyclical
- Market
- Sector
- Contrarian

The above classification system is offered to provide a framework for the discussion below. It should be pointed out that investment styles may include more than one of the above categories. For example, a growth manager may focus on firms that have either large or small capitalizations. Similarly, value investors may focus on specific sectors or capitalizations to achieve their objectives. Thus, these classifications are not mutually exclusive.

Capitalization

Historically, in terms of total return, small capitalization stocks have outperformed higher capitalization stocks on a risk adjusted basis. An increasing number of professionals are investing in small *capitalization* stocks. The stocks of smaller-sized companies are attractive investment vehicles to many professional investment managers who believe they have a comparative advantage in being among the first to identify small companies with exceptional earnings prospects. By being among the first to invest in such companies, professional managers believe their clients will enjoy substantial excess returns, adjusted for risk, on their portfolios.

Table 3.2 reports the annualized total return for large company stocks (S&P 500 Index), small company stocks (Russell 2000 Index), as well as the annual inflation rate over the last 15 years ending June 30, 2006. During this period, both large and small company stocks provided investors with

TABLE 3.2   Annualized Total Returns, 15 Years Ending June 30, 2006

Investment Category	Geometric Mean (%)	Standard Deviation (%)
S&P 500 Index	10.7	14.9
Russell 2000 Index	11.8	19.2
Inflation	2.7	1.2

returns *far* exceeding the rate of inflation. As the table reveals, small company stocks provided investors with higher annual returns than the large company stocks. However, as indicated by the corresponding standard deviations, these returns were accompanied by greater risk. Small company stocks have historically provided returns about 10% greater (11.8% versus 10.7%) than those of large company stocks. The risks in small company stocks have historically been approximately 29% higher (19.2% versus 14.9%) than those of larger company stocks. The relationship between capitalization and performance is also consistent when reviewing the historic results of companies listed on the New York Stock Exchange. Smaller capitalization stocks have been widely reported to provide returns greater than their larger capitalization counterparts.

Growth

Many professional managers strive for superior returns by focusing on growth investing. Their portfolios are concentrated in sectors, industries, and companies that are expected to grow much faster than the economy overall. The equity securities in growth portfolios would be characterized by possessing high return on equity, and accelerating growth in earnings. Historically, these securities have produced annual earnings growth rates well in excess of those achieved by the S&P 500 companies. Furthermore, these stocks tend to have a high market value to book value ratios. Current yields are low compared to the market since dividend payouts are scant as earnings often must be reinvested into the company to fuel its growth.

Table 3.3 reports the style characteristics for three categories of growth indexes: S&P 500 Growth, S&P 600 Small Growth, and S&P 400 Mid Cap together with the style characteristics of the S&P 500. The style characteristics listed in the table are: price/earnings ratio, dividend yield, five-year earnings growth rate, return on equity, and the ratio of market price to book value. As mentioned above, growth stocks are characterized by relatively

TABLE 3.3 Style Characteristics, Growth Indexes

Market Indexes	P/E Ratio	Dividend Yield	5-Year EPS Growth Rate	ROE	P/B Ratio
S&P 500 Growth	17.6	1.5	19.9	22.3	3.5
S&P 600 Small Growth	19.8	0.5	23.0	18.3	3.0
S&P 500	16.9	1.9	18.8	19.1	2.7
S&P 400 Mid Cap	20.8	1.3	17.6	15.2	2.5

Source: Standard and Poor's Corporation, Second Quarter, 2006 Data.

high price/earnings, equity growth rates, return on equity, and market price to book value. These stocks also possess relatively low dividend yields.

The historic performance of growth indexes based on size is reported in Table 3.4 for the 1988–2005 period. Column one represents the year, while columns 2, 3, and 4 represent the total rates of return for the Large Growth Index, Mid Cap Growth Index, and Small Growth Index, respectively. The final column reports the total return for the S&P 500 over this time.

The highest total rates of return for this period were achieved by the Mid Cap Growth Index (10.8%), closely followed by Large Cap Growth Index (10.7%). The return for the Small Cap Growth Index was 8.7%. The S&P 500 which achieved an annual rate of return of 12.0% outpaced all three indexes over this period.

TABLE 3.4   Growth Index Performance, 1988–2005

Year	Large Growth Index (%)	Mid Cap Growth Index (%)	Small Growth Index (%)	S&P 500 (%)
1988	11.3	16.9	20.4	16.6
1989	35.9	24.5	20.2	31.7
1990	–0.3	–12.2	–17.4	–3.1
1991	41.3	55.0	51.2	30.5
1992	5.0	5.8	7.8	7.6
1993	2.9	12.1	13.4	10.1
1994	2.6	–1.3	–2.4	1.3
1995	37.2	33.5	31.0	37.6
1996	23.1	15.1	11.3	23.0
1997	30.5	14.8	13.0	33.4
1998	38.7	3.1	1.2	28.6
1999	33.2	55.5	43.1	21.0
2000	–22.4	–16.1	–22.4	–9.1
2001	–20.4	–10.8	–9.2	–11.9
2002	–27.9	–29.1	–30.3	–22.1
2003	29.8	46.3	48.5	28.7
2004	6.3	14.6	14.3	10.9
2005	5.3	8.2	4.2	4.9
Annualized Returns	10.7	10.8	8.7	12.0

Source: Standard & Poor's Corporation and Frank Russell Company.

Value

Value investment style, as the name implies, seeks to identify stocks that are undervalued relative to an assessment of their fundamental worth. The managers use fundamental analysis to spot companies that have significant strengths, such as consistent earnings but are also characterized by relatively low market values to book value. These stocks may have a higher dividend yield than a growth stock, a lower return on equity, and a lower equity growth rate than their growth style counterparts. Hence, managers would consider such stocks as undervalued or relatively cheap securities when compared to growth stocks.

Table 3.5 reports the style characteristics of selected value indexes for the quarter ending June 30, 2006. As the table reveals, value stocks are characterized by low price/earnings, equity growth rates, return on equity, and market price to book value relative to growth stocks. These stocks provide investors with much higher dividend yields than growth stocks.

A comparison of the value style characteristics to the S&P 500 is also worth noting. The S&P 500 has a higher price to book ratio than the value index. These differences can be understood when viewing the relative growth rate of earnings and return on equity figures. For both measures, the S&P figures are higher than the value index.

Table 3.6 reports the historic performance of various value indexes for the 1988–2005 period. Column one represents the year, while columns two, three, and four report the total rates of return for the Large Value Index, Mid Cap Value Index, and Small Value Index, respectively. Column five displays the total rate of returns for the S&P 500 during this period.

The Mid Cap Value Index achieved an annualized total rate of return of 14.8%, followed by the Small Value Index return of 14.2%, while the Large Value Index earned a return of 13.0%. The relative returns of these value indexes are consistent with the findings of other studies reporting superior total return performance of smaller capitalized companies.

TABLE 3.5 Style Characteristics, Value Indexes

Market Indexes	P/E Ratio	Dividend Yield	5-Year EPS Growth Rate	ROE	P/B Ratio
S&P 500 Value	16.2	2.3	17.6	16.0	2.3
S&P 600 Small Value	21.6	1.3	15.7	10.2	2.0
S&P 500	16.9	1.9	18.8	19.1	2.7
S&P 400 Mid Cap	20.8	1.3	17.6	15.2	2.5

Source: Standard and Poor's Corporation, Second Quarter, 2006 Data.

TABLE 3.6   Value Index Performance, 1988–2005

Year	Large Value Index (%)	Mid Cap Value Index (%)	Small Value Index (%)	S&P 500 (%)
1988	23.2	27.7	29.5	16.6
1989	25.2	15.2	12.4	31.7
1990	–8.1	–17.4	–21.8	–3.1
1991	24.6	40.7	41.7	30.5
1992	13.6	24.9	29.1	7.6
1993	18.1	19.3	23.8	10.1
1994	–2.0	–1.3	–1.5	1.3
1995	38.4	29.8	25.8	37.6
1996	21.6	22.2	21.4	23.0
1997	35.2	33.1	31.8	33.4
1998	15.6	–1.9	–6.5	28.6
1999	7.4	1.5	–1.5	21.0
2000	7.0	20.8	22.8	–9.1
2001	–5.6	9.7	14.0	–11.9
2002	–15.5	–9.9	–11.4	–22.1
2003	30.0	44.9	46.0	28.7
2004	16.5	21.6	22.3	10.9
2005	7.1	7.7	4.7	4.9
Annualized returns	13.0	14.8	14.2	12.0

Source: Standard & Poor's Corporation and Frank Russell Company.

Cyclical

A cyclical style is characterized by an investment process that focuses on changing economic and market climates. The investment manager will attempt to time the market by identifying firms whose earnings are sensitive to changes in the business cycle of the economy. Industries which exhibit sensitivity to changes in the business cycle would be attractive to this type of investment manager. These would include interest sensitive sectors such as consumer durable goods and manufacturer's capital goods such as automobile, housing, and banking industries, aircraft and machine tools. For this reason, this investment approach is characterized by "sector rotation," that is, identifying how industries will perform during different segments of the business cycle and acting accordingly.

Market

Market timing was an investment style that was quite popular at one time. This approach requires the manager to identify the troughs and peaks of market cycles and change their asset allocations to coincide with these shifts. Market timers rely heavily on technical analysis to signal when to get in and out of the market. The underlying concept is that historical price and volume data convey information concerning future movements in the market. Such signaling devices as the Dow Theory and the Elliot Wave Theory, for example, have been around for years. After several studies illustrated the perils of being out of the market, this timing approach had lost much of its following.

Investment managers who are market timers seek to identify major shifts in markets and adjust their portfolios to reflect the anticipated change. Their approach to adjusting a portfolio involves changing the asset allocation as well as selecting the types of securities which are likely to benefit from the anticipated market environment. Prior to a major upswing in the market, these managers are expected to shift funds out of cash and equivalents and into stocks in anticipation of a rising market. Likewise, if these managers believe that the end of a bull market is at hand, they would likely reduce the amount of equities in the portfolio while simultaneously increasing the percentage of cash and equivalents. The remaining equities within the portfolio would likely consist of securities which possess relatively low market risk.

Sector

Sector managers concentrate their holdings in a single industry. This approach calls for investors to concentrate a portion of their holdings in a portfolio specializing in a particular industry. By focusing on one industry group, the managers can develop industry expertise and target the top prospects within that sector. The disadvantage is the lack of diversification. However, the investor would be able to gain diversification by investing simultaneously in other sectors.

In addition to reporting the performance of the S&P 500 as a whole, the relative performances of the index's sectors are recited. The index is usually broken down into the following nine sectors: Consumer Discretionary, Consumer Staples, Energy, Financials, Health Care, Industrials, Information Technology, Materials, Telecom Services, and Utilities. The performance results of each sector are then reported. Table 3.7 presents the S&P 500 performance by these sectors for the six months ended June 30, 2006.

During this period, the total rate of return for the S&P 500 was 2.7%. As the table shows, seven of the nine sectors outperformed the index. The

TABLE 3.7   S&P 500 Index Sector Performance, Year-to-Date Ended June 30, 2006

	Return (%)
Consumer discretionary	2.5
Consumer staples	4.2
Energy	13.7
Financials	3.1
Health care	−3.8
Industrials	7.1
Information technology	−5.8
Materials	7.0
Telcom services	13.9
Utilities	4.5
Total S&P 500	2.7

Source: Standard & Poor's Corporation.

Telecom Services and Energy sectors led the way with total returns of 13.9 and 13.7%, respectively. Of the sectors that achieved lower returns than the index, Information Technology was the worst performer with a total return of −5.8% for the six months ended June 30, 2006.

Contrarian

A contrarian investment style attempts to recognize stocks that are either overlooked by others or that fall out of favor. An excellent example of a contrarian investment was the health care industry whose stocks dropped during the discussions of President Clinton's health reform initiative in 1993. Health Care stocks such as Bristol Myers, Merck, and Johnson and Johnson were deeply discounted at that time by Wall Street based on expectations of lower profit margins and investment returns. More recently, the airline industry has seen its ups and downs, pardon the pun. Higher fuel costs coupled with increased security expenditures have contributed to a difficult post-9/11 environment. As a result, continued consolidation in the airline industry is expected.

Thus shocks to an entire industry or firm specific circumstances can lead to situations where stocks are below their historic values. In addition to potential turnaround situations, contrarians seek out securities which have a small following and little if any institutional interest. Low P/E multiple companies, with their price selling near book value, would be candidates for contrarian investors. Disappointing earnings, or firms that are unable to meet SEC filing deadlines due to accounting irregularities such as problems with the treatment and/or full disclosure of option arrangements would also fall into this category. Other unfavorable publicity that may not affect the bottom line would also cause securities to be viewed as undervalued by contrarian investors.

INTERNATIONAL INVESTING

A discussion of investment strategies would be incomplete without considering foreign investing. With the recent advances in foreign capital markets and heightened growth prospects around the globe, professional investors are identifying new investment opportunities. The improved opportunities to hedge in the foreign exchange arena greatly reduce the foreign exchange risk of foreign investing.

Investments can be made on a global, regional, or country basis. Furthermore, professional managers invest indirectly though mutual funds, or directly by purchasing the securities of individual firms. Passive investing employing indexes can also be utilized by investment managers. Broadly speaking professional managers classify international markets as either developed or emerging. Developed markets represent the industrialized countries. Emerging markets are made up of economies in various stages of development.

Table 3.8 reports the annualized total returns of the 21 developed markets during the 1996 to 2005 period. As shown in the table, the highest annualized rate of return was 15.94% achieved by Finland. The lowest return was recorded by Japan (0.50%).

Table 3.9 reports the performance of selective emerging markets over the same period. During this period Brazil achieved an annualized total return of 18.67%, the highest of any emerging nation followed by Mexico which recorded annualized returns of 17.89% during the 1996 to 2005 period. However, several emerging nations posted negative returns with the Philippines returning a disappointing –7.39% annualized return during the measurement period.

INVESTMENT STYLES-FIXED INCOME MANAGERS

As in the case of equities, where there are several approaches to managing monies, fixed income professionals can utilize a variety of techniques in managing their investment portfolios. They can invest in U.S. Treasury issues, U.S. government agency issues, corporate bonds, publicly traded mortgages, mortgage-backed securities, municipal bonds, and preferred and

TABLE 3.8   Developed Markets, 1999–2005

Country	US$ Return Total (%)
Australia	12.55
Austria	15.66
Belgium	11.42
Canada	13.71
Denmark	14.41
Finland	15.94
France	10.92
Germany	6.91
Hong Kong	6.02
Ireland	14.69
Italy	13.17
Japan	0.50
Netherlands	8.93
New Zealand	8.48
Norway	11.88
Singapore	1.07
Spain	12.98
Sweden	11.77
Switzerland	8.76
United Kingdom	8.94
United States	9.15

Source: Wilshire Associates.

convertible stocks. Each of these fixed income investment alternatives has an impact on the portfolio's return and risk characteristics.

Quality Considerations

The long-term performance of selected fixed income securities is presented in Table 3.10. Column 1 represents the investment category, while column 2 reports the geometric means. Column 3 reports each investment's standard deviation.

As one would suspect, long-term corporate bonds provided the highest return over the past 20 years ending June 30, 2006. Corporate bonds expose investors to credit risk or default risk. Thus this premium over long-term

TABLE 3.9 Emerging Markets, 1996–2005

Country	US$ Return Total (%)
Brazil	18.67
Chile	6.53
Greece	0.982
Indonesia	−5.27
Malaysia	−3.63
Mexico	17.89
Philippines	−7.39
Portugal	8.89
South Africa	10.08
Taiwan	2.56
Thailand	−6.97
Venezuela	7.05

Source: Wilshire Associates.

TABLE 3.10 Annual Total Returns, 20 Years Ending June 30, 2006

(1) Investment Category	(2) Geometric Mean (%)	(3) Standard Deviation (%)
Long-term corporate bonds	8.6	6.8
Long-term government bonds	8.3	9.1
U.S. Treasury bills	4.7	1.0
Inflation	3.1	1.2

government bonds is expected given this risk that is not faced by holders of government bonds. In an effort to achieve higher returns, managers can choose lower quality issues. In doing so, the manager exposes the portfolio to higher risks.

Maturity Considerations

In addition to the credit risk described earlier, fixed income securities are subject to interest rate risk. Bond values and interest rates move inversely. Interest rate risk refers to the loss of market value due to increases in market interest rates. As a general rule, fixed income securities with longer maturities have greater interest rate risk than securities with shorter maturities. Normally, yield curves are upward sloping, providing higher returns with longer maturities.

Often managers will adjust the maturity of the fixed income portfolio, in anticipation of changes in overall interest rates. If interest rates are forecasted to rise, the managers will shorten the fixed income securities' maturities to minimize losses in value. If on the other hand, rates are forecasted to fall, managers will increase the maturities of its fixed income securities in order to achieve capital gains.

A common method for determining the extent to which changes in interest rates affect the value of fixed income securities is called duration analysis. It is used by managers of fixed income securities during various phases of interest rate cycles. The duration of a bond is simply the time weighted average of its yearly cash flows divided by the current market price of the bond.

Thus duration analysis is not only useful to portfolio managers with buy and hold strategies, but also for those who wish to move in and out of positions based on expected interest rate changes. Duration analysis can be a useful tool for those managers who would like to position their bond portfolios for both rising and falling markets. During periods where interest rates are likely to rise, the portfolio manager would choose to reduce the bond's duration, while in periods where interest rate decreases are forecasted, the manager would increase the bond's duration.

SUMMARY

Investment sponsors generally are interested in growth and/or current income. In developing an investment strategy to assist investors in achieving their goals, professional managers must understand their clients' objectives, risk tolerance levels, investment time horizon, and tax status. Each of these elements must be explicitly considered as part of the investment process.

Professional managers can take either a passive or active approach when managing their sponsor's funds. Using a passive approach, the manager creates a portfolio which contains the same attributes as the index which he is replicating. If successful, the portfolio will achieve investment results identical to the underlying index.

Active managers, strive to beat the market, rather than merely match it. To accomplish this, professionals use various approaches and tactics. For equity managers, these include the following "styles": capitalization, growth, value, cyclical, market, sector, and contrarian investing. Managers will also invest within their home country, or internationally. For the latter type of investing, one can choose an array of investment vehicles in foreign countries, regions, or globally.

Fixed income managers also have choices in how they are to meet their clients' needs. They can invest in U.S. Treasury instruments, U.S. Government Agency bonds, corporate bonds, mortgage backed securities, publicly traded mortgages, municipal bonds, and preferred stock. Each of these has its advantages and disadvantages.

CHAPTER 4

Alternative Investment Vehicles

R ecent decades have seen an explosion in new financial products and services, financial markets and financial institutions. New ideas and knowledge have appeared at a rapid rate and have been quickly adopted, modified and spread across the financial sector. Financial innovation appears to be driven by a host of factors, including but not limited to research breakthroughs in the pricing and design of new financial instruments; ongoing technological advances in communications and information processing that have substantially lowered the cost of transmitting and analyzing information; the growth in global economies and commerce accompanied by attendant increases in the demand for financial products and services; and changes in national and international financial regulatory structures.[1]

Financial innovation has provided investment sponsors, investment committees, and the investment managers they employee the opportunity to expand the range of investment choices beyond the traditional vehicles of common stock, fixed income bonds, and cash equivalent securities. A wider array of financial securities with different return and risk characteristics are now available. Growth in the number and types of financial organizations and markets have provided varying degrees of depth, breadth, liquidity and efficiency for the origination and trading of new financial securities.

Allocating part of a fund's portfolio to alternative investment vehicles may improve its expected return-risk profile, result in a better matching of asset and liability maturities, lower the costs of operating a fund, enhance its flexibility, and generate preferred cash flow streams. Deciding whether or not to include alternative investment vehicles in a fund's portfolio, the types to include, and the proportion of the fund to allocate to alternative investment vehicles should be based on three interrelated issues. First, the consistency and appropriateness of the properties of the alternative investment vehicles,

---

[1] A thorough discussion of the empirical evidence on the causes of financial innovation may be found in W. Scott Frame and Lawrence J. White, "Empirical Studies of Financial Innovation. Lots of Talk, Little Action?" *Journal of Economic Literature* 42 (March 2004), pp. 116–144.

such as return, risk and liquidity features, with the investment objectives established by the investment committee and embedded in the investment policy statement. The second issue is the anticipated effects of including alternative investment vehicles on the return and risk performance of the fund's complete portfolio. The third issue is the investment committee's understanding of the properties of alternative investment vehicles. Such an understanding is critical to making informed choices, to discharging prudent investor fiduciary responsibilities, and to properly evaluating performance.

Several alternative investment vehicles are reviewed in this chapter. They are hybrid securities, derivative contracts, international securities, real estate investments, investments available only to so-called qualified investors including hedge funds, venture capital and buyout private equity funds, and commodities and collectibles. Important features of each investment vehicle are described and discussed.

HYBRID SECURITIES

As the name implies, hybrid securities contain features of several types of financial instruments such as debt, equity and derivatives. These features may give investment committees greater choices, improved flexibility and speed, and lower costs in portfolio management decisions. Convertible bonds, convertible preferred stock, and warrants attached to either equity or bonds are the most common types of hybrid securities.

Convertible Securities

The options to convert a debt security to common stock and to convert shares of preferred stock to common stock are valuable to investors. Including these options in securities is also worthwhile to their issuers. Convertible securities provide these options. Convertible bonds give to their owners the option to exchange a bond for a fixed number of shares of common stock. Convertible preferred stock gives to its owners the option to exchange preferred shares for a specified number of common stock shares.

Corporations whom investors view as somewhat risky appear to be the primary issuers of convertible securities. The perception of higher risk might arise because the company in question is relatively young; because its basic business and industry are inherently volatile; or because it is seen as very susceptible to broader economic fluctuations. The sense of higher risk would generally require the company to offer higher yields on its debt and equity securities as compensation to investors. By offering convertible securities, however, the company may reduce either its borrowing cost or cost of equity.

Convertible Bonds

Convertible bonds offer investors compensation for accepting higher risk. In the worst case scenario of a company's liquidation, convertible bondholder claims are aligned with the other bondholders and precede those of stockholders. In the best case situation, where the company prospers beyond expectations, the convertible bondholders can benefit by converting the bonds to shares of stock. Under normal conditions investors will receive an adequate return on the bonds while maintaining the option to convert.

It is important for investment committee members to understand several features of convertible bonds. The *conversion ratio* is the first noteworthy feature. The conversion ratio specifies the number of shares of common stock to be received for each bond converted. The conversion ratio is set by the issuing company. The *conversion price,* the ratio of the bond's par value to its conversion ratio, is the second important feature and can be determined once the conversion ratio is established. If the bond is exchanged for stock then the conversion price is the price paid for the stock. The third feature of note is the bond's *conversion value,* determined as the conversion ratio multiplied by the company's current stock price. Comparisons of a convertible bond's current market value to its conversion value are often the basis for deciding whether or not to exercise the conversion option. When the bond's current market value exceeds its conversion value it is generally not worthwhile to convert the bond to common stock. In contrast, when the bond's current market value is less than its conversion value then converting the bond to shares of stock is frequently profitable.

Our discussion indicates that the valuation of convertible bonds has three segments. The first segment derives from valuing the bond strictly on the basis of its *pure bond value.* Like most bonds, the pure bond value is based on the promised cash flows, that is, the coupon payments and maturity value of the bond; the frequency with which cash flows are promised and length of time over which they will be made; the risks of the issuer; and changes in the general level and structure of interest rates. The pure bond value sets a lower boundary on the value of a convertible bond in cases where conversion is unlikely. These are situations where the company's stock price is quite low relative to its conversion value.

The *conversion value,* noted above, sets a second lower boundary to the value of a convertible bond. In cases where the issuing company's stock price has been rising, conversion becomes more likely and the bond will then not sell for less than its conversion value. Otherwise, investors would buy the bond, immediately convert it to common stock at the conversion value, and then sell the stock at the higher price.

The third segment of a convertible bond's value is the value of the *embedded option to convert*. As noted above, the option to convert the bond to common stock shares expands investors' range of choices, and the expanded choices have value. Models for pricing call options can be used to determine a convertible bond's embedded option value.

Convertible Preferred Stock

Convertible preferred stock is a type of preferred stock that includes an option for the owner to convert the preferred shares into a specified number of common shares. The conversion generally can occur anytime after a predetermined date set by the issuing company.

Convertible preferred stock, like other types of preferred shares, pays to its holders a fixed dividend subject to the issuing company's financial capacity and willingness to pay. Dividends must first be paid to preferred shareholders before than can be paid to common stockholders. However, preferred stock frequently does not carry voting rights. Preferred shareholders claims, in the event of a company's liquidation, take priority over those of common shareholders but stand behind those of bondholders.

Given the features of preferred shares most analysts view and value them in a very similar fashion as they do a company's coupon bonds. This holds as well for convertible preferred stock. The same three key features of convertible bonds, (conversion ratio, conversion price and conversion value) exist for convertible preferred stock. Issuing companies set the conversion ratio for convertible preferred stock as they do for convertible bonds. A conversion price can be determined for convertible preferred stock, based on the conversion ratio and the offering price of the preferred stock rather than a convertible bond's par value. A conversion value and associated conversion premium or discount based on the differences between the conversion price and the common stock's current price also exist. One notable difference, however, is that issuers of convertible preferred stock may force conversion. This type of put option is not generally found in convertible bonds.

Warrants

A warrant is a financial instrument that gives the owner the right to purchase a specified quantity of the underlying financial security at a predetermined price for a specified period of time.[2] The specified quantity of the underlying financial security is given by the conversion ratio—the number of warrants

---

[2] Put warrants, which give the holder the right to sell shares of common stock to the issuing company, also exist. However, their use appears to be very limited and we therefore emphasize the more widely used call warrants.

required to purchase one unit of the underlying security. This conversion ratio is set by the issuing company. The predetermined or exercise price at which the underlying financial security can be purchased is also set by the issuing company and is generally set at a sizable premium to the current stock price. American style warrants can be exercised anytime up to and including their expiration date, while European warrants may only be exercised on their expiration date. Expiration dates on warrants are often set for several years after the new security is issued. The underlying financial security is most often shares of a company's common stock, but other securities such as stock indexes and bonds may also be used.

Warrants are generally attached to new offerings of either debt or equity instruments and, like other hybrid securities, are designed to make the security more attractive to investors. Warrants may be stripped from the security to which they were originally attached and then traded as separate instruments on either organized exchanges or over-the-counter markets.

Clearly, warrants are similar to options and are valued on a similar basis. Factors such as the price volatility of the underlying security, differences between the exercise price and current market price of the underlying security, length of time to maturity, and interest rates determine the prices of warrants as they do with options. Owing to the low dollar prices for most warrants, returns on them—both positive and negative—may be exaggerated when the price of the underlying security rises and falls. This is also the case with options.

There is, however, one important distinction between warrants and options. When warrants are exercised the issuing firm is required to issue additional shares of stock. This also holds true for convertible securities. In all cases the issuing firm then receives the proceeds from in essence selling additional shares of common stock. The change in the number of shares outstanding and the concurrent change in equity capital may affect a company's accounting-book value per share. Additionally, with more shares outstanding reported earning per share may also be affected. Accounting conventions require firms with sizable amounts of hybrid securities to report their financial results on an unadjusted or primary basis and on an adjusted or fully diluted basis.

DERIVATIVE CONTRACTS

Of the many innovations that have swept across the financial sector in recent decades none have been more widely accepted than derivative contracts. For example, in 1990, the notional principle value of all outstanding financial derivative contracts stood at close to $6.0 trillion. By 2005, this amount had soared to about $339 trillion.[3]

Financial derivative contracts are contracts whose value is derived from and dependent upon the value of an underlying financial security, collection-index of securities or interest rate. The value of the underlying security or index, unless it is another derivative contract, is based in turn on underlying operational, industry and national and global macroeconomic factors.

The widespread use of derivative contracts underscores their importance as an alternative investment vehicle and highlights the necessity for investment committee's to clearly articulate appropriate policies regarding their use. Derivative contracts are often an effective vehicle as part of a fund's overall risk management policy. However, they may also be beyond the scope of a fund's investment policy. In either event an informed decision requires a basic understanding of the characteristics of derivative contracts.

Uses of Derivative Contracts

Fundamentally, derivative contracts can be employed for one of two purposes: risk management or hedging and speculation. Risk management refers to the process of managing the volatility of a portfolio's return, especially downside returns below those of some specified target return or benchmark. Derivative contracts can be used to manage the downside risk.

The basic idea in employing derivatives for risk management purposes is that the market value of the derivative contract will change in the opposite direction from that of the underlying part of the portfolio being hedged. Gains (losses) on the derivative contracts at least partially offset any declines (increases) in the securities being hedged. Consequently, the return on the underlying portfolio is less volatile than without the use of derivative contracts in the risk management strategy.

Limitations exist in employing derivative contracts as part of a risk management strategy. These limitations may prevent risk from being reduced to some desired, specified level. One such risk may arise because an appropriate derivative contact simply does not exist to hedge the underlying security. In a related vein the features of an existing derivative contract, such as its maturity or value, may not provide the extent of risk management desired. In such situations portfolio managers attempt to construct synthetic hedges,

---

[3] The notional amount refers to the gross dollar value of outstanding contracts, adjusted for double counting and is widely used as a measure of market size. Data sources are: Stephen O. Morrell, "Trends in the Market for Financial Derivatives," *Derivatives Risk Management Service* 1, no. 1 (February 1996), pp. 1–22; and "OTC Derivatives Market Activity in the Second Half of 2005," Bank for International Settlements, Monetary and Economics Department, May 2006.

using derivative contracts whose price movements are expected to be highly correlated with the securities being hedged.

The problem of incomplete markets for hedging with derivatives, however, appears to be abating at a rapid rate. For example, three of the largest and best-known organized derivative exchanges—the Chicago Mercantile Exchange, the Chicago Board of Trade, and the Chicago Board Options Exchange—offer a combined total of almost 160 separate and distinct financial derivative contracts. These products include a wide and expanding range of equity index, interest rate and foreign exchange rate futures, and options contracts.[4]

A second limitation in the use of derivative contracts for hedging purposes arises from basis risk. Basis refers to the spread between the value of the derivative contract and the current market value of the financial asset being hedged. Occasionally, the basis may widen resulting in a smaller decline in volatility, that is, a lesser reduction in risk than planned. During periods of extreme events, such as country debt defaults, foreign exchange rate crises, and sudden equity market collapses basis risk appears to be particularly severe.

Counterparty risk, the likelihood that the opposite party in the derivatives contract will not execute their contractually stipulated part of the agreement, may also be present in derivatives contracts. Counterparty risk is minimized for exchange traded derivatives as the exchange itself serves as the intermediary or counterparty for all contracts. Various forms of insurance may be available to reduce counterparty risk for over-the-counter derivative contracts, and derivative product companies, separately capitalized special purpose clearinghouses, as well as other types of clearinghouses for reasonably standardized over-the-counter derivative contracts have emerged.

Derivative contracts can also be employed for speculative purposes. Speculators find derivatives an attractive investment vehicle for two reasons. First, margin requirements on exchange traded derivative contracts are often substantially lower than those on purchases and sales of the underlying security. The lower margin requirements allow speculators to take larger positions for any amount of their own equity capital allocated to the position. If the value of the derivative contract changes as expected, then speculators' returns on equity will be magnified as a consequence of the leverage they have assumed. The second reason derivative contracts are a preferred investment vehicle of speculators is that they allow them to participate in so-called price discovery markets. Markets for increasing numbers of derivative contracts are extremely broad, deep, liquid, and highly competitive. If prices change more rapidly and completely on derivative markets

---

[4] These data do not include the approximate 1,500 options contracts on individual stocks and 460 long-term maturity options (LEAPS) offered on the CBOE.

in response to new information than other markets, then speculators may earn higher returns via these markets.

Derivative Markets and Types of Derivative Contracts

Derivative contracts are originated and traded on both organized exchanges and over-the-counter markets. Contracts originated and traded on organized exchanges have standardized specifications, such as notional contract sizes, expiration dates, margin requirements, minimum price changes or 'tick' sizes, daily limits on price changes, set hours of operation, and established settlement procedures to name but a few. As noted previously, organized derivative exchanges assume the counterparty risk. They are also supervised and regulated by external governmental agencies. These characteristics of organized exchanges generally provide hedgers and speculators with relative anonymity; allow trades to occur with relatively low transactions cost; and make for highly liquid markets. They tend to be best suited for hedging and speculation of marketwide, systematic types of risk.

In contrast, derivative contracts originated and traded on over-the-counter markets provide for hedging and speculative vehicles customized to the end-users unique needs. Contract terms and specifications are often individually determined, and the trading of contracts may be privately negotiated between the parties involved. Hedgers and speculators have less anonymity. Over-the-counter derivatives markets tend to be self-regulated rather than by external authorities. These characteristics tend to make them best suited for hedging and speculation of more firm-specific, idiosyncratic risk.[5]

Table 4.1 presents data on the size and composition of the global derivatives market at five-year intervals from 1990 to 2005. Data are presented for both over-the-counter and exchange traded markets; for the three primary classes of underlying securities (interest rate-bonds, foreign currency, and equity indexes); and for the four primary types of derivative contracts (forwards, futures, options and swaps).

Several points are worth noting from the data in Table 4.1. The first, as mentioned previously, is the soaring size of the markets for financial derivative contracts. The market has accelerated from a $6 trillion one in 1990 to a size of $339 trillion by 2005—a stunning increase in market size of some $333 trillion. The second noteworthy point is that interest rate derivate products, whether originated and traded on organized or over-the-counter markets, were and remain the dominant investment vehicle for hedgers and speculators. In

---

[5] The Commodities Futures Trading Commission and the Securities and Exchange Commission are the primary federal regulatory agencies for U.S. organized derivatives exchanges. The International Swaps and Derivatives Association is one of the major self-regulatory authorities for over-the-counter derivatives markets.

TABLE 4.1 Financial Derivatives: Market Size and Composition, 1990–2005: Notional Principal Outstanding (billions of dollars)

	1990	1995	2000	2005
Over-the-Counter Contracts				
Total	$3,451	$17,713	$94,538	$281,211
Interest Rate Contracts	2,873	16,516	64,667	215,237
Forward rate agreements	NA	NA	6,423	14,483
Swaps	2,312	12,811	48,768	172,869
Options	561	3,705	9,476	27,885
Foreign Exchange Contracts	578	1,197	15,666	31,609
Forwards and Forex swaps	NA	NA	10,134	15,915
Currency swaps	578	1,197	3,194	8,501
Options	NA	NA	2,338	7,193
Equity Contracts	NA	NA	1,891	5,057
Forwards and swaps			335	1,111
Options			1,555	3,946
Other contracts	NA	NA	12,313	29,308
Credit default swaps	NA	NA	NA	13,698
Exchange-Traded Contracts				
Total	$2,339	$9,282	$20,905	$57,817
Interest rate contracts	2,050	8,618	12,642	52,297
Futures	1,455	5,876	7,908	20,709
Options	595	2,742	4,734	31,588
Foreign Exchange Contracts	126	154	95	174
Futures	69	34	74	108
Options	57	120	21	66
Equity Contracts	163	510	8,168	5,346
Futures	69	172	4,283	803
Options	94	338	3,885	4,543

Sources: Bank for International Settlements. *BIS Quarterly Review* (December 2005 and May 2006). Full publication available free of charge on www.bis.org.

1990, interest rate products represented about 85% of the notional value of all derivative contracts. By 2005, the market share of interest rate products had slipped somewhat, but still stood at a robust 75% of the total. The third point worth noting is the enlargement in the total market share accounted for by over-the-counter derivatives markets and contracts. In 1990, over-the-counter derivative contracts represented about 60% of the total notional value of all outstanding derivative contracts. By 2000, the over-the-counter market share had jumped to about 82% and had inched-up to roughly 83% by 2005. The fourth noteworthy point is that over-the-counter markets appear especially dominant in providing interest rate and foreign exchange rate contracts, while organized exchanges dominant the market for equity contracts. Over-the-counter markets supply nearly 82% of all interest rate derivative contracts and close to 99% of all foreign exchange derivative contracts. In contrast, organized exchanges provide about 60% of all equity contracts.

There are four generic types of derivative contracts: forward, futures, options and swaps. The variations on these contracts are almost innumerable, including growing numbers of derivative contracts where the underlying security is another derivative contract. Options on futures contracts and options on swap contracts are just two examples. New financial derivative contracts are appearing with a high frequency, such as credit derivatives and credit default swaps whereby one party makes a periodic payment to another in return for a payment should a specified event, such as a default, occurs. Definitions of the four generic types of derivative contracts follow.

Forward Contract

A customized, tailor-made agreement for the future delivery or receipt of a financial security where one party aggress to purchase and the other party agrees to sell a specified amount of the financial security at a specified date in the future at a price agreed upon today. Forward contracts originate and trade on over-the-counter markets.

Futures Contract

Futures contracts are the same as forward contracts except futures contracts have standardized specifications and are originated and traded on organized derivatives markets.

Options Contracts

Options provide the holder with the right, but not the obligation, to either purchase (call) or to sell (put) a specified amount of a specified financial security at a predetermined price within a specified period of time. Writers of options contracts, if the contracts are exercised, are obligated to either sell in the case of a call option or buy in the case of the put option the specified financial security at the predetermined price. Options contracts originate and trade on both organized and over-the-counter derivatives markets.

Swaps

Swap contracts are agreements between two parties to exchange cash flow streams for a specified time period on a specified notional amount. Swap contracts originate and trade on over-the-counter markets.

INTERNATIONAL INVESTMENT VEHICLES

The explosive progress in new financial products and services, financial institutions and financial markets has certainly not been limited to the United States. Developed and emerging economies in all parts of the globe have experienced substantial growth, sometimes at breathtaking speed, in the size of their financial sectors. Financial sector enlargement has not only contributed to the progress of many nations, especially in the so-called emerging markets, but also reflects the potential for sustainable, healthy long-term economic growth throughout much of the world.

International securities offer considerable opportunity for investment committees and the portfolio managers they select to support the achievement of the fund's investment objectives. Returns may be increased and portfolio risk reduced via allocations to international securities. At the same time, additional issues may be present when investing in international securities.

The International Bank for Reconstruction and Development, more commonly known as the World Bank, reported that the market capitalization for all the world's equity markets, excluding mutual fund shares, totaled approximately $43.6 trillion in 2005. Equity market capitalization in the U.S. represented about 40% of the world total or roughly $17.6 trillion, leaving some $26 trillion of international equity securities for investors. Emerging market equities are estimated to account for close to 12% or $5 trillion of the 2005 world equity market capitalization.[6]

In a similar vein the International Monetary Fund reported that the size of the global fixed income market, in terms of market value, was almost $58

---

[6] www.web.worldbank.org. The World Bank also provides a global breakdown on equity market capitalizations by regions and countries. The data on equity market capitalization in emerging economies are from the International Financial Corporation, the private sector arm of the World Bank.

trillion in 2004. U.S. corporate and public sector debt securities accounted for about $22 trillion or 38% of the world total, leaving some $36 trillion of international debt securities for investors. Emerging market economies were responsible for issuing roughly $9.3 trillion or about 16% of the total global fixed income securities outstanding.[7]

The universe of stocks and bonds outside the United States thus totaled approximately $62 trillion in 2005, and it is estimated this capitalization is expanding at a 15% annual rate. International investors, however, have been somewhat slow to capture the prospective benefits of global investing. For some time financial researchers have been analyzing the so-called 'home country bias'—the propensity of investors to underweight the proportion of global securities in their portfolios relative to the proportions predicted by standard portfolio theory.[8] For a wide range of U.S. investors, standard portfolio theory indicates about 38% of total equity holdings should be allocated to international equities. Actual allocations to international equities by U.S. investors, however, hovered closer to 8% until recently.[9]

Table 4.2 gives an indication of the potential benefits from international investments. The table presents historic return and risk measures for 13 distinct asset classes, ranging from one-year maturity Treasury bills, the proxy for cash equivalent investments, to a variety of U.S. and international stock and bond asset classes, to commodities, to real estate investment trusts, the proxy for real estate investments (discussed next in this chapter). Annual return and risk measures from 1996 through 2005, based on monthly return data on indexes of the respective asset classes, are contained in the table. Two return measures are employed: the geometric mean/average return (GMR) which is also the compound annual growth rate; and the simple arithmetic mean/average return (AMR). Risk is measured via three statistics: (1) the standard deviation of annual returns; (2) the semistandard deviation of annual returns below the arithmetic mean return; and (3) the mean shortfall or average return below the arithmetic mean return. The latter two measures of risk focus on downside risk relative to the average return. Additionally, a measure of return relative to risk, the arithmetic mean return divided by the standard deviation of the return, is listed in Table 4.2.

---

[7] International Monetary Fund: Global Financial Stability Report: Market Developments and Issues: September, 2005.

[8] Karen K. Lewis, "Trying to Explain the Home Bias in Equities and Consumption," *Journal of Economic Literature* 37 (June 1999), pp. 571–608.

[9] Kenneth French and James Poterba, "Investor Diversification and International Equity Markets," *American Economic Review* 81 (June 1991), pp. 222–226. The International Monetary Fund reports that allocations to global equities by international investors have steadily risen in recent years.

TABLE 4.2 Return anf Risk Measures for 13 Asset Classes, 1996–2005

Year	T-Bills	S&P Lg Cap 500	S&P Mid Cap 400	S&P Small Cap 600	Nikkei	FTSE	EAFE	S&P/ IFC	Lehman Corp/Tr Bond	MLynch CMBI	Morgan GGB	GSCI	REIT
1996	0.053	0.184	0.160	0.183	0.115	0.129	0.043	0.089	-0.005	0.015	0.073	0.339	0.3135
1997	0.055	0.270	0.266	0.219	-0.237	0.244	0.002	-0.159	0.145	0.043	0.091	-0.141	0.1789
1998	0.053	0.236	0.163	-0.021	-0.105	0.077	0.167	-0.249	0.129	0.036	0.096	-0.357	-0.1967
1999	0.050	0.178	0.125	0.109	0.225	0.061	0.225	0.513	-0.090	-0.008	-0.012	0.409	-0.0591
2000	0.062	-0.107	0.150	0.105	-0.240	0.016	-0.086	-0.382	0.187	0.038	0.080	0.498	0.2414
2001	0.039	-0.140	-0.016	0.056	-0.313	-0.198	-0.159	0.018	0.045	0.044	0.051	-0.319	0.1503
2002	0.017	-0.266	-0.168	-0.166	-0.033	-0.370	-0.098	0.066	0.161	0.042	0.082	0.321	0.0575
2003	0.011	0.234	0.293	0.318	0.083	0.209	0.302	0.452	0.033	0.035	0.022	0.207	0.3330
2004	0.013	0.087	0.141	0.195	0.075	0.084	0.162	0.143	0.078	0.023	0.048	0.220	0.2901
2005	0.036	0.034	0.209	0.067	0.411	0.167	0.163	0.385	0.043	0.057	-0.024	0.264	0.0904
Return													
GMR	0.033	0.055	0.124	0.098	-0.025	0.023	0.062	0.048	0.070	0.032	0.050	0.101	0.1273
AMR	0.039	0.071	0.132	0.106	-0.002	0.042	0.072	0.088	0.073	0.032	0.051	0.144	0.1399
Risk													
Variance	0.000	0.031	0.016	0.017	0.047	0.032	0.021	0.080	0.006	0.000	0.002	0.084	0.0264
Standard Deviation	0.018	0.176	0.128	0.129	0.217	0.180	0.146	0.284	0.081	0.017	0.040	0.289	0.1625
Semi–standard deviation	0.020	0.218	0.193	0.138	0.210	0.275	0.150	0.283	0.084	0.026	0.051	0.427	0.2013
Mean Shortfall	-0.016	-0.191	-0.152	-0.099	-0.184	-0.226	-0.132	-0.229	-0.067	-0.023	-0.042	-0.416	-0.1669
Return/Risk													
Arithmetic Mean/Stan-dard Deviation	2.1680	0.4050	1.0340	0.8250	-0.0080	0.2330	0.4920	0.3090	0.9010	2.9120	1.2510	0.4980	0.8609

Columns 3 to 9 of Table 4.2 present historic return and risk data for three well known U.S. stock market indexes—asset classes and four widely followed international stock market indexes. The three U.S. stock market indexes are the Standard and Poor's 500, the Standard and Poor's Mid Cap 400, and Standard and Poor's Small Cap 600, respectively. These are equity market capitalization weighted indexes of the largest 500 stocks, the next largest 400 companies and the smallest 600 stocks in the S&P universe. The international indexes are: the Nikkei 225—a price-weighted index of 225 companies traded on the Japanese stock market; the FTSE or Financial Times Stock Exchange 100—an index of the 100 largest traded companies by equity market capitalization on the London Stock Exchange; the Morgan Stanley Capital International EAFE (Europe, Australia, Far East) stock index designed to measure a broad collection of stocks in developed countries outside the U.S.; and the S&P/IFC (Standard and Poor's/International Financial Corporation) index of stock prices in 21 emerging markets.

The benefits from investing in international equities are not obvious from quickly inspecting the return and risk data for the seven stock market indexes in Table 4.2, but can be seen in some investment vehicles upon further analysis. For example, the GMR on the S&P 500 of 5.50% trailed that on the EAFE of 6.20%. One dollar invested in the S&P 500 at the beginning of 1996 would have grown to $1.71 by the end of 2005. In contrast, the same dollar invested in the EAFE would have grown to $1.82, a difference of 11%. At the same time, average returns on the S&P Mid Cap and Small Cap indexes were higher than those on any of the international market indexes as well as the S&P 500. Money invested in asset classes represented by the S&P Mid Cap and Small Cap indexes would have grown to larger amounts than the same amount of money invested in any of the international markets as well as the market for large capitalization U.S. stocks.

Turning to the three measures of risk, all are noticeably higher for the S&P 500 index than again, for example, the EAFE index. Examining the Mean Shortfall as an illustration, when annual returns are below the AMR for the S&P 500 they have averaged 19% less than the average. In contrast, for the EAFE, they have averaged only 13% below the AMR. Like the return data, however, all the measures of risk for the S&P Mid Cap and Small Cap indexes are better—in this case smaller—than for the international equity indexes and the S&P 500. The return-to-risk ratios tell a similar story.

International equities, as noted, are only part of the universe of international investment vehicles and are overshadowed in size by the global bond markets. Three indexes of return and risk for U.S. and international bond asset classes are presented in columns 10 to 11 of Table 4.2. They are: (1) the Lehman Brothers Corporate–Treasury Bond Index, and index of high grade U.S. corporate and U.S. Treasury bonds; (2) the Merrill Lynch Corporate Master Bond Index, a measure of returns on U.S. corporate bonds; and (3) the JP Morgan Global Government Bond Index, an index of returns on developed country sovereign bonds. The latter is our proxy for international bond investments.[10]

The return data for the bond markets reveals that the Lehman Corporate/Treasury index outperformed the other bond market measures by a substantial margin, and that bond market returns in general compared favorably to several of the stock market returns. Global government bond returns as represented by the JP Morgan index exceed those of U.S. corporate bonds as represented by the Merrill Lynch index. With regard to risk, the Merrill Lynch Corporate Master Index showed considerably less risk, regardless of the risk measure, than the other two bond market indexes. Moreover, all three measures of risk for all three classes of bonds were lower than for all of the equity asset classes. The data reaffirm the notion that bonds are less risky than equities. Additionally, in terms of return-to-risk ratios, the Merrill Lynch Corporate Master Bond Index demonstrated the best performance of all the bond and stock market classes, followed by the JP Morgan Global Government Bonds Index.

Investment committees rarely design investment policies calling for a fund to be allocated to only one asset class such as equities or fixed income instruments. Instead, funds are allocated across several asset classes. To appreciate the prospective benefits of international investment vehicles we have to look beyond the return and risk measures assessed above and address a critical question. Namely, what are the anticipated effects of including international securities on the return and risk characteristics of the fund portfolio? Undoubtedly, international securities should be included in the fund if they improve its expected return and/or risk features.

Two items of information are required to answer this salient question. First, we need estimates of the expected return(s) and risk(s) for the prospective international securities such as those presented in Table 4.2. The second and more important item is the expected movements of the returns on the international asset classes with those of the fund as it is presently constituted. These comovements in returns, commonly measured by the correlations of returns, are the key to the diversification benefits of international investment vehicles.[11]

---

[10] The Morgan Global Bond Index has a weighting of about 24% in U.S. government bonds and is therefore not entirely an international index.

[11] Correlation among asset class returns may be subject to instabilities over longer time horizons, necessitating a measure of the long-term comovements in asset prices. Cointegration measures provide for this and can be used for a dynamic analysis of correlations in returns.

Table 4.3 presents a correlation matrix for the thirteen assets classes listed in Table 4.2. The correlations are based on the annual return data in Table 4.2. For each asset class the pair-wise correlations of returns with every other asset class are depicted. Table 4.3 lists 78 distinct pairwise return correlations. The positive or negative sign of the correlation coefficient indicates whether or not the returns on the two asset classes rise and fall in tandem (a positive sign), or rise and fall in opposite directions (a negative sign). The numerical value of the correlation coefficient indicates the extent to which the returns rise and fall together or in the opposite directions. Ideally, the most substantial diversification benefits are derived from the addition of asset classes with large, negative correlations of returns to the return on the existing portfolio. Realistically, such assets classes are somewhat rare and so diversification benefits are more often obtained by including assets classes with positive but low correlations of returns to the existing portfolio.

The correlation matrix of Table 4.3 suggests that a variety of international securities are likely to enhance the diversification of a portfolio comprised of just U.S. asset classes. Consider first the return correlations of the three U.S. stock market indexes with the international equity indexes. Correlations with the Nikkei Japanese stock market are all positive but relatively low, ranging from about 0.10 with the S&P Small Cap 600 index to about 0.24 with the S&P 500. Slightly larger but nonetheless low positive correlations also are present among the S&P/IFC emerging stock market index and the three U.S. equity indexes. Including either Japanese equities or emerging market stocks in a portfolio of U.S. stocks is likely to lower overall portfolio risk.[12] On the other hand, the correlations of returns with the FTSE–U.K. stocks and, to a lesser degree, with the EAFE index are positive but relatively high. Noticeable improvements in diversification are not highly likely from adding these equities to a portfolio of U.S. equities. Finally, global bond returns have a negative correlation with U.S. equity returns, ranging from –0.09 to –0.22 with the S&P 500 and the S&P Mid Cap 400 and S&P Small Cap 600, respectively.

We next examine the return correlations among the U.S. bond asset classes, as represented by the Lehman Corporate/Treasury and Merrill Lynch Corporate bond indexes, and the international assets classes. The data in Table 4.3 reveal that the returns in U.S. bond markets are rather highly, negatively correlated with returns in international equity markets. The correlations are as large as –0.80 between the Lehman Corporate/Treasury index returns and those on the S&P/IFC emerging markets returns, and as low as –0.06 between the Lehman Corporate/Treasury index returns and

---

[12] The correlation between the Nikkei and S&P/IFC is 0.78 indicating these markets are reasonably close substitutes in providing diversification benefits to a U.S. equity portfolio.

TABLE 4.3 Correlation Matrix of Returns for 13 Asset Classes

	T-Bills	S&P 500	S&P 400	S&P 600	Nikkei	FTSE	EAFE	S&P/ IFC	Lehman Corp/ Tr Bond	MLynch CMBI	Morgan GGB	GSCI	REIT
T-Bills	1												
S&P Lg Cap 500	0.216	1											
S&P Mid Cap 400	0.218	0.830	1										
S&P Small Cap 600	−0.043	0.665	0.814	1									
Nikkei	−0.290	0.241	0.232	0.104	1								
FTSE	0.234	0.871	0.982	0.793	0.324	1							
EAFE	−0.275	0.717	0.635	0.475	0.683	0.657	1						
S&P/IFC	−0.525	0.192	0.122	0.264	0.784	0.167	0.626	1					
Lehman	0.058	−0.368	−0.181	−0.338	−0.604	−0.250	−0.512	−0.801	1				
MLynch CMBI	−0.147	−0.360	−0.050	−0.236	−0.265	−0.128	−0.369	−0.348	0.657	1			
Morgan GGB	0.270	−0.090	−0.223	−0.223	−0.768	−0.242	−0.546	−0.862	0.715	0.192	1		
GSCI	−0.109	−0.210	−0.021	0.100	0.506	0.009	0.141	0.338	−0.188	−0.371	−0.358	1	
REIT	−0.303	−0.022	0.263	0.660	−0.047	0.235	−0.089	0.079	0.010	0.066	0.012	0.368	1

the returns on the Nikkei stock market index. Adding international equities to a U.S. fixed income portfolio will clearly reduce the portfolio's risk. This is not necessarily the case with international bonds. The correlations among U.S. and international bond returns are positive and reasonably high at 0.71 between the Lehman Corporate/Treasury index and the Morgan Global Government bond index, but positive and quite low at 0.19 between the Merrill Lynch Corporate and Morgan Global Government bond indexes.

As few portfolios are comprised solely of just stocks or only bonds a final illustration of the potential benefits of international investments considers a simple domestic, U.S. portfolio comprised of stocks as represented by the S&P 500 index, bonds as represented by the Lehman Corporate/Treasury index, and cash equivalents as represented by Treasury bills. Employing the return, risk, and correlation data from Tables 4.2 and 4.3, the optimal complete portfolio—the portfolio with the highest return-to-risk ratio—comprised of these two risky asset classes and the so-called risk free security, when short sales are permitted, has an expected return of 10.00% and a risk as measured by standard deviation of 10.99%. Its return-to-risk ratio is 0.91.[13]

International investment vehicles can improve the performance of this simple, hypothetical U.S. portfolio if they improve its return-to-risk ratio. Accomplishing this improvement depends on the return-to-risk ratio of the international asset class and its correlation with the U.S. portfolio. In particular, if the return on the international investment vehicle divided by the product of its standard deviation times its correlation with the U.S. portfolio is greater than the return-to-risk ratio on the U.S. portfolio then the international investment vehicle should be added. This is summarized in equation 4.1.[14]

$$E(R_i)/\sigma_i \times \rho_{i,\text{us}} > E(R_{\text{us}})/\sigma_{\text{us}} \qquad (4.1)$$

where:

$E(R_i)$ = expected return on the international asset class

σ_i = the standard deviation of the return on the international asset class

$\rho_{i,\text{us}}$ = correlation of returns between the international and U.S. asset classes

$E(R_{\text{us}})$ = expected return on the U.S. portfolio

σ_{us} = risk of the U.S. portfolio

---

[13] This portfolio has an allocation of 46% to the S&P 500, 137% to the Lehman Corporate Treasury index, and an 83% short position in Treasury Bills.
[14] The discussion in this section is based on Robert Hodrick, "The Logic That Lies Behind Oversees Diversification," in James Pickford (ed.), *Mastering Investment* (London: Pearson Education, 2002).

Applying the data from Tables 4.2 and 4.3 we see that the ratios from equation (4.1) for the Nikkei/Japanese stock market; the S&P/IFC emerging stock market index; and the JP Morgan Global Government Bond Index are (in absolute values) 3.84, 1.63, and 1.42 respectively. Adding these assets classes would clearly improve the return-to-risk performance of the hypothetical U.S. portfolio. In contrast, the ratios for the EAFE and FTSE indexes are 0.69 and 0.27, respectively. Adding these international asset classes would not necessarily improve the performance of the hypothetical U.S. portfolio.

The average correlation between the U.S. portfolio return and the returns on the three international asset classes that would improve the return-to-risk measure on the U.S. portfolio is only 0.11. For the two international assets classes, whose addition may not improve performance, the average correlation of returns was 0.48. It is this low correlation that is responsible for improving the return-to-risk trade-off.

The number and variety of international investment vehicles has expanded rapidly in recent years in concert with the growth of the international financial sector, the expansion of the global economy, and the increased recognition of the potential benefits of international investing. New investment vehicles are frequently introduced, and existing ones are finding wider acceptance.

Investors seeking to purchase equity and bonds in one or a few international companies or countries can purchase securities directly in the financial markets of these countries. The transactions and administrative costs of such direct purchases may be relatively high, however, and the rules, regulations and operations of foreign securities exchanges may be significantly different from those of U.S. stock exchanges. American Depository Receipts (ADRs) are a popular alternative investment vehicle to direct international security investments. ADRs are claims to one or more shares of stock in foreign domiciled companies. ADRs are U.S. dollar-denominated claims listed and traded on U.S. stock markets. The foreign domiciled company agrees to conform to U.S. accounting conventions, and disclosure rules as set forth by the U.S. Securities and Exchange Commission. Moreover, some foreign domiciled companies have bypassed the ADR route and had their shares primarily or exclusively listed and traded on U.S. stock markets, making them readily available to U.S. investors. Equity and debt securities of U.S. multinational companies whose earnings and cash flows are highly dependent on international commerce also provide a vehicle for international investment.

In addition to the vehicles already mentioned, a growing number of closed-end, open-end, and exchange-traded international mutual funds exist. These funds may invest in stock and bond market indexes of foreign countries such as those discussed in Table 4.2; collections of companies in

one or more foreign countries; specific foreign industries; and single countries and regions of the world. Finally, for qualified investors private equity
and hedge funds offer international investment vehicles.

Investors in international securities may confront a range of additional risks not faced when they invest in U.S. markets and securities. Some
international security market indexes may be dominated by just a handful
of companies, tying their performance to a few stocks. Investors in these
markets are therefore exposed to *firm-specific risk*. Broad, macroeconomic
conditions in a country or region may unexpectedly deteriorate, exposing
investors to *economic/market risk*. In a related vein, nascent international
securities markets, especially in emerging economies, may be thinly capitalized and relatively illiquid exposing investors to wider price fluctuations, a
diminution in flexibility, and higher transactions costs. Moreover, the legal,
regulatory, and financial reporting standards may be appreciably different
in foreign countries. Institutions, systems and conventions for such thing as
corporate governance and the protection and enforcement of shareholder
rights may also vary considerable. These *country risks* are an incremental
risk to investing in international securities.

Dramatic shifts in government regimes, government programs, and policies may also be present in international investing. Debt defaults, currency
controls, taxes on repatriated gains, and industry and firm nationalizations
are a few examples of *political risk*. Changes in the foreign exchange value of
the U.S. dollar, whether they are nominal (inflation based) or real (adjusted
for inflation) are a further source of risk from investing in international securities. *Currency risk* may affect an investor's total return as the dollar based
returns from international investing depend on two fundamental factors.
First, returns depend on the net-of-expenses cash flows, such as dividends
and capital gains, derived from the investment. These returns are frequently
denominated in the foreign currency of the country where the investments
were made. The second factor is any exchange rate change between the time
the investment was made and the time investment performance is evaluated.
Depreciations in the foreign exchange value of the dollar, such that units
of the foreign currency can be translated into greater dollar amounts, will
boost the investment's U.S. dollar total return. Appreciations in the U.S. dollar will have the opposite effect.

Risks of international investing can be increasingly mitigated via the
use of derivative contracts discussed previously. The growth in the number,
types, market size and composition of the global derivatives market has
both encouraged international investing by providing vehicles for managing
the risks associated with it, and contributed to the expansion in the number
and variety of international investment vehicles.

REAL ESTATE INVESTMENT VEHICLES

Real estate is sometimes viewed by investment committees as a relatively illiquid and, therefore, unsuitable investment vehicle. It is argued that real estate's lack of liquidity arises because transactions occur less frequently, transactions costs of trading real estate might be notably higher than for financial assets, and real estate markets are thin compared to markets for many financial securities in that there are far fewer buyers and sellers. In addition, local knowledge such as an understanding of zoning regulations, property tax rates, building codes, and traffic patterns might be critical in making real estate investments.

Liquidity and local knowledge issues notwithstanding, there are a number of methods for investing in real estate. In the first instance, investment committees may approve direct real estate investments. Portfolio managers may then directly purchase undeveloped land, commercial properties, and residential structures or lend to others for these purposes. The investment committee may also permit joint ventures such as investments in master limited partnerships. Investment committees may also allow for less direct real estate investments via the purchase of equity and debt securities of companies whose assets, cash flows and market values are substantially tied to real estate market conditions.

Alternatively, investment committees may permit investments in real estate investment trusts (REITs). REITs are a type of closed-end mutual fund (discussed in Chapter 10). REIT closed-end mutual funds issue a limited number of shares to the general investing public. The shares are then listed and traded on either organized or over-the-counter securities markets, enhancing their liquidity. The proceeds from the share offering are used to acquire the REITs investments in real estate assets. Cash flows generated from the underlying assets as well as their risk then drive the demand for and the valuation of the REITs shares. As with mutual fund investments in general, REITs may provide a lower transactions cost means of investing in real estate or achieving diversification with it.

REITs are typically organized per the types of real estate assets they own. Equity REITs, as the term implies, hold ownership claims in real estate such as office properties, shopping centers, apartment buildings and other commercial ventures. Revenues are generated by way of a variety of fee and rental incomes from the properties. Mortgage REITs, in contrast, act as lenders to finance the acquisition, development and construction of commercial projects as well as to provide longer term financing for completed projects. Revenues are generated from the fees and interest income on the mortgages they hold. Hybrid REITs, a combination of equity and mortgage REITS, are another form of REITs.

REITs are not treated as corporations for income tax purposes. Earnings of REITs distributed to shareholders are taxed at the shareholder level, but not at the firm level. The tax code requires that 95% of a REITs taxable income be distributed to shareholders. Moreover, the tax code stipulates that at least 75% of a REITs gross income must come from real estate activities, and no more than 30% of it from real estate owned less than four years. Tax laws regarding the depreciation of commercial real estate are also an important feature of REITs as depreciation schedules can significantly affect the amounts and timing of cash flows.

Table 4.4 presents annual information on REIT returns and risk, based on monthly data from 1996 through 2005. Data are presented for Equity, Mortgage, and Hybrid REITs as well as for a Composite index. The return data show that, based on the Composite index, REITs have provided an average annual return of almost 14% from 1996 through 2005. Average returns ranged from a low of 9.43% per year on Hybrid REITs to a high of 14.54% per year on Equity REITs. The risk information, with risk measured as standard deviation about the annual average returns, show Mortgage REITs have the highest risk with a standard deviation of almost 32%, and Equity REITs with the lowest risk of about 16%. Returns on Mortgage REITs appear especially sensitive to changes in the level and structure of

TABLE 4.4   REIT Return and Risk Measures, 1996–2005

Year	Equity (%)	Mortgage (%)	Hybrid (%)	Composite (%)
1996	31.01	42.43	26.34	31.35
1997	19.15	4.96	10.73	17.89
1998	−18.24	−28.52	−37.65	−19.67
1999	−3.99	−35.19	−41.24	-5.90
2000	24.55	15.31	11.96	24.14
2001	13.68	60.04	43.31	15.03
2002	4.44	29.09	21.75	5.75
2003	32.31	47.10	46.00	33.30
2004	29.80	22.05	23.70	29.01
2005	12.66	−24.56	−10.56	9.04
Average return	14.54	13.27	9.43	13.99
Standard deviation	15.70	31.79	28.84	16.25
Return-to-risk	0.93	0.42	0.33	0.86

Source: National Association of Real Estate Investment Trusts.

interest rates. Returns on Equity REITs appear especially sensitive to trends in the inflation rate and overall macroeconomic conditions.

Interestingly, the data in Table 4.3 indicate that returns on the Composite REIT index are almost completely uncorrelated with returns on the S&P 500 and the Lehman Corporate/Treasury bond index. REIT returns have a low, positive correlation of 0.26 with the S&P Mid Cap 400 and a moderate-to-high correlation of 0.66 with the S&P Small Cap 600 index. The implication is that REITs may help to diversify a portfolio of large and mid-sized capitalization equities and U.S. bonds.

INVESTMENT VEHICLES FOR ACCREDITED INVESTORS

Regulation 230.501 of the U.S. Securities and Exchange Commission as used in its Regulation D specifies eight classes of accredited investors:[15]

(1) Any bank as defined in section 3(a)(2) of the Act, or any savings and loan association or other institution as defined in section 3(a)(5)(A) of the Act whether acting in its individual or fiduciary capacity; any broker or dealer registered pursuant to section 15 of the Securities Exchange Act of 1934; any insurance company as defined in section 2(13) of the Act; any investment company registered under the Investment Company Act of 1940 or a business development company as defined in section 2(a)(48) of that Act; any Small Business Investment Company licensed by the U.S. Small Business Administration under section 301(c) or (d) of the Small Business Investment Act of 1958; any plan established and maintained by a state, its political subdivisions, or any agency or instrumentality of a state or its political subdivisions, for the benefit of its employees, if such plan has total assets in excess of $5,000,000; any employee benefit plan within the meaning of the Employee Retirement Income Security Act of 1974 if the investment decision is made by a plan fiduciary, as defined in section 3(21) of such Act, which is either a bank, savings and loan association, insurance company, or registered adviser, employee benefit plan has total assets in excess of $5,000,000 or, if a self-directed plan, with investment decisions made solely by persons that are accredited investors;
(2) Any private business development company as defined in section 202(a)(22) of the Investment Advisers Act of 1940;
(3) Any organization described in section 501(c)(3) of the Inter-

---

[15] www.sec.gov Regulation D is entitled "Rules Governing the Limited Offering and Sale of Securities without Registration Under the Securities Act of 1933."

nal Revenue Code, corporation, Massachusetts or similar business trust, or partnership, not formed for the specific purpose of acquiring the securities offered, with total assets in excess of $5,000,000;

(4) Any director, executive officer, or general partner of the issuer of the securities being offered or sold, or any director, executive officer, or general partner of a general partner of that issuer;

(5) Any natural person whose individual net worth or joint net worth with that person's spouse, at the time of his purchase exceeds $1,000,000;

(6) Any natural person who had an individual income in excess of $200,000 in each of the two most recent years or joint income with that person's spouse in excess of $300,000 in each of those years and has a reasonable expectation of reaching the same income level in the current year;

(7) Any trust, with total assets in excess of $5,000,000, not formed for the specific purpose of acquiring the securities offered, whose purchase is directed by a sophisticated person as described in § 230.506(b)(2)(ii); and

(8) Any entity in which all of the equity owners are accredited investors.

As can be seen, the accredited investor designation pertains to a broad range of institutional investors and a reasonably wide array of individual investors, including most of the investment sponsors discussed in Chapter 1. These accredited investors are viewed, in the eyes of the SEC, to be sufficiently knowledgeable and sophisticated about investments such that they can consider allocating parts of their portfolios to investment vehicles that less knowledgeable and sophisticated investors can not consider.

Investment committees of accredited investment sponsors may want to consider these investment vehicles. They have been among the vanguard of the financial innovations that have been a theme of this chapter. We examine two types of investment vehicles available to accredited investors. They are hedge funds and private equity funds—the latter including venture capital funds and buyout funds.

While there are several notable differences between hedge funds and private equity funds, to be discussed below, there are also several important similarities we first present.

1. *Organizational form.* Hedge funds and private equity funds are generally organized as limited partnerships. The general partners are the fund's organizers and managers, and often invest a substantial portion of their own wealth in the fund resulting in a closer alignment of part-

ners' economic interest. Accredited investors are the limited partners. The partnerships generally have a fixed life that can range from 3 to 10 years. Limited partners may cede substantial control of their investments to the general partners. The general partners usually charge a management fee to the limited partners, and also receive performance-based fees which can further align partner incentives and interests.[16]

2. *Regulatory oversight.* Hedge funds and private equity funds are largely exempt from the reporting and regulatory requirements of the SEC, the Investment Company Act of 1940, and the Investment Advisors Act of 1940 that apply to most other investment vehicles. This exempt legal status is one of their defining characteristics, and provides them a range of investment strategies and tactics as well as a flexibility not found in other investment vehicles.[17]

3. *Use of leverage.* While data are not available, it is generally thought that hedge funds and private equity funds employ appreciable amounts of leverage or borrowed funds in addition to the equity funds contributed by the general and limited partners.

4. *Diversification and liquidity.* By their nature hedge funds and private equity funds tend to concentrate their investments in asset classes, trading strategies and tactics, industries and firms. As a result they tend not to be highly diversified investment vehicles. Also, the investments of the limited partners are generally expected to remain for the life of the partnership making such investments somewhat illiquid. Provisions for early redemption of funds are often a feature of the partnership agreement, and these features may make the investments more liquid but they may also be accompanied by various fees or penalties.

Hedge Funds

The often-cited history of hedge funds is that the first was started by Albert W. Jones in 1949. Jones's investment strategy employed a long (ownership) position in equities buttressed with leverage and a simultaneous short (sale) position in equities to "hedge" the underlying equity portfolio. Jones's fund also employed a performance based fee structure.[18] From this beginning hedge funds as an investment vehicle experienced a somewhat uneven re-

---

[16] The partnership organizational form avoids the double taxation found in corporate organizations making it particularly well-suited to hedge funds and private equity funds. This issue is discussed in William Fung and David A. Hsieh, "A Primer on Hedge Funds," *Journal of Empirical Finance* 6 (1999), pp 309–331.

[17] Hedge funds have come under greater regulatory scrutiny in recent years, but as of this writing no new regulations applying to hedge funds have been adopted.

[18] See Fung and Hsieh, "A Primer on Hedge Funds," pp. 314–315.

ception from accredited investors, marked by periods of growth and decline in their popularity and use. Starting in roughly the mid-1990s, however, this uneven reception changed markedly. In 1996, there were 1,076 hedge funds with $59.4 billion of assets under management. By 2005, these numbers had soared to about 7,000 hedge funds with more than $1.0 trillion of partner-invested assets under management.[19] Moreover, the total invested assets of hedge funds are likely substantially more than $1.0 trillion owing to their widespread use of leverage.

The investment goals of hedge funds are to provide 'absolute' returns to their partners and to provide diversification to the returns on portfolios comprised of typical equity and debt securities. Absolute returns have come to mean positive returns regardless of overall returns and conditions in the equity and debt markets. Hedge funds seek absolute returns by exploiting market inefficiencies as well as the mispricing of securities, and employing investment strategies and tactics other investors are unable to pursue because of regulatory constraints. As Edwards and Gaon note, "They [hedge funds] can trade any type of security or financial instrument, operate in any market anywhere in the world, make unlimited use of any kind of derivative instrument, engage in unrestricted short selling, employ unlimited amounts of leverage, hold concentrated positions in any security without restriction, pursue any investment strategy, hold long and short positions, use dynamic instead of buy and hold tactics, ..."[20] Hedge funds flexibility with regard to their investment strategies and tactics are thought to be a key advantage over other institutional investors.

Hedge Fund Research, a company specializing in data, information, analysis and research on the hedge fund industry, categorizes hedge funds by 20 distinct investment strategies. They are presented in Table 4.5 along with a brief description of each strategy. Most of the strategies employ leverage and rely on the use of derivative contracts. While other researchers may present fewer or more categories of hedge fund investment strategies, the salient point is that the universe of investment strategies for hedge funds is sizable and expanding.

The explosive growth in the number of hedge funds and the amount of assets they manage have focused the attention of a growing number of researchers on their return-risk performance and the diversification benefits they might provide. Performance evaluation has been complicated by

---

[19] The data are from Hedge Fund Research, www.hfr.com and exclude commodity trading pools, organizations similar to hedge funds but operated by commodity trade advisors (CTAs) who invest and trade via futures contracts. CTAs are required to register with the Commodities Futures Trading Commission.

[20] Franklin R. Edwards and Stav Gaon, "Hedge Funds: What Do We Know?," Columbia University Business School, 2002.

TABLE 4.5 The Variety of Hedge Fund Investment Strategies

Strategy	Description
Convertible arbitrage	Purchase of convertible securities, generally bonds, and hedge portion of equity risk.
Distressed securities	Purchase and/or short sales of securities of companies affected by distressed situations.
Emerging markets	Invest in securities of companies and sovereign debt of developing countries.
Equity hedge	Core holdings of long equities hedged with equity short sales and equity derivatives.
Equity market neutral	Exploit pricing inefficiencies among related securities and neutralizing market risk by combining long and short positions.
Equity nonhedge	Long equity–"stock picking" funds. May or may not hedge long positions.
Event driven	Investing in opportunities created by significant transactional "corporate life cycle" events.
Fixed income: Arbitrage	Investing to exploit pricing inefficiencies between related fixed income securities while neutralizing exposure to interest rate risk.
Fixed income: Convertible bonds	Long-only convertible bonds.
Fixed Income: Diversified	Investing in a variety of fixed income securities employing multiple strategies.
Fixed income: High yield	Investments in non-investment grade debt.
Fixed income: Mortgage-backed	Investments in mortgage-backed securities.
Macro	Invest based on expected shifts in global, regional, and national economic conditions and associated security price movements.
Market timing	Shifts among assets classes and securities based on anticipated uptrends and downtrends in prices and returns.
Risk arbitrage	Purchase of securities of companies expected to be acquired, and short sales of securities of acquiring companies.
Regulation D	Negotiated purchase of private security offering prior to public offering.
Relative value arbitrage	Investing to take advantage of relative price discrepancies across securities.
Sector	Investing in specific market sectors such as energy, financials, health care, technology.
Short selling	Sale of borrowed securities to take advantage of expected price declines.
Fund of funds	Investing with multiple hedge fund managers to obtain diversification of investment strategies.

Source: Hedge Fund Research.

a number of factors, some of which are not unique to hedge funds but are relevant to newer investment vehicles in general. These may include a survivorship bias where return data do not include returns for hedge funds that no longer exist owing to poor performance. A selection bias may also be present where, because performance results are voluntarily reported, poorly performing hedge funds will not report results. New hedge funds with only a short or 'instant history' of strong performance may also bias upwards the reported average returns for the group. Finally, traditional statistical models for capturing the sources of hedge fund returns may simply not work as well as they do for other investment vehicles, such as mutual funds, owing to the complex and dynamic nature of many hedge fund strategies.

The research on hedge fund performance indicates that many, but not all, of the investment strategies pursued by hedge funds provide the potential for diversification benefits. Hedge fund returns in many cases have low correlations with returns on stocks and bonds. For example, researchers at the University of Massachusetts report correlations of returns for hedge funds and the S&P 500 as low as 0.35 for hedge funds pursuing convertible arbitrage strategies, and as high as 0.76 for hedge funds following equity long-short investment strategies. The average correlation between the eight classes of hedge funds analyzed in the University of Massachusetts research and the S&P 500 was 0.50. Correlations of hedge fund returns with the Lehman Corporate/Treasury index were found to be considerably lower-averaging just 0.15 and ranging from a high correlation of 0.28 with the global macro investment strategy to a low of 0.06 with the event driven investment strategy.[21]

More importantly, this same research demonstrates that hedge funds have yielded notable improvements to the return-risk profile of stock and bond portfolios. A portfolio comprised of 40% stocks, 40% bonds and 20% hedge funds had an annualized return that was 119 percentage points higher and a risk that was 52 percentage points lower than a portfolio made up of 50% stocks and 50% bonds. Additionally, Franklin and Gaon report that, based on the research they reviewed, many hedge funds earn excess returns.[22]

---

[21] "The Benefits of Hedge Funds: 2006 Update," Center for International Securities and Derivatives Markets, Isenberg School of Management, University of Massachusetts, May 2006. The data in the study cover the period from 1990 to 2005. Eight separate hedge fund investment strategies are considered as well as a composite index of hedge fund returns.

[22] Edwards and Gaon also note (p. 21) that ". . . it is clear that still more (research) needs to be done before we can be reasonably certain that hedge funds do in fact earn excess returns."

Private Equity Funds: Venture Capital and Buyout Funds

Qualified investors have allocated substantial amounts to private equity funds, especially Buyout funds, in recent years. In discussing private equity funds, we make a distinction between Venture Capital funds and Buyout funds. While both types of private equity funds are similar in many important respects, there are also sufficient differences to merit a distinction.

Venture Capital funds are limited partnerships that generally make early-stage, equity investments in companies. The funds of the limited partners are pooled in a specific fund. Larger venture capital organizations may operate more than one fund. Most venture capital funds are independent partnerships, but they may also be affiliates of a larger financial services organization.

Although venture capital funds may occasionally make investments at later times in a company's history, they typically invest close behind so-called angel investors when a company is still young and its future is far from certain. As such, their investments are risky and higher expected returns are required to compensate for the additional risk.

Venture capital funds are involved or active investors in the firms receiving their funds. Their skills are in identifying, analyzing, evaluating and selecting—among thousands of young firms—the handfuls with the best chances of success. Additionally, venture capitalists will actively participate in the firm's growth and development. They may provide executive management and operating support to the companies in which they invest and almost always are involved in the firm's strategic decisions and direction by sitting on the company's board of directors.

Investments of venture capital funds are typically concentrated in a relatively small number of firms, diminishing diversification as the fund assumes firm specific risk. The fund's active involvement is one way they manage this risk. Also, firms receiving venture capital support often are in the same industry allowing the venture capital fund to take advantage of the industry-specific knowledge and skills they have accumulated. Moreover, venture capital funds may co-invest with other venture capital funds as a risk management strategy. Prospective investors in venture capital funds may also obtain some diversification via investing in so-called 'funds of funds,' which are a collection of venture capital funds.

Investor in venture capital funds obtain their returns in one of several alternative ways, but rarely before the life of the fund expire. One occurs when another private investment group purchases the equity stake of the venture capital fund. A second occurs when the firm in which the venture capital fund has invested is merged or acquired with another firm, including publicly traded firms. A third method is when the firm in which the venture capital fund has invested is brought public via an initial public offering of its stock.

Private equity "buyout" funds, like venture capital funds, are organized as limited partnerships and make equity investments in companies. A second similarity is that buyout funds are highly skilled in the identification, analysis, evaluation, selection, monitoring, and development of companies in which they invest.

One notable difference, however, is that buyout funds may more often invest in somewhat older, more established companies than venture capital funds. Because the investments are in somewhat better established firms, the risks and expected returns of investments in private equity buyout funds may not be as great as those in private equity venture capital funds. Moreover, the companies in which investments are made already may be publicly traded. In this case the buyout fund uses its equity investment to 'take the company private' by retiring its outstanding, publicly traded shares. The buyout fund may also employ substantial leverage in a process known as a leveraged buyout.

Once the company has become a privately held one, it then has greater flexibility to make organizational, managerial and operational changes designed to improve its profitability. Existing, underperforming assets and divisions may be sold; low demand product lines discontinued; and unprofitable markets may be exited. Investments in new assets, divisions, product lines and markets may be made. As the company's profitability improves, any leverage used in the buyout will magnify the buyout fund's return on equity.

Investors in private equity buyout funds receive their returns in much the same ways as do investors in private equity venture capital funds; namely via mergers, acquisitions, initial public offerings and the investments of new private equity partnerships. Buyout firms may also exit by recapitalizing the firms in which they have invested.

Annual return and risk data for venture capital and buyout private equity funds are presented in Table 4.6. The data are from Cambridge Associates, the leading financial and investment counseling firms on investment consulting, performance reporting, and research to nonprofit endowments and private clients.[23] Cambridge Associates annual data base on venture capital returns starts in 1981, while its data base on buyout firms dates from 1986. The "vintage year" is the year in which the fund started making investments. Vintage year funds formed since 2002 are excluded from the results as they are considered too young to have produced meaningful results. The "pooled mean net return to limited partners" is net of fees, expenses, and carried interest (profits to the general partners).

As can be noted from the table, annual returns to qualified, limited partner investors in venture capital funds have averaged a substantial 23%

---

[23] www.cambridgeassociates.com.

TABLE 4.6 Return and Risk Data for Venture Capital and Buyout Private Equity Firms

Vintage Year	U.S. Venture Capital Pooled Mean Return to Limited Partners (%)	U.S. Buyout Pooled Mean Return to Limited Partners (%)
1981	8.47	
1982	7.37	
1983	10.23	
1984	8.84	
1985	12.83	
1986	14.59	18.96
1987	18.31	10.84
1988	22.02	13.56
1989	19.23	23.17
1990	33.04	17.32
1991	33.66	27.21
1992	34.51	24.95
1993	47.52	24.91
1994	54.45	9.18
1995	87.84	13.15
1996	95.41	10.19
1997	85.90	5.63
1998	12.36	6.77
1999	−4.74	12.80
2000	−3.22	17.78
2001	−1.96	30.61
2002	3.69	25.08
2003	0.16	19.01
2004	−2.37	9.43
2005	−18.66	−7.88
GMR	20.07	15.28
AMR	23.18	15.64
Std. Deviation	30.16	9.15
Semi Standard Deviation	17.38	6.06
Mean Shortfall	−15.04	−5.48
Correlation of Returns	−0.06	

Source: Cambridge Associates. Data are as of October 2006.

per year over the 25 years ending in 2005. The range of these returns has been wide, varying from a whopping high return of 95.41% in 1996 to a low of –18.66% in 2005. The standard deviation of returns has been in excess of 30%. In contrast, annual returns to qualified, limited partner investors in buyout funds have averaged almost 16% per year. The range of returns in buyout funds has been much narrower than the range for venture capital funds; the highest return of 31% was recorded in 2001 and the lowest return of –7.88% occurred in 2005. The standard deviation of returns has been roughly 9%. The data are entirely consistent with our view that venture capital private equity funds are a higher risk–higher expected return investment vehicle than buyout private equity funds. Finally, it is interesting to note that the correlation between venture capital fund and buyout private equity fund returns from 1986 to 2005 was –0.06. The implication is that one type of private equity funds provides investors diversification benefits to the other.

COMMODITIES AND COLLECTIBLES

Commodities and collectibles are the final classes of alternative investment vehicles that investment committees might consider as appropriate for their funds. Commodities and collectibles both refer to tangible, physical assets. The distinction for purposes of investment consideration is that commodities refer to extractive resources such as oil, natural gas, precious and industrial metals, timber, and agricultural products that are often further processed and refined, while collectibles refer to human-made physical objects that are rarely further refined and processed once made. Art, antiques, stamps, coins, war relics are just a few examples of collectibles.

Financial innovations have affected the markets for commodities and collectibles in recent years, as has been the case with all of the alternative investments examined in this chapter. New products and markets exist for the purchase and sale of commodities and collectibles. Mutual funds for trading diverse baskets of commodities or specific groups of commodities now exist. New over-the-counter and exchange traded derivative contracts have been developed for hedging and speculating in commodities. Hedge funds may base investment strategies on expected developments in commodities markets, and private equity funds may consider investments in commodity processing and refining companies. Electronic markets for trading of collectibles may improve the accuracy and timeliness of information and lower the cost of trading, expanding the size and liquidity of collectible markets. These innovations are in addition to the traditional means of trading commodities and collectibles which include direct transactions on spot and futures markets and indirect methods such as the purchase of securities of companies involved in the operations of commodities and collectibles.

Investment committee decisions to permit fund allocations to commodities and collectibles should be grounded on the same criteria as with all other alternative investments: namely, the anticipated effects on the return and risk characteristics of the portfolio; their liquidity and transactions costs; the efficiency of the markets in which they are traded; and the investment committee's knowledge of the investment vehicle.

Investments in commodities are often thought to carry higher risk than investments in traditional debt and equity financial securities. The markets for many commodities are global in scope, and variations in prices and returns may be highly sensitive to small changes in market demand conditions. The production of commodities may involve high fixed cost, resulting in substantial operating leverage for commodity producing companies whereby earnings and cash flows are highly sensitive to variations in production and sales. Natural disasters, weather, climatic changes and a host of other shocks may significantly affect returns on commodity markets.

The Goldman Sachs Commodity Index provides excellent insights into return, risk and potential diversification benefits of commodities as an investment vehicle. The index is designed to be a reliable and publicly available benchmark of commodity markets comparable to equity indexes such as the S&P 500. A broad, diversified spectrum of 24 liquid commodities including energy products, industrial and precious metals, and agricultural and livestock products comprise the index.[24]

Returning to Table 4.2, the Goldman Sachs Commodity Index has the highest average annual return (14.40%) from 1996 to 2005 of all the 13 asset classes surveyed. The risk measures (standard deviation, semi-standard deviation, mean shortfall) for the commodity index are also among the highest of all the asset classes. Looked at in isolation, commodities are a high risk–high return investment.

Table 4.3 presents the correlations of returns between the Goldman Sachs Commodity Index and the 12 other asset classes. Returns on commodities have notably low to negative correlations with the returns on all the equity indexes, with the possible exception of the Japanese stock market. To an even greater degree than equities, returns on commodities have sizable negative correlations with bond market returns. The clear implication is that commodities as an investment vehicle offer the potential for substantial diversification benefits if added to portfolios of stocks and bonds.

As an investment vehicle collectibles may require highly specialized knowledge, skills and information. Markets may be quite thin, illiquid, localized in nature and the investments under consideration may require

---

[24] www.goldmansachs.com.

costly verification and safekeeping. Research on collectibles as an investment vehicle suggest that the majority yield lower returns and higher risks than equities, and often lower returns than bonds. Moreover, the research indicates the return on collectibles is subject to short-run kurtosis, that is, markets for some collectibles may exhibit boom and bust patterns. Finally, this research finds that returns on collectibles often fall as equity market returns rise, but that returns on collectibles remain flat as equity market returns diminish. [25]

SUMMARY

Financial innovation has profoundly changed the investing landscape, particularly with regard to the number, variety, types and markets for alternative investment vehicles. Alternative investments that in the not-to-distant past may have been considered inappropriate by many investment committees now may merit renewed analysis and evaluation. The effects of alternative investments on achieving a sponsor's investment objectives, especially as they apply to a fund's return and risk characteristics and to its liquidity are key criteria in evaluating the appropriateness of alternative investment vehicles.

---

[25] Benjamin J. Burton and Joyce Jacobs, "Measuring Returns on Investing in Collectibles," *Journal of Economic Perspectives* 13, no. 4 (Fall 1999), pp. 193–212.

CHAPTER 5

Return Measures and Reporting Techniques

S electing a money manager requires careful consideration of a variety of factors. The candidates' investment philosophy and style, risk tolerance, quality of service, and organizational support among other factors, requires the sponsors to make judgments as to the fit. One factor that should lend itself to ease of comparison is the relative performance of the money manager candidates. Unfortunately, this is not normally the case. Even after the selection process is completed, sponsors are still finding the task of evaluating investment performance challenging.

Traditionally, individuals responsible for monitoring investment performance are faced with difficulties in measuring accurately the returns achieved by funds and in evaluating the performance of the fund's manager. These difficulties are even more bothersome when the performance results of one fund manager are compared to those of other managers, composites, and/or indexes. Often the performance measures of the fund managers and the comparison group are based on divergent calculation methodologies. This prevents meaningful comparisons.

The investment community has long recognized this short-coming. As a result, investment professionals have adopted the *dollar-weighted rate of return* as a uniform measure of investment performance. Unfortunately, this measure has significant weaknesses. The actual performance results are distorted when the fund experiences inflows (contributions) and/or outflows (withdrawals) at any time during the measurement period. In these instances, investment performance is systematically overstated or understated, depending on the nature of the flows, (i.e., inflows or outflows).

DOLLAR-WEIGHTED RATE OF RETURN

An example will be used to illustrate the impact of cash inflow and outflows on this rate of return measure. The dollar-weighted rate of return (RR_{DW})

simply calculates the percentage of increase/decrease that the fund has experienced over a given investment horizon. This dollar-weighted rate of return is calculated as follows:

$$RR_{DW} = \frac{(MV_1 - MV_0)}{MV_0}$$

where:

RR_{DW} = the dollar-weighted rate of return

MV_1 = the market value of the fund at the end of the measurement period

MV_0 = the market value of the fund at the beginning of the measurement period

The calculation of return using this formula is straightforward. Let us assume that at the beginning of an investment period, a fund had a market value of $1,000,000. At the end of that same investment period, the market value of the fund was $1,030,000. The dollar-weighted rate of return would be calculated as follows:

$$RR_{DW} = \frac{(\$1,030,000 - \$1,000,000)}{\$1,000,000} = 3\%$$

As shown above, the dollar-weighted rate of return equals 3%. This rate of return appears to be a proper indicator of performance. In fact, the fund's assets increase from the initial value of $1,000,000 to $1,030,000, or by 3% over the measurement period. Thus, in this instance, the dollar-weighted rate of return correctly reflects the fund's performance. Please keep in mind that no contributions and/or withdrawals are made to the fund during the measurement period. The dollar-weighted rate of return measure, while simple to calculate, is not a suitable method for calculating performance in most cases. This is especially true when the amount of funds available for investing changes during the measurement period.

Impact of Cash Withdrawals on Return

For funds which either disburse funds and/or receive cash contributions, the dollar-weighted rate of return will produce misleading results. To illustrate the impact that contributions (or withdrawals) have on investment returns using the dollar-weighted rate of return, consider two index funds, both invested fully in the S&P 500 at the beginning of the investment period. Both funds remain fully invested in the S&P 500 throughout the period. However, Fund B is required to disburse $30,000 midway through the measurement period while Fund A experiences no increases or decreases during this time.

TABLE 5.1 Comparison of Investment Performance Dollar-Weighted Rate of Return Measure Cash Withdrawal Scenario

		Fund A	Fund B	
Date	S&P 500	Market Value (no withdrawal)	Market Value Prior to Withdrawal	Market Value after Withdrawal
1/1	$1,212	$1,000,000	$1,000,000	$1,000,000
7/1	$1,191	980,000	980,000	950,000[a]
12/31	$1,248	1,030,000		998,470

[a] Reflects $30,000 withdrawal on July 1 from Fund B.

Table 5.1 presents key data for both funds. Since both fund managers are pursuing the identical investment strategy, (i.e., invested in the S&P 500), their investment performance results should be the same. Yet, using the dollar-weighted rate of return method, Fund A's performance is 3%, while Fund B's is –0.15%. The cash withdrawal from Fund B is the only difference between the two Funds. All other factors are the same. Yet, in terms of the dollar-weighted rate of return measure, Fund B be would appear to have underperformed Fund A. This is clearly not within the control of the fund manager. Therefore, Fund B's performance results should not be influenced by the withdrawal of funds during the measurement period.

Using the above information, the dollar-weighted rate of return calculation is shown for both funds.

For Fund A,

$$RR_{DW} = \frac{(\$1,030,000 - \$1,000,000)}{\$1,000,000} = 3\%$$

For Fund B,

$$RR_{DW} = \frac{(\$998,470 - \$1,000,000)}{\$1,000,000} = -0.15\%$$

Impact of Cash Contributions on Return

This time we assume that one of the funds receives a cash contribution during the measurement period. Specifically, this time Fund B receives contributions of $50,000 (instead of the cash withdrawal in the previous example) midway through the measurement period. Table 5.2 presents key data for both funds.

As before, Fund A's performance as measured by the dollar-weighted rate of return does not change. The new calculation (with the contribution) for Fund B is as follows:

TABLE 5.2   Comparison of Investment Performance Dollar-Weighted Rate of Return Measure Cash Contribution Scenario

		Fund A	Fund B	
Date	S&P 500	Market Value (no contribution)	Market Value Prior to Contribution	Market Value after Contribution
1/1	$1,212	$1,000,000	$1,000,000	$1,000,000
7/1	$1,191	980,000	980,000	1,030,000[a]
12/31	$1,248	1,030,000		1,082,530

[a] Reflects $50,000 cash contribution on July 1 to Fund B.

$$RR_{DW} = \frac{(\$1,082,530 - \$1,000,000)}{\$1,000,000} = 8.25\%$$

Using the dollar-weighted rate of return formula, Fund B's $50,000 cash contribution results in an 8.25% return. Again, the managers of Fund A and B followed identical investment strategies. However, Fund B's $50,000 cash contribution results in a higher dollar-weighted rate of return, than Fund A. Thus the use of this return measure will provide misleading results when cash contributions and/or withdrawals are considered.

Obviously, in circumstances where funds were either added or withdrawn from the portfolio, the dollar-weighted rate of return provides misleading information. This is because the dollar-weighted rate of return is directly affected by the size and timing of these contributions and withdrawals. Since money managers cannot control these adjustments, their performance should not be evaluated on a basis of a measure which is affected by cash contributions and withdrawals.

TIME-WEIGHTED RATE OF RETURN

The previous illustrations demonstrate the limited usefulness of the dollar-weighted rate of return when evaluating the performance of money managers. Investment managers often experience cash inflows and outflows throughout the measurement period. Hence, the *time-weighted rate of return* (RR_{TW}) is the standard method employed to evaluate the performance of money managers. This performance measure, also referred to as the *unit rate of return*, considers explicitly the impact that the timing of contributions and withdrawals has on investment performance. Thus it allows for a fair evaluation of the fund manager's performance free from the distortions associated with the use of the dollar-weighted rate-of-return method.

This approach requires that periodic returns are calculated prior to any cash contribution or withdrawal. Each time a cash contribution and/or withdrawal occurs, the market value of the fund is adjusted by the amount of the cash flow. The new "adjusted" market value is then used as the base from which the next return is measured. This process is repeated when additional contributions and/or withdrawals occur throughout the remaining measurement period. The measure of calculation is as follows:

$$RR_{TW} = \left(\frac{MV_1}{MV_0} \times \frac{MV_2}{MV_1 + C_1} \right) - 1$$

where:

RR_{TW} = the time weighted rate of return
MV_0 = market value of fund at the end of period 0
MV_1 = market value of fund at the end of period 1
MV_2 = market value of fund at the end of period 2
C_1 = net contribution in period 1

The calculation of the time-weighted rate of return will be illustrated using the earlier example, Fund A and B. For Fund A, the return would be

$$RR_{TW} = \left(\frac{\$980,000}{\$1,000,000} \times \frac{\$1,030,000}{\$980,000} \right) - 1 = 0.03 = 3\%$$

The return for Fund A, using the time-weighted rate of return, is 3%. (Note that the result is the same as calculated earlier using the dollar-weighted rate of return. This is because the two methods yield the same results when there are no inflows or outflows during the measurement period.)

Fund B calculations will first be illustrated assuming that the fund experienced a $30,000 cash withdrawal (see Table 5.1).

$$RR_{TW} = \left(\frac{\$980,000}{\$1,000,000} \times \frac{\$998,470}{\$950,000} \right) - 1 = 0.03 = 3\%$$

Using the time-weighted measure, the return for Fund A (3%) is identical to the return for Fund B (3%), even though Fund B experienced a $30,000 withdrawal during the measurement period. Next, the time-weighted rate of return for Fund B is calculated under the assumption that a $50,000 contribution (Table 5.2) is made during the measurement period. The return for Fund B is

$$RR_{TW} = \left(\frac{\$980,000}{\$1,000,000} \times \frac{\$1,082,530}{\$1,030,000} \right) - 1 = 0.03 = 3\%$$

ANNUALIZED RATES OF RETURN

Typically, fund sponsors are concerned with investment performance over a multitude of time horizons. Indeed, it is not uncommon for sponsors to ask to see the performance results during several business cycles. Performance during both up and down markets can provide the sponsors insight as to the capabilities of investment managers. In fact, investment performance may be measured on a daily, monthly, quarterly, semiannual, or annual basis. Furthermore, investment performance can be reported over periods of 3, 5, 10, and 20 years if the data are available. Investment companies marketing their expertise regularly provide these return measures to potential customers.

Investment professionals recommend that performance measured over time periods of one year or longer be presented on an annualized basis. Providing this information requires that short-term performance measures be annualized or restated as average annual rates of return. The measurement of investment performance over more than one period is straightforward. To illustrate, consider the quarterly investment returns of Fund C which are presented in Table 5.3.

In order to annualize quarterly returns, the data must first be converted into returns relative. This is accomplished by adding 1.00 to the quarterly percentage return. For example, the first quarter (Q_1) return of 3.5% would have a return relative of 1.035 (1.00 + 0.0350 = 1.0350). The quarterly returns and returns relative are reported in Table 5.4.

Fund C's annualized return for 200X is found by simply multiplying the return relative for each quarter together (1.035 ×1.027 × 1.013 × 1.003

TABLE 5.3   Fund C Quarterly Returns

Quarter	Return
Q_1	3.5%
Q_2	2.7
Q_3	1.3
Q_4	0.3

TABLE 5.4   Fund C Returns Relative 200X

Quarter	Return	Return Relative
Q_1	3.5%	1.035
Q_2	2.7	1.027
Q_3	1.3	1.013
Q_4	0.3	1.003

= 1.07999), producing a 7.999%. Thus, $1,000 invested in Fund C at the beginning of the year would be worth $1,079.99 by the end of the year.

This process is also used for developing average annualized returns for longer periods. For example, the average annualized returns for a two-year period can be found by multiplying the eight quarterly returns relative. The five-year return would be found by multiplying the 20 quarterly returns relative during that period.

GEOMETRIC MEAN

The geometric mean is commonly used when estimating investment performance in terms of growth rates. Using the arithmetic mean, a more commonly understood measure, would be inappropriate. To see why, consider the investment performance of Fund D as presented in Table 5.5.

As the figures in Table 5.5 indicate, an initial investment of $100,000 invested in Fund D increases to $200,000 in one year (doubled). The $200,000 grew to $1,000,000 in the second year (increased fivefold). Using the arithmetic mean, the first-year growth rate of 2 is added to the second year growth rate of 5. The sum of these is then divided by 2, yielding an arithmetic mean growth annual rate of 3.5 times per year.

Table 5.6 reports the results of using the arithmetic mean as an estimate of investment growth rate. As the table shows, the growth rate of 3.5% computed above is applied to the initial investment of $100,000. At the end of one year, the initial investment grows to $350,000 ($100,000 × 3.5). If one applies the same growth rate to the $350,000 in the fund at the beginning of year two, then one would expect $1,225,000 ($350,000 × 3.5) at

TABLE 5.5 Fund D Market Values

Year	Market Value	Growth
0	$100,000	–
1	200,000	2X[a]
2	1,000,000	5X[b]

[a] Year 1 growth = $200,000/$100,000 = 2.
[b] Year 2 growth = $1,000,000/$200,000 = 5.

TABLE 5.6 Arithmetic Mean Growth Calculation

Year	Beginning Value	Growth Rate Value	Ending
1	$100,000	3.5X	$350,000
2	350,000	3.5X	1,225,000

TABLE 5.7   Geometric Mean Growth Calculation

Year	Beginning Value	Growth Rate	Ending Value
1	$100,000	3.1623X	$316,232
2	$316,232	3.1623X	$1,000,014

the end of the investment period. Clearly, the arithmetic mean provides an estimated value of the portfolio at the end of year two which is $225,000 greater than the actual value as reported in Table 5.6. Thus, the arithmetic mean's estimate overstates the actual value by 22.5%.

Next, the estimated growth rate is calculated using the geometric mean. Under this method, the first year's growth rate (2×) is multiplied by the second year's growth rate (5×). Then, the square root of the product (10) provides a 3.1623 geometric growth rate.

Table 5.7 applies the geometric mean growth rate to the $100,000 initial investment. As before, the growth rate is then applied to the initial investment of $100,000. This yields $316,230 ($100,000 × 3.1623) at the end of the first year. If one applies this growth rate to the $316,230 available at the beginning of year two, it will result in an estimated ending portfolio value of $1,000,014 ($316,230 × 3.1623). The slight difference ($14) is due to the rounding of the geometric growth rate.

This illustration demonstrates the superiority of the geometric mean as compared to the arithmetic mean when estimating the average growth rates of an investment portfolio. It is for this reason that the geometric mean is the preferred method for analyzing investment performance and is used by professionals.

TOTAL RETURN AND ITS COMPONENTS

The discussion of rates of return relates to the change in the portfolio's value over measured periods of time. This process involves the comparison of the fund's market value at the end of a specified period with its market value at the beginning of the same period. The percentage of increase or decrease represents the fund's total return. Return performance is then based on this measure.

Although performance measured in this manner is useful, decomposing the total return measure into its current income and capital gain (loss) components can provide valuable insight into how the total return is achieved. This is especially helpful in evaluating portfolios that have different goals. For example, a fund with an income objective would need to pay careful attention to the current yield component of the total return measure since it may be required to payout a specified amount periodically. Then the money manager would be limited to the amount of funds that may be committed to nonincome producing investments. In this instance, the performance should be compared to portfolios with similar goals and constraints.

On the other hand, for those fund managers where current income is not a factor, the capital appreciation component of total return would be of particular interest. Thus investment performance of these funds would require a comparison with portfolios that have similar objectives.

In any event, the partition of investment of portfolio performance in terms of capital gain (loss) and income is important to consider. The breakdown of total return into its components is as follows:

$$\text{Total return} = \text{Capital gain (loss)} + \text{Income}$$

The capital gain (loss) component is measured by calculating the percentage gain or loss in the fund's principal, that is, the percentage increase (decrease) in the market value of its assets. The income component is found by dividing the sum of dividends and/or interest income by the beginning market value of the fund.

Table 5.8 presents the total return and their components for Fund E and Fund F, each having an initial value of $10,000,000. Total returns are stated in terms of both percentages and dollars. Fund E is an income-oriented portfolio and Fund F is a growth-oriented portfolio. As the table indicates, Fund E's total return equals 10% and is primarily comprised of income (7.5%), with the additional return due to the appreciation of the fund's market value. Thus, Fund E has income equaling $750,000 available to distribute to its investors.

In contrast, the total return of Fund F is comprised mainly of capital gains or increases in its market value of its assets (9.5%), and to a much

TABLE 5.8   Total Return Components

Portfolio	Total Return	Capital Gain (Loss)	Income
In percent:			
Fund E	10%	2.5%	7.5%
Fund F	12%	9.5%	2.5%
In dollars:			
Fund E	$1,000,000	$250,000	$750,000
Fund F	$1,200,000	$950,000	$250,000

lesser extent, its income component (2.5%). While Fund F's total return is greater than Fund E, its income component is only $250,000 or 1/3 of that available to investors in the income-oriented fund. While total returns of each type of fund will vary based on market conditions, growth-oriented funds are designed to provide less current income to its investors than are income-oriented funds.

Dividend Reinvestment

No discussion would be complete without exploring the impact of dividend reinvestment on the growth of investment portfolios. Portfolio growth rate is not only a function of its investment appreciation (or decline for that matter). It is also affected by whether the income earned on the fund's assets is reinvested or disbursed. Therefore, funds which require that part or all of their income be distributed will experience a lower growth rate (assuming that the fund is appreciating) than if this constraint were not present. Consider the total return of Fund G in Table 5.9. The total return and its capital gain and income components are shown in the table.

Assume that Fund G has a policy requiring that all of its income be distributed each year. While the total return for the year is 10%, the fund's growth rate will only be 2.5%. If the fund is charged with distributing 5% of its total return, then the fund will grow at 5%. The 5% growth rate is found by adding the 2.5% capital gain to the 2.5% of income retained (i.e., 7.5% minus 2.5%) by the fund. Thus the growth rate of the fund is directly affected by its income distribution requirements.

As the previous example demonstrates, dividend/interest reinvested assumptions play a significant role in the calculations of returns. It is therefore necessary, when comparing performance between managers, that income reinvestment is treated in a consistent manner.

In addition to the size of cash distributions, the timing of the distributions will also influence growth measurements. Funds vary in the timing of distribution requirements. For example, distribution may be made on a monthly, quarterly, or an annual basis. These timing distributions may slightly alter the performance. Therefore this aspect of dividend/interest reinvestment should not be overlooked when evaluating the performance of portfolios and/or their managers.

TABLE 5.9   Total Return Components

	Total return	=	Capital gain (loss)	+	Income
Fund G	10%	=	2.5%	+	7.5%

FIGURE 5.1 S&P 500 Stock Index, Study of Total Returns

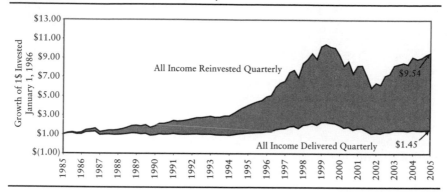

COMPOUND GROWTH

The effect of compound growth and the decision to reinvest income can have a profound impact on the value of a portfolio over a period of time. This consequence can be demonstrated by viewing the performance of the S&P 500 over a period of 20 years.

Figure 5.1 reports the value of one dollar invested in the S&P 500 over a period of 20 years beginning on January 1, 1985. As the graph illustrates, a dollar invested at that time would have grown to $1.45 by the end of 2005, assuming that dividends were distributed. If dividends were reinvested, the growth of the portfolio would have been even more dramatic. In this instance, the same dollar invested would be worth $9.54 at the end of this twenty year period. This represents an increase of more than 9.5 times the original investment, or more than 6.5 times the amount that would have resulted if dividends were distributed. The reinvestment of income is the key to achieving growth.

Gross versus Net of Fees

The issue of how to treat management fees when reporting investment performance is of particular interest to those responsible for evaluating fund managers. Some investment advisors report performance net of fees, while others provide investment performance figures without adjusting for fees. This gross fees approach is the preferred way of evaluating investment performance, since it is free from distortions due to varying fee schedules.

Consider the performance results and fees charged by the two money managers presented in Table 5.10. Fund manager H's investment perfor-

TABLE 5.10   Comparison of Money Managers Investment Performance (Gross Fees versus Net Fees)

	Fund H	Fund I
Return (Gross)	14.2%	13.9%
Fees	0.9	0.4
Return (Net)	13.1%	13.5%

mance during the measurement period was 14.1%, compared to 13.9% for the manager of Fund I. Over the measurement period, Fund G earned a higher return. However, if the comparison is made on a net fee basis, Fund Manager I's lower fees result in a return of 13.5%, as compared to 13.1% for Fund H, in spite of the fact that Fund I earned a higher return as measured by investment performance. Obviously, it is also important for evaluators to consider the cost of investment portfolio management services. Currently, the investment community recommends that portfolio managers present returns on a gross fee basis. The CFA Institute also recommends that returns be reported gross of fees (both Investment Management and Administrative Fees,) but before the deduction of taxes.[1] Portfolio evaluators may request performance figures on both a gross and net of fee basis.

Mutual Funds

Mutual funds are held to a different reporting standard as defined by the Securities and Exchange Commission (SEC). They require the deduction of investment and administrative fees from the funds' net asset value (NAV) therefore mandating a net of fee calculation in the reporting of fund performance.

Alternative Investments

Private Equity

A special treatment is necessary when one evaluates private equity deals. Unlike public equity securities, investing in private equity funds normally command a fixed commitment to the agreed investment principal. Another important difference between public and private funds centers on the timing of cash flows. Under private equity funds the timing of the cash flows are perfectly under the control of the manager. In fact, the timing and amount of cash flows must be factored in using the discounted cash flow method for

---

[1] 2005–06, CFA Institute—Provisions of *The Global Investment Performance Standards*. CFA® and GIPS® are trademarks owned by CFA Institute.

calculating the private equity funds' internal rate of return. As noted early in this chapter, the internal rate of return (IRR) is a dollar-weighted rate of return calculation. Further, we already know that for public equity security portfolios, the time-weighted rate of return is the preferred method of reporting those results.

Alternative investments as a vehicle is becoming increasingly popular, if not demanded, for endowments, foundations and retirement plans. Indeed, this asset class can offer greatly enhanced returns, albeit at greater volatility (risk) in the achievement of those returns, but still a reality that investment committees, investment managers, and investment consultants must reconcile in reporting total portfolio performance results. When evaluating a client's portfolio, one must ask, what return should be reported?

The problem arises because thus far, we have discussed the reporting of only time-weighted rates of return and it is relatively easy to composite several managers' returns when they are all of similar publicly traded status. However, in private equity investments, it is often several years (as many as five to seven) before the investor's original capital begins to be returned. Also, in the first several years of the investment life, capital is continually invested, thus showing negative cash flows on the part of the investor.

There are specific requirements associated with the reporting of investment performance for private equity funds. The CFA Institute indicates that private equity investments should be kept in separate composites and even should be segregated by vintage year of the private equity fund presenting investment results for this investment type.[2] Therefore, keeping in this spirit, is it appropriate that the calculations should omit the values and cash flows associated with the private equity fund(s) when reporting total portfolio performance return for the latest period? Further, with regard to private equity funds, the should the evaluator refrain from reporting any returns until a significant portion of the investment's life has expired? This is questioned because the IRR calculated can be misleading as it won't include a significant portion of the investment's cash flow and any projection of remaining cash flows is speculative until the last portion of the life cycle.

We also realize, however, the desire for investment committees to determine if the private equity investment added value. The investment committee could decide to include in the total portfolio return calculation, the private equity market values and cash flows. However, the user of this practice should recognize that there will be periods of skewed returns both negatively and positively depending on the life cycle of the private equity investment. It is also possible to calculate a weighted return, based on market value, of the final IRR of the private equity Investment and the marketable securities

---

[2] 2005–06, CFA Institute—Provisions of *The Global Investment Performance Standards*. CFA® and GIPS® are trademarks owned by CFA Institute.

TABLE 5.11   Private Equity Funds

Calculation	Valuation	Percent of Total	Return		Weighted Return
Marketable securities	$50 million	90.9% ×	8.5%	=	7.73%
Private equity fund	$5 million	9.1% ×	21.0%	=	1.91%
Total portfolio	$55 million	100.0%	Total		9.64%

portfolio in the following manner, as shown in Table 5.11, for a hypothetical private equity fund that existed for 12 years:

Marketable securities portfolio: Market value = $50 million
12-year annualized time-weighted return = 8.5%
Private equity fund: Total investment returned = $5 million
12-year internal rate of return = 21%

While this should be noted as only an approximation of the total portfolio's accomplishment including the private equity fund, it will give the investment committee a fairly good feel for the overall result.

SUMMARY

The success of a portfolio is ultimately determined by the rate of return that it has achieved over a specified period of time, given an acceptable risk level. This rate of return is compared with a predetermined index and/or "goal" to determine if the portfolio has earned an acceptable return. The actual target set must be consistent with the investment and risk objectives of the portfolio as spelled out in the investment policy statement. For example, if the investment objectives require the portfolio to assume a specified risk level, then an index and/or required return which reflects that level of risk must be used.

In addition to the appropriate level of return, the portfolio measurement period must be established. A portfolio's performance typically is measured on a quarterly, semi-annual, or annual basis. Over the long term, it is useful to measure performance over a given market cycle. The latter measurement period is important when comparing portfolios with differing investment approaches. Evaluation of investment performance over a full market cycle provides vital information as to the portfolio's sensitivity to varying market conditions. Furthermore, it affords investment managers an opportunity to focus on the long-term, rather than being overly preoccupied with short term results. To be sure, the choice of investment target returns and measurement periods are important. It is equally important that the appropriate return measure be used.

CHAPTER 6

Return-Risk Measurement

In the preceding chapter, a number of measures of investment return were presented as criteria to aid in the evaluation of investment performance. These performance measures are important to understand. However, judging investment performance solely on the basis of return measures is incomplete and will likely result in poor decisions. Risk must also be considered when evaluating portfolio performance. In essence, the art of investing requires the fund manager to balance the returns in risk in a multitude of investment climates. It is equally imperative that those individuals charged with investment oversight, have an equal grasp of these performance measures. This chapter is designed to provide the reader with a better understanding of return measures in the context of risk.

Risk is the probability or likelihood that the actual investment performance will be different from the desired or expected investment performance. The greater this likelihood, the higher are the risks. Risk aversion typifies most investors. That is, risk is undesirable and, as a consequence, most investors must be compensated for assuming higher risks with the expectations of higher returns. Given two portfolios with identical returns, the portfolio with lower risk is more desirable. Likewise, at a given level of risk, the portfolio with the higher return is preferred. Thus portfolio performance must be evaluated on a return-risk basis. In this chapter, the return-risk measures typically used to evaluate portfolio performance results are presented and discussed.

RETURN RELATIVE

In the last chapter, the return relative was developed to measure investment performance over specific time periods. Table 6.1 presents quarterly returns, return relatives, and cumulative return relatives for both the Index and Fund I for a 20 quarter period. Recall from Chapter 5 that the return relative is simply the quarterly return plus one. As shown in the table, the Index's return relative for the first quarter is 0.97 (i.e., −0.030 + 1.00). The cumulative return relative is found by linking (i.e., multiplying) the individual return relatives. For period two, the cumulative return relative for the Index is 1.0309, or 0.970 times 1.0628.

Using the information contained in this table, the annualized return for the entire 20 quarters or 5 years for the Index and Fund I can be found. The five-year average annualized return for the Index is 1.0865 (i.e., $[1.5143^{(0.2)}]$), or 8.65%, while the five-year average annualized return for Fund I is 1.1236 (i.e., $[1.7907^{(0.2)}]$), or 12.36%. An investment in the Index would have provided an average annualized return of 8.65%, whereas, an investment in Fund I would have generated a significantly higher average return of 12.36% over this same time period. Thus, on the basis of return,

TABLE 6.1 Index and Fund I Return Relatives

	Index			Fund I		
Period	Quarterly Return	Return Relative	Cumulative Return Relative	Quarterly Return	Return Relative	Cumulative Return Relative
1	−0.0300	0.9700		−0.0302	0.9698	
2	0.0628	1.0628	1.0309	0.0750	1.0750	1.0425
3	−0.1372	0.8628	0.8895	−0.1500	0.8500	0.8862
4	0.0891	1.0891	0.9687	0.0950	1.0950	0.9703
5	0.1449	1.1449	1.1091	0.1500	1.1500	1.1158
6	−0.0019	0.9981	1.1069	−0.0001	0.9999	1.1158
7	0.0535	1.0535	1.1662	0.0750	1.0750	1.1995
8	0.0831	1.0831	1.2631	0.1050	1.1050	1.3254
9	−0.0254	0.9746	1.2310	−0.0260	0.9740	1.2909
10	0.0194	1.0194	1.2549	0.0310	1.0310	1.3309
11	0.0308	1.0308	1.2936	0.0440	1.0440	1.3895
12	0.0508	1.0508	1.3593	0.0580	1.0580	1.4701
13	0.0427	1.0427	1.4173	0.0550	1.0550	1.5510
14	0.0052	1.0052	1.4247	0.0350	1.0350	1.6053
15	0.0255	1.0255	1.4610	−0.0050	0.9950	1.5972
16	0.0230	1.0230	1.4946	0.0560	1.0560	1.6867
17	0.0986	1.0986	1.6420	0.1560	1.1560	1.9498
18	−0.1206	0.8794	1.4440	−0.1600	0.8400	1.6378
19	0.0490	1.0490	1.5147	0.1100	1.1100	1.8180
20	−0.0003	0.9997	1.5143	−0.0150	0.9850	1.7907

the investment results of Fund I were superior to the Index over this five-year period.

STANDARD DEVIATION

While Fund I is more attractive from a return standpoint, how attractive is it from a risk perspective? As shown in the table, the Index's quarterly returns ranged from a low of −13.72% to a high of 14.49%. Fund I's lowest quarterly return was −16%, while its highest quarterly return was 15.6%. Thus, the range of quarterly returns for Fund I appear to be greater than that for the Index.

Rather than visually estimating the range of variability of returns, a more accurate method of measuring risk, called the standard deviation is generally used. The standard deviation provides a precise measure of the volatility of actual quarterly returns relative to the average quarterly return. The resulting statistic provides the evaluator with a numeric estimate of risk.

Table 6.2 demonstrates this technique using the Index quarterly data from Table 6.1. Columns 1 and 2 represent the period and quarterly return obtained in the period, respectively.

Column three is the average quarterly return over the five-year period. Column 4, labeled difference, is found by subtracting column 3 from column 2. Finally, column 5 represents the squared difference.

When using annualized returns, it is customary to present standard deviations on an annualized basis. The formula for annualized standard deviation is as follows:

$$\sigma = \left(\left(\left(\left(\Sigma x_i - \mu \right)^2 \right) / n \right) 4 \right)^{0.5} \tag{6.1}$$

where:

σ = annualized standard deviation

x_i = quarterly returns

μ = average quarterly returns

n = number of quarters

Using the above formula and the data from Table 6.2, the Index's annualized standard deviation is also obtained.

$$\sigma = \left(\left(\left(\left(0.08600 \right)^2 \right) / 20 \right) 4 \right)^{(0.5)} = 13.11\%$$

TABLE 6.2   Index Standard Deviation

(1)	(2)	(3)	(4)	(5)
Quarter	Actual Return	Average Return	Difference (2) − (3)	Squared Difference
1	−0.0300	0.0232	−0.0532	0.0028
2	0.0628	0.0232	0.0397	0.0016
3	−0.1372	0.0232	−0.1604	0.0257
4	0.0891	0.0232	0.0660	0.0043
5	0.1449	0.0232	0.1218	0.0148
6	−0.0019	0.0232	−0.0250	0.0006
7	0.0535	0.0232	0.0304	0.0009
8	0.0831	0.0232	0.0600	0.0036
9	−0.0254	0.0232	−0.0485	0.0024
10	0.0194	0.0232	−0.0037	0.0000
11	0.0308	0.0232	0.0077	0.0001
12	0.0508	0.0232	0.0277	0.0008
13	0.0427	0.0232	0.0196	0.0004
14	0.0052	0.0232	−0.0179	0.0003
15	0.0255	0.0232	0.0024	0.0000
16	0.0230	0.0232	−0.0001	0.0000
17	0.0986	0.0232	0.0755	0.0057
18	−0.1206	0.0232	−0.1438	0.0207
19	0.0490	0.0232	0.0259	0.0007
20	−0.0003	0.0232	−0.0235	0.0005
			Sum =	0.08600

Fund I's standard deviation calculations are presented in Table 6.3. As before, Columns 1, 2, and 3 represent the period, quarterly return, and average quarterly return, respectively. Columns 4 and 5 represent the difference and squared differences, respectively. Using equation (6.1) and the data from Table 6.3, Fund I's annualized standard deviation is found as follows:

$$\sigma = ((((0.06600)^2)/20)4)^{(0.5)} = 16.26\%$$

A comparison of the annualized standard deviations reveals that the Index has less risk than that of Fund I. The annualized standard deviation of the Index is 13.11%, while it is 16.26%% for Fund I. Therefore, on this basis, Fund I exposes its investors to more risk than the Index.

TABLE 6.3 Fund I Standard Deviation

(1)	(2)	(3)	(4)	(5)
Quarter	Actual Return	Average Return	Difference (2) – (3)	Squared Difference
1	−0.0302	0.0329	−0.06314	0.003986
2	0.0750	0.0329	0.04201	0.001769
3	−0.1500	0.0329	−0.18294	0.033465
4	0.0950	0.0329	0.06207	0.003852
5	0.1500	0.0329	0.11707	0.013704
6	−0.0001	0.0329	−0.03304	0.001091
7	0.0750	0.0329	0.04207	0.001769
8	0.1050	0.0329	0.07207	0.005193
9	−0.0260	0.0329	−0.05894	0.003473
10	0.0310	0.0329	−0.00194	0.000004
11	0.0440	0.0329	0.01107	0.000122
12	0.0580	0.0329	0.02507	0.000628
13	0.0550	0.0329	0.02207	0.000487
14	0.0350	0.0329	0.00207	0.001439
15	−0.0050	0.0329	−0.03794	0.001439
16	0.0560	0.0329	0.02307	0.000532
17	0.1560	0.0329	0.12307	0.015145
18	−0.1600	0.0329	−0.19294	0.037224
19	0.1100	0.0329	0.07707	0.005939
20	−0.0150	0.0329	−0.04794	0.002298
			Sum =	0.00660

TABLE 6.4 Index versus Fund I Return-Risk Profile

	Index	Fund I
Five-year annualized return	8.65%	12.36%
Standard deviation	13.11%	16.26%

Table 6.4 summarizes the return-risk characteristics of the Index and Fund I. The Index provided investors with both a lower return and lower risk than those who invested in Fund I.

PORTFOLIO RISK MEASURE

Standard deviation provides an accurate assessment of the risk for individual securities. Risk measures for portfolios of securities also use variance, and its square root, the standard deviation. However, the computation of a portfolio's risk is more complicated than that for individual securities. This added complication provides the key to efficiently reducing risk via diversification.

Consider a portfolio of only two securities, stock 1 and stock 2. The actual return on this portfolio will depend on the returns obtained by each stock and the weights of each stock, that is the percent of the portfolio represented by each stock, in the portfolio as given by

$$R_p = w_1 r_1 + w_2 r_2 \tag{6.2}$$

where:

R_p = the portfolio's rate of return
w_1 = the percent of the portfolio invested in stock 1
w_2 = the percent of the portfolio invested in stock 2
r_1 = the return on stock 1
r_2 = the return on stock 2

The variance of this security portfolio is given by.

$$\sigma^2 = w_1^2 \sigma_1^2 + w_2^2 \sigma_2^2 + 2 w_1 w_2 \text{Cov}(r_1, r_2) \tag{6.3}$$

where:

σ^2 = portfolio variance
σ_1 = variance of stock 1
σ_2 = variance of stock 2
w_1 = the percent of the portfolio invested in stock 1
w_2 = the percent of the portfolio invested in stock 2
$\text{Cov}(r_1, r_2)$ = the covariance of returns between stocks 1 and 2

Equation (6.3) tells us that a portfolio's risk is determined by three items: (1) The risk associated with each individual security as measured by its variance; (2) the percent of the portfolio invested in each security as measured by its weight; (3) and the weighted covariance of the security's return. The covariance is the most critical of the three determinants. Covariance provides a measure of the degree to which returns on the two securities move together, that is, covary. Covariance measures the interaction of security returns. In our hypothetical two stock portfolio there will be two covariance; the covariance of the return of stock 1 with stock 2 and the covariance of the return of stock 2 with stock 1. While the numerical values of this covariance will be the same, both covariances are employed in the measurement of portfolio variance. This is the reason the third term on the right-hand side of equation (6.3) starts with 2. Hence, portfolio risk is comprised of the risk associated with each separate security plus twice the interaction of the security's returns as measured by their covariance.

To comprehend how important the covariances are in determining the risk of a portfolio of securities, consider an equity portfolio of 30 stocks. The risk of this portfolio will be determined by the:

1. Weight assigned to each stock, of which there are 30.
2. Risk or variance of each stock, of which there are 30.
3. Covariance of the returns on each pair of stocks, of which there are $N(N-1)/2$. In our portfolio of 30 stocks, there would be 435 covariances.

We can therefore conclude that it is the interactions of the returns on the securities in a portfolio, the covariances, which have the greatest influence on the portfolio's risk. This fundamental principle can be applied to reducing a portfolio's risk.

One practical shortcoming of using covariance as a measure of the interactions of security returns is that, in concept, the numerical values of covariance are unbounded, that is, they can assume any values. As an alternative, the correlation coefficient of security returns is used. The relationship between the covariance and correlation coefficient is given by

$$\rho_{1,2} = \frac{Cov(r_1, r_2)}{\sigma_1 \sigma_2} \tag{6.4}$$

where:

$\rho_{1,2}$	= the correlation coefficient of the returns on securities 1 and 2
$Cov(r_1, r_2)$	= the covariance of the returns on securities 1 and 2
σ_1, σ_2	= the standard deviations of the returns on securities 1 and 2

Correlation coefficients have the property of assuming values from a minimum of −1 to a maximum of +1. A correlation coefficient between the return on securities 1 and 2 of +0.5 would tell us two things. First, the positive sign indicates that the returns on securities 1 and 2 move in the same direction. When the return on security 1 is rising (falling), the return on security 2 is also rising (falling). Second, the magnitude of the correlation coefficient reveals the degree to which the securities' returns move. In our example of a correlation coefficient of +0.5, this would indicate that for every percentage point change in the return on security 1, the return on security 2 changes by one-half (0.5) of a percentage point.

The formula for portfolio risk can now be modified by substituting the expression for correlation coefficient for covariance to obtain

$$\sigma_p^2 = w_1^2\sigma_1^2 + w_2^2\sigma_2^2 + 2w_1w_2\sigma_1\sigma_2\rho_{1,2} \tag{6.5}$$

This equation for portfolio risk can now be used to illustrate how the adroit selection of securities with different correlation coefficients can alter the riskiness of a portfolio. We use the following numerical example:

w_1 = 0.50–50% of the portfolio is invested in security 1
w_2 = 0.50–50% of the portfolio is invested in security 2
σ_1 = 0.20–security 1 has a risk measured by standard deviation of 20%
σ_2 = 0.30–security 2 has a risk measured by standard deviation of 30%
$\sigma_{1,2}$ = +1, 0, –1 three cases for the correlation coefficient of returns on securities 1 and 2 will be presented:

Case 1: Perfect positive correlation between the returns on securities 1 and 2, ρ = +1.

$$\sigma_p^2 = (0.5)^2(0.2)^2 + (0.5)^2(0.3)^2 + (2)(0.5)(0.5)(0.2)(0.3)(1) = 0.0625$$
$$\sigma_p = 0.25 \text{ or } 25\%$$

Case 2: No correlation between the returns on securities 1 and 2, ρ = 0.

$$\sigma_p^2 = (0.5)^2(0.2)^2 + (0.5)^2(0.3)^2 + (2)(0.5)(0.5)(0.2)(0.3)(0) = 0.0325$$
$$\sigma_p = 0.18 \text{ or } 18\%$$

Case 3: Perfect negative correlation between the returns on securities 1 and 2, ρ = –1.

$$\sigma_p^2 = (0.5)^2(0.2)^2 + (0.5)^2(0.3)^2 + (2)(0.5)(0.5)(0.2)(0.3)(-1) = 0.0025$$
$$\sigma_p = 0.05 \text{ or } 5\%$$

Table 6.5 clearly reveals how including securities in a portfolio with the lower correlation coefficients reduces portfolio risk. In case 1, where the return on securities 1 and 2 were perfectly positively correlated the portfolio

TABLE 6.5 Impact of Correlation Coefficients on Portfolio Risk

Case	Correlation Coefficient	Portfolio Risk
1	+1	25%
2	0	18%
3	−1	5%

TABLE 6.6 Correlations of Historical Returns (15 years ending June 30, 2006)

Series	Large Company Stocks	Small Company Stocks	Long-Term Corporate Bonds	Long-Term Government Bonds	U.S. Treasury Bills
Large company stocks	1.00				
Small company stocks	0.84	1.00			
Long-term corporate bonds	0.08	0.03	1.00		
Long-term government bonds	−0.17	−0.22	0.88	1.00	
U.S. Treasury bills	0.10	−0.05	0.07	0.13	1.00
Inflation	−0.25	−0.17	−0.31	−0.18	0.02

risk was 25%. If the securities selected for the portfolio had been chosen so that their returns were completely uncorrelated, case 2, portfolio risk would have fallen to 18% or by about 28%. In case 3 where the returns on the securities had a hypothetical correlation of −1, perfectly negative correlation, portfolio risk would be only 5%, a situation where the portfolio would have shown 80% less risk than in case 1.

The lesson should be abundantly clear. To reduce portfolio risk, include securities whose correlation of returns is as low, ideally negative, as possible.

Professional investment managers seeking to reduce risk of their client's portfolios spend considerable effort identifying the correlation coefficients of individual securities or asset classes of securities. Table 6.6 provides a matrix of correlation coefficients for a number of asset groups. Such tables are used to choose assets to include in a portfolio so as to minimize its risk.

SCATTER DIAGRAM

The previous return-risk relationships are often compared to other indexes and/or portfolios using a scatter diagram. Figure 6.1 plots the return-risk

FIGURE 6.1   Return versus Risk

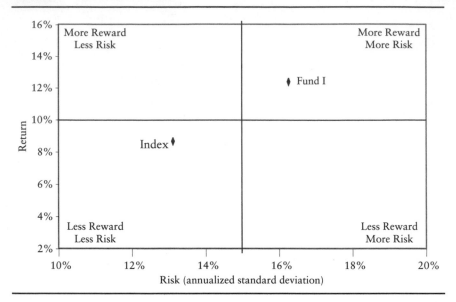

characteristics of the Index and Fund I, as well as other hypothetical funds (making up the universe) on a scatter diagram. The vertical axis represents the annualized rate of return, while the horizontal axis measures risk (standard deviation). The scatter diagram is divided into four quadrants, with the origin representing the median annualized rate of return and risk measures. Data points for both the Index (8.65%, 13.11%) and Fund I (12.36%, 16.26%) are plotted on the scatter diagram.

The actual points plotted will lie in one of the four quadrants. Portfolios lying in the northwest quadrant are the most desirable since they provide the investor with returns greater than the median level, and risks lower than the median fund reporting. In contrast, portfolios residing in the southeast quadrant are the least desirable, since these funds provide both lower returns and higher risks than the median portfolios.

COEFFICIENT OF VARIATION

The *coefficient of variation* (COV) provides a direct comparison between a fund's return and risk characteristics. The coefficient of variation is simply the fund's standard deviation divided by its return (arithmetic). This ratio allows the analyst to normalize risk relative to return. The higher the ratio, the greater the risk in proportion to return. Table 6.7 presents the coef-

TABLE 6.7 Index versus Fund I Coefficients of Variation

	Index	Fund I
Quarterly return	2.32%	3.29%
Standard deviation	6.55%	8.13%
Coefficient of variation	2.823	2.471

ficients for the Index and Fund I. As shown in Table 6.7, the coefficient of variation is 2.823 for the Index and 2.471 for Fund I. These data mean that for every one percentage point of return earned in the Index, 2.823 percentage points of risk were assumed; while to obtain one percentage point of return on Fund I, 2.471 percentage points of risk were taken. The coefficient of variation suggests that Fund I is more attractive as less risk is taken per-percentage point of return.

REGRESSION ANALYSIS

The investment performance of a particular portfolio is often compared to the performance of the overall market as represented by an index such as those presented in Chapter 2. Portfolio managers frequently compare their portfolio's return and risk attributes to those associated with a relevant market index. This allows inferences to be drawn regarding the performance of a fund relative the overall market itself. The evaluator can compare the investment performance of the fund relative to the risk being taken by the fund's managers.

Regression analysis is a valuable tool used by investment professionals in the evaluation of portfolio performance. The regression analysis yields the following equation:

$$Y_t = \alpha + \beta X + e_t \tag{6.6}$$

where:

Y_t = portfolio return in time period t

X = index return in time period t

α = regression intercept

β = regression slope

e = residual term

The above equation provides an estimate of beta, which measures the sensitivity of the portfolio's return to the market return. It measures the relative riskiness or volatility of the portfolio to the index. A portfolio with a beta equal to 1 suggests that the volatility of the portfolio is equal to that of the index, while a beta greater than 1 would indicate that the portfolio possesses more volatility than the market. Conversely, a beta less than 1 indicates that the portfolio's volatility is less than that of the market. The formula for beta is as follows:

$$\beta = \left[N(\Sigma x_i y_i) - (\Sigma x_i)(\Sigma y_i) \right] / \left[N(\Sigma x_i^2) - (\Sigma x_i)^2 \right] \qquad (6.7)$$

where:

β = portfolio's beta

N = number of observations

x_i = measured return of index at time I

y_i = measured return of portfolio at time I

The regression's intercept, alpha, measures the excess of the portfolio's return to that of the index. Alpha or the Jensen Index (JI), as it is commonly referred to, is an indicator of management's contribution to investment performance. A positive alpha indicates that the portfolio achieved a superior return to that of the index on a risk-adjusted basis. Conversely, a negative alpha would indicate that the investment manager under performed the market on a risk-adjusted basis. The formula for obtaining alpha (α) is as follows:

$$\alpha = (\Sigma y_i - (\beta\Sigma x_i))/N \qquad (6.8)$$

R^2, commonly referred to as the *coefficient of determination*, measures the degree to which the variability of the portfolio's returns is associated with the variability of the index. The formula for R^2 is as follows:

$$R^2 = \frac{N(\Sigma x_i y_i) - (\Sigma x_i)(\Sigma y_i)}{\left((N(\Sigma x_i^2) - (\Sigma x_i)^{2(0.5)})((N(\Sigma y_i^2) - (\Sigma y_i)^2)^{(0.5)}) \right)^{(2)}} \qquad (6.9)$$

This measure indicates the degree of diversification achieved by the portfolio, and can assume a value from zero to one. For example, an R^2 of 0.0 would indicate that none of the portfolio's variability is explained by the variability of the index. An R^2 of 0.9 would indicate that 90% of the variability in the portfolio's return is explained by the index. A portfolio with an R^2 of 1.0 is considered to be a fully diversified portfolio in that the only source of portfolio risk is the risk associated with the market index itself.

The residual terms, e_t, represent the difference between the actual return earned on the portfolio for a particular time period and the return predicted by the regression equation for that specific period. The residual term represents, therefore, so-called "forecast errors." These residuals also offer insight into the value of the regression equation. Ideally, these forecast errors are distributed such that episodes where actual returns on the fund are greater that the forecasted returns are canceled or offset by episodes where the opposite occurs. In short, the average forecast error is ideally zero. Moreover, ideally these forecast errors should have unchanging variability. In cases where these conditions fail to hold, the investment evaluator should look to other evaluation criteria, for their presence suggests that alpha and beta statistics are likely highly misleading.

PORTFOLIO SIZE AND DIVERSIFICATION LEVELS

Total risk or the amount of variability in a fund's return consists of systematic and unsystematic risk. Systematic risk refers to risk attributed to changes in the market index, while unsystematic or unique risk is that specific to an individual security's return. In essence, the R^2 measure provides information concerning the amount of portfolio variability which is explained by the market index. This portion of the variability in return is referred to as systematic risk. If the regression equation indicates that the R^2 is 0.9, then 90% of total variability is related to the market and the other 10% is unrelated, or unsystematic.

Studies have shown that by increasing the number of securities in a portfolio, the level of unsystematic risk decreases. Figure 6.2 illustrates this

FIGURE 6-2   Portfolio Size and Risk

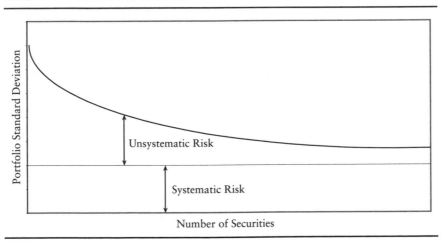

relationship. In fact, the drop off in risk is greatest in the early stages of securities additions. Furthermore, as more securities are added, the overall portfolio risk will decline at a decreasing rate. In concept, by adding additional securities, the total portfolio risk could decrease to the point where only systematic risk remains. At this point, the portfolio's R^2 will be 1.00.

REGRESSION ANALYSIS OF FUND I

Table 6.8 presents the calculations required in order to estimate Fund I's alpha, beta, and R^2. Using the quarterly returns, Fund I's alpha is estimated to be 0.512% (quarterly basis) or 2.05% annualized. Thus, Fund I's stock selection provides an annual return independent of the market. Likewise, Fund I's beta is estimated to be 1.2015. This indicates that the fund has

TABLE 6.8   Quarterly Returns of Index Versus Fund I

Quarter	Return (x_i)	Return (y_i)	x^2	y^2	$x*y$
1	-3.00%	-3.02%	0.0009	0.0009	0.0009
2	6.28%	7.50%	0.0039	0.0056	0.0047
3	-13.72%	-15.00%	0.0188	0.0225	0.0206
4	8.91%	9.50%	0.0079	0.0090	0.0085
5	14.49%	15.00%	0.0210	0.0225	0.0217
6	-0.19%	-0.01%	0.0000	0.0000	0.0000
7	5.35%	7.50%	0.0029	0.0056	0.0040
8	8.31%	10.50%	0.0069	0.0110	0.0087
9	-2.54%	-2.60%	0.0006	0.0007	0.0007
10	1.94%	3.10%	0.0004	0.0010	0.0006
11	3.08%	4.40%	0.0009	0.0019	0.0014
12	5.08%	5.80%	0.0026	0.0034	0.0029
13	4.27%	5.50%	0.0018	0.0030	0.0023
14	0.52%	3.50%	0.0000	0.0012	0.0002
15	2.55%	-0.50%	0.0007	0.0000	-0.0001
16	2.30%	5.60%	0.0005	0.0031	0.0013
17	9.86%	15.60%	0.0097	0.0243	0.0154
18	-12.06%	-16.00%	0.0145	0.0256	0.0193
19	4.90%	11.00%	0.0024	0.0121	0.0054
20	-0.03%	-1.50%	0.0000	0.0002	0.0000

FIGURE 6.3   Regression Equation Line

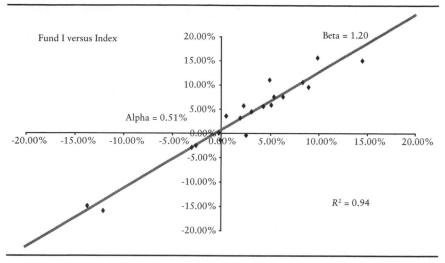

greater risk than the market as a whole. Finally, Fund I's R^2 is 0.936. This indicates that more than 93% of the variability in Fund I's returns is explained by the market.

Figure 6.3 presents the market characteristic line for Fund I. The results of the above regression analysis suggest that the fund has performed well on a risk-adjusted basis. The fund can be characterized as being well diversified and having more volatility than the market as a whole.

ADDITIONAL PERFORMANCE INDEXES

In addition to the performance evaluation techniques illustrated previously, there are two additional measures which are used frequently. The first measure, the Sharpe Index, is a measure of the fund's reward to variability. The Sharpe Index (*SI*) measure is defined as follows:

$$SI = \frac{(R_j - R_f)}{sd_j} \qquad (6.10)$$

where:

   R_j = the average return of portfolio j
   R_f = the risk free rate of return using Treasury bills
   sd_j = the standard deviation of returns of portfolio j

Note that the numerator of the Sharpe Index (i.e., $R_j - R_f$) measures the so-called excess return of a fund, while the denominator measures the fund's overall variability. In essence, the numerator provides the evaluator with a measure of the additional return or "premium" earned by taking on risk, while the denominator reports the level of risk taken during the measurement period. The higher the Sharpe Index, the greater return premium per unit of risk.

Another performance measure, the Treynor Ratio (TR), is similar to the Sharpe Index, except that it compares the fund's excess return to the fund's market risk, as measured by its beta. The formula is as follows:

$$TR = \frac{(R_j - R_f)}{\beta_j} \qquad (6.11)$$

where β_j = portfolio j's beta.

The Treynor Ratio relates the tradeoff between the additional return earned (i.e., above the risk-free rate) and the fund's exposure to market risk. The higher the ratio, the greater the benefit from the tradeoff. Each of these measures provides a basis for evaluating performance on a risk adjusted basis and can be useful in the evaluation process.

Yet another performance measure is the appraisal ratio (AP). This measure is the ratio of the portfolio's alpha to the nonmarket or unique risk of the portfolio. Recall that a portfolio's alpha measures the average return over and above that predicted by the market return, given the portfolio's beta. The unsystematic risk is that risk which, in principle, can be eliminated via diversification. Hence the appraisal ratio indicates abnormal return per unit of diversifiable risk.

The Appraisal Ratio formula is as follows:

$$AP = \frac{\alpha_p}{\sigma_{(ep)}} \qquad (6.1)$$

where:

AP = Appraisal Ratio
α_p = Alpha of the portfolio
$\sigma_{(ep)}$ = Diversifiable risk of the portfolio

SUMMARY

Investment performance must be evaluated on the basis of not only the returns, but also on the level of risk taken to achieve these returns. Along these lines, there are several tools available to properly gauge performance on a return-risk basis. These measures include the fund's standard deviation, its alpha, beta and coefficient of determination. Additional measures, such as the Sharpe Index, Treynor Ratio, and the Appraisal Ratio can assist one in evaluating portfolio performance. These and other similar measures allow for the viewing of performance results in the context of the risk associated with the fund. As such, they are important evaluation tools and should be relied upon as a part of the normal evaluation process.

CHAPTER 7

Portfolio Performance Evaluation

In this chapter, we focus on evaluating the overall portfolio performance, and the manager's asset allocation decisions. The chapter concludes with an examination of the cash and equivalent component of the portfolio. Chapters 8 and 9 will examine the performance of the equity and fixed income components, respectively.

Performance evaluation typically starts with an examination of the overall portfolio's total return and risk during a specific period. The evaluation process cannot be conducted in a vacuum. Rather investment performance must be compared to a predetermined set of goals in order to judge the effectiveness of the portfolio's manager. This requires the evaluator to compare the actual investment results with predetermined established benchmarks. These benchmarks, or performance requirements, are generally stated in terms of achieving returns relative to an index or selected universe as stipulated in the investment policy statement. The evaluator's role is simply to compare fund performance against these criteria. Furthermore, the evaluator must understand the underlying factors affecting performance results.

A portfolio's investment performance over a given period of time is the result of two important decisions made on the part of its management. First, the manager has to decide within the constraints of the portfolio's policy guidelines the appropriate allocation of assets among equities, fixed income, and cash equivalents. Second, the manager is responsible for the securities selected within each category. In evaluating the manager's investment performance, both of these factors must be considered.

Over time, the relative performance of the components alters the investment mix. For example, if equities out perform the other components, then its market value and therefore, relative weight, increases. If unadjusted, the investment mix shifts over time. To safeguard against the unintended shift in relative weighting, managers monitor this shift and rebalance the portfolio when necessary, to ensure that the actual asset mix is within the guidelines of the investment policy statement.

PERFORMANCE RESULTS

In order to illustrate the methods used to evaluate the performance of a given fund, a hypothetical balanced portfolio, Fund XYZ, is used. Table 7.1 reports the quarterly performance results for this fund over the 2001 (3rd Q) to 2006 (2nd Q) time period. Column 1 identifies the quarter, while columns 2, 3, and 4 report the investment returns for the Fund's equity, fixed income, and cash and equivalent components, respectively. Finally, column 5 represents the total quarterly return for XYZ Fund.

Typically, the investment policy statement allows professional managers to decide how assets are allocated between equities, fixed income securities, and cash and equivalents. Specifically, as discussed in Chapter 2 the policy

TABLE 7-1   Fund XYZ Quarterly Returns (%)[a]

(1) Quarter		(2) Equities	(3) Fixed Income	(4) Cash	(5) Composite
2001	3Q	−14.50	4.92	0.92	−7.13
	4Q	10.71	0.25	0.66	6.57
2002	1Q	0.20	−0.30	0.45	0.08
	2Q	−15.50	4.35	0.43	−7.95
	3Q	−19.00	6.25	0.42	−9.48
	4Q	8.90	2.25	0.36	6.05
2003	1Q	−2.00	2.65	0.32	−0.37
	2Q	16.00	4.10	0.29	10.86
	3Q	3.10	−0.75	0.26	1.66
	4Q	11.50	−0.10	0.25	6.90
2004	1Q	2.50	2.75	0.24	2.35
	2Q	2.25	−1.75	0.27	0.85
	3Q	−1.30	2.94	0.35	0.14
	4Q	8.50	0.95	0.46	5.43
2005	1Q	−1.75	−0.75	0.65	−1.21
	2Q	1.63	3.75	0.71	2.17
	3Q	4.20	−1.25	0.82	2.23
	4Q	2.25	0.75	0.93	1.67
2006	1Q	5.10	−0.85	1.08	2.91
	2Q	−0.90	−0.30	1.21	−0.51

[a] Portfolio weights: equity 60%, fixed income 30%, cash 10%.

statement specifies acceptable ranges for each asset component. For illustration purposes, we will assume that the portfolio is allocated over the measurement period as follows: 60% equities, 30% fixed income securities, and 10% cash and equivalents. These weights are assumed for both XYZ Fund and in computing the composite index.

In our illustration, we "rebalance" the portfolios each quarter, to maintain the initial 60% equities, 30% fixed income securities, and 10% cash and equivalents relationship. Thus portfolio performance is a result of these predetermined asset allocation choices. Later, we investigate the impact of the manager's asset allocation and securities selection decisions on the overall portfolio performance.

XYZ funds' total quarterly returns are derived by multiplying the individual asset class returns by their corresponding weights. These weights are the same as for Fund XYZ. For example, the total composite index return for the third quarter of 2001 is found as follows:

$$(-14.5\%)(0.6) + (4.92\%)(0.3) + (0.92\%)(0.1) = -7.13\%$$

COMPOSITE INDEX

Well, how did XYZ portfolio investment managers fare? To answer this question the results presented above in Table 7.1 must now be compared to the portfolio's investment objectives. One approach to evaluate the portfolio's performance will be to compare its measures with that of a composite index, consisting of equity, fixed income, and cash and equivalent indexes. As described in Chapter 2, there are large numbers of indexes from which to choose. The investment policy statement identifies the indexes to be used to evaluate investment performance. The selection of indexes must be consistent with the overall goals and objectives of the portfolio. This, in turn, gives the money managers a clear understanding of how their work will be evaluated.

For illustration purposes, the S&P 500 is used as the equity component, while the Lehman Brothers Government/Corporate index is used as a benchmark for the fixed income portion of the portfolio. Finally, the Lehman Brothers three-month Treasury bill index is used to evaluate the fund's cash and equivalent component.

The quarterly return for these three indexes over the five-year period is presented in Table 7.2. Column 1 represents the investment quarter. The investment returns of the equity, fixed income, and cash indexes are reported in columns 2, 3, and 4, respectively. Column 5 represents the composite index.

TABLE 7.2 Composite Indexes Quarterly Returns (%)[a]

(1) Quarter		(2) S&P 500	(3) LB Gov/Corp	(4) 90 T-Bill	(5) Composite
2001	3Q	−14.68	4.76	0.91	−7.29
	4Q	10.69	0.06	0.65	6.49
2002	1Q	0.28	−0.47	0.44	0.07
	2Q	−13.40	3.75	0.44	−6.87
	3Q	−17.28	5.70	0.43	−8.61
	4Q	8.44	1.73	0.39	5.62
2003	1Q	−3.15	1.65	0.30	−1.37
	2Q	15.39	3.52	0.28	10.32
	3Q	2.65	−0.50	0.25	1.46
	4Q	12.18	−0.03	0.24	7.32
2004	1Q	1.69	3.08	0.23	1.96
	2Q	1.72	−3.17	0.24	0.11
	3Q	−1.87	3.56	0.32	−0.02
	4Q	9.23	0.80	0.44	5.82
2005	1Q	−2.15	−0.67	0.57	−1.43
	2Q	1.37	3.44	0.69	1.92
	3Q	3.61	−0.96	0.80	1.95
	4Q	2.09	0.60	0.91	1.52
2006	1Q	4.21	−1.01	1.03	2.32
	2Q	−1.44	−0.14	1.16	−0.79

[a] Composite Index weights: equity 60%, fixed income 30%, cash 10%.

A comparison of Tables 7.1 and 7.2 provide the evaluator with quarterly performance of both the XYZ funds and the composite index. The data can now be used to quantify the risk and return measures for both portfolios.

RETURN-RISK ANALYSIS

Table 7.3 reports the return-risk characteristics of Fund XYZ and the composite index for the period from 2001 (3Q) to 2006 (2Q.) As the table reveals, Fund XYZs return of 4.22% exceeds that of the composite index (3.70%). In evaluating Fund XYZs performance relative to the other funds the quantification of its risk is also required. A common measure of risk, the

TABLE 7.3   Return-Risk Profile XYZ Fund Five-Year Measures

Performance Measure	Fund XYZ	Composite Index
Annualized return	4.22%	3.70%
Annualized standard deviation	10.09%	9.70%
Coefficient of variation	2.391	2.622

standard deviation, which we discussed in Chapter 6, compares the quarterly returns with the average returns over the period selected. Please note that Fund XYZs standard deviation is higher (10.09%) than the composite index (9.70%). Thus, while the comparison of a fund's return with other funds and indexes serves as an indication of its overall performance, it is also important to compare the degree of risk taken relative to other funds in achieving a given return. The resulting measure indicates the riskiness of the fund relative to its return. In the current case, the XYZ Fund has both a higher return and a higher risk than the composite index. Since this is the case, the evaluator must evaluate both funds by their returns relative to their risks.

In these instances, a statistical measure, called the *coefficient of variation* (the ratio of standard deviation to average return) can be used as a method of comparing return-risk measures. A larger coefficient of variation indicates that the portfolio has a higher exposure to risk per unit of return. A comparison of the coefficients of variation indicates that the composite index has a higher coefficient of variation (2.622) than Fund XYZ (2.391.)

UNIVERSE COMPARISON

The comparison between XYZ Portfolio and the composite index provides useful information. There are limitations however. Remember that the manager of XYZ portfolio must incur transaction costs during the measurement periods, due to commissions and other fees while the Index is a "pure" measure, not affected by fees. Furthermore, there may be additional costs borne by the investment manager associated with increasing the portfolio's scale of holdings.

Given the shortcomings of using composite indexes as a sole source for evaluation, investment performance can be compared to funds with similar investment objectives and constraints. These other portfolios are referred to as the investment universe. The comparison of investment results is often depicted graphically, to give a better picture of the range of performance among the universe participants. Figure 7.1 illustrates this approach using the bar chart form. Performance results for a universe of balanced accounts are reported for 1-, 2-, 3-, 4-, and 5-year periods. For each period examined, the range of returns is illustrated by the use of a bar.

FIGURE 7.1   Balanced Accounts (US$), Periods Ending June 30, 2006

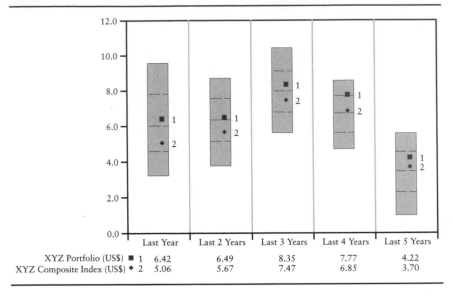

	Last Year	Last 2 Years	Last 3 Years	Last 4 Years	Last 5 Years
XYZ Portfolio (US$) ■ 1	6.42	6.49	8.35	7.77	4.22
XYZ Composite Index (US$) ◆ 2	5.06	5.67	7.47	6.85	3.70

Consider the rate of return data presented in year one. During this period, Fund XYZs return is 6.42% (square), while the composite index's return is 5.06% (diamond). Thus, for the one-year period, Fund XYZ outperformed the composite index in terms of return. In addition, it ranks within the 2nd quartile of all funds comprising the selected universe during the periods. Furthermore, it ranks in the top quartile during one out of five measurement periods. Fund XYZ falls within the 2nd quartile for all other periods measured. Fund XYZ outperforms the composite index for all periods measured.

The bar chart approach focuses on the return performance of funds. As mentioned earlier, it is important to view return relative to risk in order to measure performance properly. Once again, universes can be used to evaluate a fund's performance over time. A common technique utilized to compare a fund's return-risk measure to those of a universe is to graphically segment funds into quadrants. Figure 7.2 illustrates this technique, again using balanced accounts as the fund's universe. The composite is also plotted in this chart. Annualized rates of return are represented along the vertical axis, while annualized standard deviations are represented along the horizontal axis. The return-risk performance of each fund is then plotted on the chart. The chart is divided into four quadrants. The return and risk of the median funds within the universe are used to delineate these quadrants. Quadrant I (upper right-hand square) represent funds with high-return and

FIGURE 7.2 Balanced Accounts (US$), Five-Year Period Ending June 30, 2006

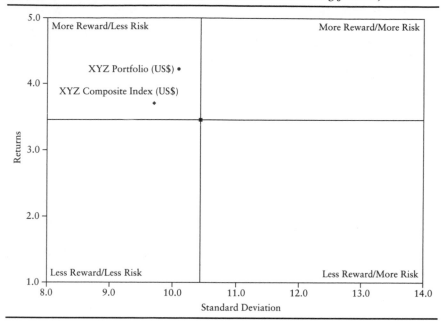

high-risk attributes. Funds found in Quadrant II (lower right-hand square) would represent low return/high risk, while funds in Quadrant III (lower left square) would be labeled as having low return/low risk. Finally, funds which are located in Quadrant IV (upper-left hand square) would represent high return/low risk portfolios. Ideally, fund managers would strive to have their funds located in the "northwest" or quadrant IV.

As indicated by the circle in Figure 7.2, Fund XYZ and the composite index are located in quadrant four. Thus Fund XYZ and the composite index compare favorably to other balanced accounts on a return-risk basis. Specifically, these two portfolios provide investors with a return higher than the median fund, while simultaneously exposing investors to lower risk than the median firm of balanced accounts.

EVALUATING THE ASSET ALLOCATION DECISION

Total portfolio performance will be affected by both the manager's asset allocation decision and the performance of the securities within each asset category. Significant insight into the evaluation process can be accomplished by separating the impact of the asset allocation and security selection decisions on performance results. The evaluator should examine the effect of asset allocation and security selection on a quarter by quarter basis. This technique is demonstrated using Fund XYZs and the composite index's most recent quarterly returns (Tables 7.1 and 7.2).

Let us assume that Table 7.4 represents the asset allocation parameters of the Fund XYZ. According to these guidelines, Fund XYZ's "optimal target" would be a portfolio that consists of the following weights: 75% in equities, 10% in fixed income securities, and 15% in cash and equivalents. This "optimal target" would be derived after considering the long-term performance of each securities class as well as the portfolio's goals, objectives and investment constraints.

Individual money managers typically are also permitted to allocate assets within a specified "range" around the portfolio's target percentage. In the current illustration, it is assumed to equal between 40% and 80% in equities, between 5% and 40% in fixed income securities, and between 0% and 20% of its assets in cash and equivalents.

Table 7.5 reports the actual asset allocation as well as the returns for each of the components. During the 2nd quarter, 60% of its assets were invested in equities, 30% were in fixed income securities, and the remaining 10% was in cash equivalents. Column 1 in the table represents the asset type, while column two reports the asset allocation weights used by the investment manager, and column three lists the second quarter return for each asset type. Finally, column 4 which is the weighted return is found by

TABLE 7.4   Fund XYZ Asset Allocation Parameters

Investment Type	Target	Range
Equity securities	75%	40–80%
Fixed income securities	10%	5–40%
Cash and equivalents	15%	0–20%

TABLE 7.5   Fund XYZ (2nd Quarter 2006) Actual Fund Performance

(1) Asset Category	(2) Actual Allocation Percentage	(3) Actual Quarterly Return (%)	(4) Weighted Return (%)
Equities	60%	−0.9	−0.54
Fixed income	30%	−0.3	−0.09
Cash and equivalents	10%	1.21	0.12
	100%	Actual portfolio total return	−0.51

multiplying the weights in column 2 by the individual component's return in column 3. Fund XYZs quarterly return is –0.51%.

As the table reveals, during the 2nd quarter, cash and equivalents provide the highest return (1.21%), followed by fixed income (–0.3%), while equities yielded the lowest return (–0.9%) during this period. This type of decomposition allows for an examination of the various asset categories' effect on investment performance (i.e., –0.51%).

Obviously, had the investment manager been fully invested in cash and equivalents during this period, total portfolio return would have been 1.21% rather than –0.51%. However, the portfolio manager was not free to invest 100% of the portfolio in cash and equivalents, but was limited according to the investment guidelines. Instead, a maximum of 20% was allowed to be invested in cash and equivalents. The next highest performance component for the period was fixed income securities. The maximum allowable invested in this component was 40%. The remaining 40% of the portfolio's assets could have been invested in the equities, the lowest performing component. While hindsight is always 20/20, it is nearly impossible to determine which asset class will be dominant during short term periods. However, the investment policy statement will define a "target" weighting for a given portfolio. Therefore, it is more appropriate to evaluate performance given the constraints placed upon the investment manager. Referring to Table 7.4, the "target" weights are as follows:

Equities	75%
Fixed income	10%
Cash/equivalents	15%
	100%

The maximum returns possible given the "target asset allocation constraint and securities selected within each investment category are presented in Table 7.6. As the table reports a total return of –0.52% would have been obtained if Fund XYZs asset allocation had been 75% in equities, 10% in fixed income, and 15% in cash and equivalents, while holding the identical securities within each category.

The portfolio's total return during this period would have decreased by less than 2% (i.e., –0.52% versus –0.51%) if the fund manager's allocation decision mirrored the targeted weights. It should be pointed out that this strategy exposed the fund to more risk, since equities are regarded as riskier than fixed income securities and cash equivalents. Nevertheless, this approach illustrates one can evaluate the effectiveness of the money manager's decision in terms of asset allocation contribution to investment returns.

TABLE 7.6   Fund XYZ (2nd Quarter 2006) Portfolio Return Assuming Optimal Asset Allocation

(1) Asset Category	(2) Allocation Percentage	(3) Quarterly Return (%)	(4) Weighted Return (%)
Equities	75%	−0.9	−0.68
Fixed income	10%	−0.3	−0.03
Cash and equivalents	<u>15%</u>	1.21	<u>0.18</u>
	100%		−0.52

TABLE 7.7   Index Fund Asset Selection Analysis

(1) Asset Category	(2) Allocation Percentage	(3) Quarterly Return (%)	(4) Weighted Return (%)
Equities	60%	−1.44	−0.86
Fixed income	30%	−0.14	−0.04
Cash and equivalents	<u>10%</u>	1.16	<u>0.12</u>
	100%		−0.79

Now that the influence of asset allocation on investment performance has been determined, we can now measure the contribution that each asset category had on the overall portfolio return. Table 7.7 report a "hypothetical" total return using index returns while retaining the fund manager's actual asset allocation percentages. The table reveals that given the fund's asset allocation, the fund's overall security selection fared well compared to the composite index.

The portfolio's total return during this period would have decreased by about 55% (i.e., −0.79% versus −0.51%) based on security selection. A closer look reveals that for the most recent quarter, the fund's equity performance (−0.9%) was better than the S&P 500 (−1.44%), while its fixed income performance (−0.3%) fared poorer than the Lehman Brothers Government/Corporate index (−0.14%). Finally, the fund's cash and equivalent component (1.21%) fared slightly better than the index's three-month treasury securities index (1.16%).

Finally, the impact of both the asset security selection decisions is examined in Table 7.8. The data in this table shows the portfolio's total return assuming:

1. The target asset allocation percentages previously displayed in Table 7.6 and

TABLE 7.8 Index Fund Evaluation-Asset Allocation and Selection

(1) Asset Category	(2) Allocation Percentage	(3) Quarterly Return (%)	(4) Weighted Return (%)
Equities	75%	−1.44	−1.08
Fixed income	10%	−0.14	−0.01
Cash and equivalents	<u>15%</u>	1.16	<u>0.17</u>
	100%		−0.92

TABLE 7.9 Fund XYZ Range of Possible Returns 2nd Quarter 2006

Investment Choices	(%)
Actual fund return (Table 7.5)	−0.51
Return if optimal asset allocation had been made (Table 7.6)	−0.52
Return if optimal security selection had been made (Table 7.7)	−0.79
Return if both optimal asset allocation and security selection had been made (Table 7.8)	−0.92

2. The quarterly returns achieved by the market indexes as reported in Table 7.7.

Note that the combination of the target asset allocation and the use of the index as a performance measure results in a total return of −0.92% compared to the −0.51% achieved by the investment manager. Thus the quarterly return is lower than the Fund XYZs actual return.

Table 7.9 summarizes the range of returns under various investment choices cited previously. Column 1 represents alternative securities selection and asset allocation choices available to money managers, while column 2 reports quarterly return associated with each choice. As the table reports, the highest quarterly return (−0.51%) was achieved by the money manager. Indeed, the target asset allocation percentage would have resulted in a slightly lower return (−0.52%), while substituting the index returns for the actual returns would have decreased the quarterly returns (−0.79%) even further. Finally, the use of the target asset allocation percentage along with the index returns would have produced the worse scenario, or a quarterly return of −0.92%.

The above analysis provides insight into the performance of Fund XYZ. The impact of the investment manager's asset allocation decision as well as security selection decision can be evaluated relative to assumed asset allocations and investment in appropriate indexes. In the previous example the investment manager invested less in equities than permitted (i.e., 60% versus 75%).

Portfolio Decomposition Analysis

The professional manager's decision regarding the portfolio's asset allocation as well as the selection of securities within these components determines the fund's relative performance. As Table 7.5 reported, the return on Fund XYZ was –0.51% during the second quarter of 2006. This return was due to the Fund's securities favorable performance relative to the individual benchmark indexes. At the same time, the actual asset allocation led to better returns than the target allocation. As Table 7.8 recounts, the benchmark portfolio was –0.92%. Recall that this return is based on a combination of the individual indexes' returns (i.e., S&P 500 total return index, Lehman Brothers Government/Corporate Index, and three-month Treasury bills) and the "target" weights (i.e., 75% equities, 15% cash and equivalents, and 10% fixed incomes securities. The difference between Fund XYZs actual performance results and "benchmark" portfolio is as follows:

Fund XYZ Return	–0.51%
Composite Index Return	<u>–0.92</u>
Deviation	0.41%

Thus Fund XYZs returns were 0.41% above the benchmark.

The relative impact of the manager's asset allocation, security selection and interaction can be separated to identify the source of this deviation. Table 7.10 reports the percent deviation caused by the suboptimal asset allocation decision. Column 1 represents the asset class, while columns 2 and 3 are the portfolio weights and composite weights, respectively. Column 4 represents the difference between the portfolio weights (column 2) and composite index weights (column 3). Column 5, labeled Return Difference, is found by subtracting the aggregate benchmark return (i.e., –0.92% [Table 7.8] from each of the benchmark's component returns (i.e., in the case of equities –1.44% minus –0.92%, or –0.52%). The same procedure is used for the fixed income and cash and equivalent return difference measures.

As the table reports, the manager's asset-allocation decision alone, resulted in 0.13% return increase from the benchmark. However, the total deviation between the Fund and benchmark index was 0.41%. Thus the manager's security selection and interaction had to increase the overall deviation by 0.28% (i.e., 0.28%).

This positive deviation can be isolated using Tables 7.11 and 7.12. In Table 7.11 (Security Selection Deviation) Column 1 presents the asset type, while columns 2 and 3 report the fund's return and the benchmark's return,

TABLE 7.10 Asset Allocation Deviation (Second quarter 2006)

(1) Asset Type	(2) Portfolio Weight	(3) Composite Weight	(4) Weight Difference	(5) Return Difference	(6) Asset Allocation Contribution
Equity	60%	75%	–15%	–0.52%	0.08%
Fixed income	30%	10%	20%	0.78%	0.16%
Cash and equivalents	10%	15%	–5%	2.08%	<u>–0.10%</u>
					0.13%

TABLE 7.11 Security Selection Deviation (Second Quarter 2006)

(1) Asset Type	(2) Portfolio Return	(3) Benchmark Return	(4) Difference	(5) Benchmark Weights	(6) Selection Contribution
Equity	–0.90%	–1.44%	0.54%	75%	0.41%
Fixed income	–0.30%	–0.14%	–0.16%	10%	–0.02%
Cash and equivalents	1.21%	1.16%	0.05%	15%	<u>0.01%</u>
					0.40%

respectively. Column 4 represents the difference between the portfolio's component returns (column 2) and the benchmark's component returns (column 3). Column 5 depicts the benchmark's actual asset allocation percentages. Finally, column 6 reports the Fund XYZs components influence on the security selection contributor.

As the table indicates, the manager's security selection had a positive impact on the fund's investment performance.

The final impact can be described as the interaction effect, the combination of asset allocation and security selection together and can be measured in the manner presented in Table 7.12. In Table 7.12 (Interaction Deviation), column 1 presents the asset type, while columns 2 and 3 report the fund and benchmark's return, respectively. Column 4 represents the difference in the portfolio's component returns (column 2) and the benchmark's component returns (column 3). Column 5 reports the portfolio's component asset class weight and column 6 reports the benchmark's weight. Column 7 reports the difference between the portfolio and benchmark's weight within the respective asset classes. Finally, column 8 reports the interaction effect which is simply the product of the difference in returns for the asset classes for the portfolio versus benchmark (column 4) and the difference in weights

TABLE 7.12 Interaction Deviation (Second Quarter 2006)

(1) Asset Type	(2) Portfolio Return	(3) Benchmark Return	(4) Difference	(5) Portfolio Weights	(6) Benchmark Weights	(7) Difference	(8) Interaction Contribution
Equity	-0.90%	-1.44%	0.54%	60%	75%	-15.00%	-0.08%
Fixed income	-0.30%	-0.14%	-0.16%	30%	10%	20.00%	-0.03%
Cash and equivalents	1.21%	1.16%	0.05%	10%	15%	-5.00%	0.00%
							-0.12%

for the asset classes for the portfolio versus benchmark (column 7). The summed effect for interaction contribution equals –0.12%.

The results of Tables 7.10, 7.11, and 7.12 are summarized as follows:

Asset allocation difference	+0.13%
Security selection difference	+0.40%
Interaction difference	–0.12%
Deviation of return	+0.41%

Thus the Fund's superior performance return (0.41%) was a result of its asset allocation decision (0.13%), manager's security selection decision (0.40%) and interaction impact (–0.12%). This approach can be employed by the investment committee to isolate the relative impact of the manager's asset allocation, security selection and interaction investment decisions on investment performance.

Nonnormally Distributed Asset Classes

In the previous chapter, alternative measures of risk for nonnormally distributed returns were identified. Before turning our attention to the evaluation of cash and equivalents, it may be useful to consider the impact of nonnormally distributed assets classes on portfolio performance. It has been proven statistically that investing in no, or low, correlated asset classes can lower a portfolio's overall risk, or, standard deviation, even if those newly included asset classes have higher risks when measured in isolation. Over time, asset classes' correlations have grown closer to one than moving lower.

Historically, investing in the international markets meant exposing your portfolio to more assets classes whose returns were either low or noncorrelated with those of a typical domestic equity portfolio. However, in recent years, as the economy has become more global, return correlations have increased therefore moderating the diversification benefits of international investing. For example, as we presented in Chapter 4 the correlation of returns between the S&P 500 and the EAFE indexes is about +0.71, indicating a reasonably low likelihood of diversification benefits from adding developed country stocks to a portfolio of large capitalization U.S. stocks. On the other hand, the correlation of returns between the S&P 500 and the S&P/IFC emerging markets index is only +0.19, suggesting adding emerging markets equities to the portfolio have the potential for reducing the risk when included in a portfolio of large capitalization U.S. stocks.

Investors have also turned to alternative asset classes to both achieve higher returns, but also lower overall portfolio risk as they are typically lower or noncorrelated to their typical marketable securities portfolio. This practice creates a new problem. These alternative asset classes typically have nonnormal return distributions. For instance, hedge funds depending on interest rate volatility will perform much better in periods of rising and falling interest rates influenced by Fed actions impacting interest rates. However, they will experience very unexciting returns during periods of interest rate stability.

These nonnormal return distributions make it very difficult to decide how much of a nonnormally distributed asset class to include in overall asset allocations. For example, typical mean-variance optimization models derive efficient portfolios based on means, risks, and return correlations of an asset classes. With alternative asset classes, however, they may have risk-and-return measures that are not comparable to more traditional asset classes. Inclusion of these asset classes may actually create concerns on the part of investment committees when their inclusion cause actual portfolio returns over short periods of time (one quarter, six months, one year) to be anything but normal. However, it is important to note that use of alternative assets are on the rise and those portfolios not including them may actually find themselves deficient when in comes time to measure their long-term return accomplishments. For instance, very large endowments (such as Yale) are using alternative investments in as much of 40% to 50% of their overall portfolios. Even endowments of less than $100 million are typically using at least 15% allocations to alternative assets classes.

The difficulty in modeling these nonnormally distributed asset classes is that we are still for the most part using traditional models (mean-variance optimization). There are models currently on the market that actually incorporate the skewness of returns created by these alternatives. These new models offer an approach to distinguish between upside potential and downside risk therefore better assessing each asset classes' risk-return trade-off.

The challenge, however, in including nonnormally distributed asset classes is the unpredictable nature of the alternatives' returns. For instance, how many absolute hedge fund managers predicted losing so much when hedge fund Amarenth Investors lost billions of dollars recently due to its extensive holdings in the natural gas commodity market? However, this asset class typically generates very smooth rates of return over long periods of time when compared to typical classes.

On a different front, investing in venture and private equity type investments typically offer far greater returns than traditional asset classes; and do so with typically higher than normal risk. The risk is not the problem, the timing of the returns are the problem for modeling purposes however. The normal life cycle of a private equity or venture investment is that your capital contribution is called over a five-year horizon. It is usually at least five to seven years before you typically receive any return of capital and even longer before you see full return of profit. Investors in this asset class should expect at least a 10-year horizon if investing in this type of alternative. Modeling this type of class in any asset allocation analysis is a great challenge, especially if the client has liquidity needs or concerns during the initial funding years.

The problem of course is that a small number of extreme return results can dramatically affect an asset classes' skewness while not affecting the overall mean or variance over a long period (typically used for modeling purposes). The bottom line is that more and more investors are including these asset classes anyway because they tend to be very low or noncorrelated to their existing portfolio. Therefore their inclusion can indeed lower the overall observed risk while actually increasing realized returns.

Evaluation of Cash and Equivalent Component

The next step in the evaluation of investment results is to examine the performance characteristics of the individual components. In this section, we will begin this process by evaluating the cash and equivalent component of the portfolio. An in-depth evaluation of the equities and fixed income components will be conducted in Chapters 8 and 9, respectively.

The cash is evaluated in the same manner as the other two components. Specifically, the comparison index and universe are selected based on the investment guidelines contained in the policy statement. For illustration purposes, the Citi three-month Treasury bills will be used as a surrogate for Short-Term Investment Funds (STIF) and Cash Accounts Index. Using these data, Figure 7.3 was prepared.

The squares contained in the bar chart represent the annualized rate of return for the fund's cash and equivalent component, while the diamonds represent the Citi three-month Treasury Bill Index's return during each period. Again, the top of each bar represents the highest return for a given fund within the investment universe, while the bottom of the bar reflects the lowest return of a fund within the universe. The 25th percentile, median, and 75th percentile is represented by horizontal lines drawn across the bar chart. Supporting data is contained at the bottom of the chart for each period measured.

As the chart indicates, the cash and equivalent component performs well in all periods. In fact, its return is greater than the Treasury bill index's in every period. In comparison with the universe, cash and equivalents were in the top quartile for the latest one-, two-, and three-year period. During the last four- and five-year periods, performance fell into the 2nd and 3rd quartile respectively.

FIGURE 7.3   STIF and Cash Accounts (US$), Period Ending June 30, 2006

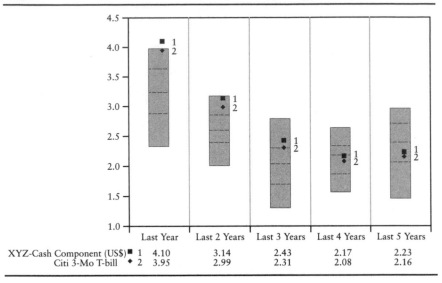

		Last Year	Last 2 Years	Last 3 Years	Last 4 Years	Last 5 Years
XYZ-Cash Component (US$) ■	1	4.10	3.14	2.43	2.17	2.23
Citi 3-Mo T-bill ♦	2	3.95	2.99	2.31	2.08	2.16

Figure 7.4 reports the performance results incorporating risk into the analysis. The scatter diagram presented in this chart is very revealing. Although the five-year annualized return is low, so is the risk. The cash component's return-risk position is indicated by a circle, and is located in the southwest quadrant. Citi three-month T-bills is depicted by a diamond and is also in the southwest quadrant. Each had lower return and risk than the median portfolios. Using a risk-return criterion, the cash component has a slightly higher return and higher risk than the index.

Table 7.13 presents the summary statistics corresponding to Figure 7.4. The maximum five-year annualized is 3.95%. In addition, the median return is 3.25%. The 25th and 75th percentiles were 3.60% and 2.80%, respectively. Fund XYZ's Cash and Equivalent component has a return of 4.10% and a standard deviation of 0.60% compared to a return of 3.95% and standard deviation of 0.59%, respectively. Thus, in terms of its return-risk characteristics, the cash portion of the portfolio is above the universe's Median. Finally, the cash and equivalent component generates a slightly greater return than the index, but also incurred slightly greater risk.

The component analysis illustrated above suggests that both the equity and fixed income portions of Fund XYZ performed well. This is true when examining performance results using both the return measures and return-risk measures. In both instances, these components fared well when compared to selected indexes and universes. The cash and equivalent component's per-

FIGURE 7.4   STIF and Cash Accounts (US$), Five-Year Period Ending June 30, 2006

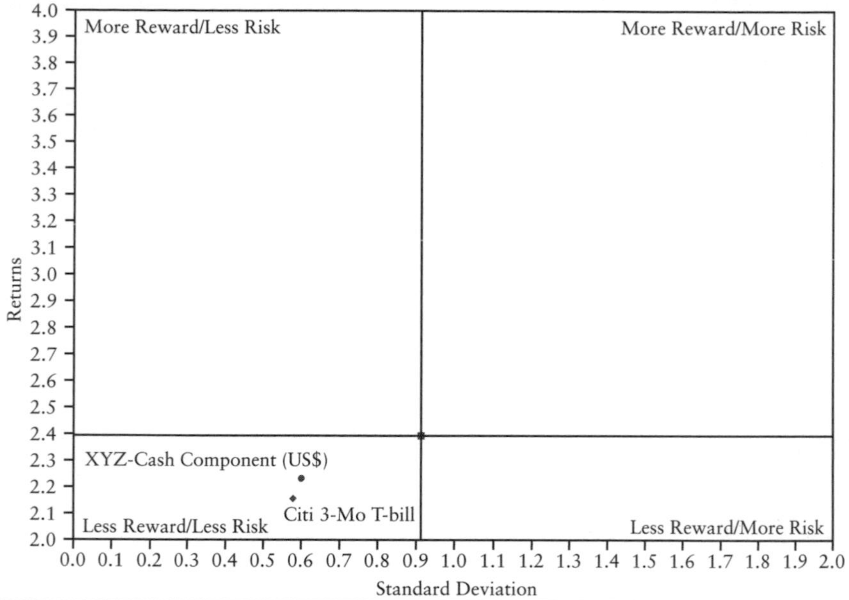

TABLE 7.13   Return-Risk Analysis, Cash and Equivalent Component, Five-Year Annualized Measures

Performance Measure	Return (%)	Standard Deviation (%)
Maximum	3.95%	NA
25th percentile	3.60%	NA
Median	3.25%	0.91
75th percentile	2.80%	NA
Minimum	2.30%	NA
Cash component	4.10%	0.60
Three-month Treasury bills	3.95%	0.59

formance results are compared favorably to the index and had a lower return and risk than the universe's median.

SUMMARY

The evaluation of portfolio performance must be based on specific, measurable criteria. Performance can be measured against an index or an investment universe. In selecting an index or indexes, the evaluator must be careful that the measure selected matches the desired characteristics of the fund to be evaluated. Even so, the evaluator must recognize that indexes do not reflect the transaction costs and fees, which are reflected in managed investment accounts.

Given this problem, evaluators should also use investment universes as a means of comparison. These universes or grouping of funds with desired characteristics provides a better means of comparison. These benchmarks can be used to evaluate overall portfolio performance and/or their components. Regardless of the comparison method, performance should be evaluated on the basis of return and risk.

As part of the evaluation process, the relative impacts on performance of security selection and asset allocation should be examined. The impact of each decision on overall performance will provide the evaluator with proper insight as to the origins of the fund's investment performance. This then aids in the identification of factors influencing the success of the fund.

CHAPTER **8**

Equity Performance Evaluation

In the preceding chapter, performance results of Fund XYZ were evaluated. In addition to examining the fund's overall return, the effect of the fund manager's asset allocation decision was examined. The chapter concluded with an evaluation of the cash and equivalent component of the fund. In this chapter, equity performance characteristics will be examined in more depth. The next chapter will focus on the evaluation of fixed income portfolios.

There are several methods used to evaluate the equity portion of a port-folio, and for funds comprised primarily of equity securities. For example, the equity results can be compared to an index possessing similar charac-teristics. In this instance, managers might be required to achieve investment results consistently better than the selected index. In addition, performance results can be evaluated in terms of an investment universe. Here, portfolio managers might be expected to achieve a ranking within the top quartile of the universe.

In addition, insights into the performance of the fund may be obtained by employing a *sector approach*. This approach allows the investment policy committee to identify the causes for differences in returns between the per-formance of the fund's equity component and the comparison index. This technique separates the return deviations into sector and selection *sector approach*. This approach allows the investment policy committee to identify the causes for differences in return between the performance of the fund's equity component and the comparison index. This technique separates the return deviations into sector and selection categories.

Greater insight into the return-risk characteristics of a portfolio can be achieved by examining the market characteristics of the equity portfolio. Specifically, the alpha, beta, and R^2 can be calculated to evaluate perfor-mance results. Additionally, other performance measures such as the Sharpe Index, Jenson Index, Treynor Measure, and Appraisal Ratio, which were discussed in Chapter 6, can also be used to further the evaluation process.

Another approach, *attribution analysis*, can be helpful. Different invest-ment styles are marked by unique financial characteristics. For example, an income-oriented portfolio and a growth-oriented portfolio would be expected to have different attributes. The financial characteristics of these two diverse equity portfolios should differ significantly in terms of capi-talization, price/earnings ratios, earning growth rates, dividend yields, and betas. *Attribution analysis* allows the investment committee to compare the characteristics of their fund with those of funds with similar objectives.

EQUITY PERFORMANCE CRITERIA

Typically, the equity component of a portfolio is compared to an index and/ or universe as provided in the investment policy statement. The investment committee selects the appropriate benchmarks based on the portfolio's ob-jectives, risk tolerances as well as other characteristics that are unique to the fund. The S&P 500 and Frank Russell's Equity Accounts universe will be used to illustrate this technique.

Table 8.1 reports the quarterly return of the S&P 500, Fund XYZ, and the three-month Treasury bills from the third quarter of 2001 through the second quarter of 2006. Column 1 lists the period, while columns 2, 3, and four report the corresponding quarterly returns of the S&P 500, Fund XYZ, and three-month Treasury bills. This data will be used to illustrate the tech-niques available for equity performance evaluation.

Figure 8.1 compares the performance of the Fund XYZ's equity com-ponent with the S&P 500 and portfolios with similar objectives which will constitute an investment universe for illustration purposes. These bar charts display the one-year, two-year, three-year, four-year, and five-year annual-ized rates of return for Fund XYZ and the S&P 500. The squares contained in the bar chart represent the annualized rate of return for the fund's equity component, while the diamonds indicate the S&P 500 return over each period. The top of each bar represents the highest return for a given port-folio within the universe, while the bottom of the figure reflects the lowest return of a portfolio within the investment universe. In addition, the hori-zontal lines contained in the bar chart represent the 25th percentile, median, and 75th percentile ranking within the universe. The bottom portions of the figure presents the return data used in construction of each bar chart.

As this figure reveals, the equity component's return ranks within the first quartile for all periods measured. Additionally, Fund XYZ's equity component provides investors with a higher return than the S&P 500 dur-ing each measurement period as well. Thus overall performance in terms of return measures is satisfactory. But what led to these performance results?

TABLE 8.1   Quarterly Returns (%)

Quarter		S&P 500 Index	Fund XYZ	Three-Month Treasury Bill
2001	3Q	−14.68	−14.50	0.91
	4Q	10.69	10.71	0.65
2002	1Q	0.28	0.20	0.44
	2Q	−13.40	−15.50	0.44
	3Q	−17.28	−19.00	0.43
	4Q	8.44	8.90	0.39
2003	1Q	−3.15	−2.00	0.30
	2Q	15.39	16.00	0.28
	3Q	2.65	3.10	0.25
	4Q	12.18	11.50	0.24
2004	1Q	1.69	2.50	0.23
	2Q	1.72	2.25	0.24
	3Q	−1.87	−1.30	0.32
	4Q	9.23	8.50	0.44
2005	1Q	−2.15	−1.75	0.57
	2Q	1.37	1.63	0.69
	3Q	3.61	4.20	0.80
	4Q	2.09	2.25	0.91
2006	1Q	4.21	5.10	1.03
	2Q	−1.44	−0.90	1.16

SECTOR ANALYSIS

To answer this question, performance will now be examined on the basis of individual sector investment results as well as the concentration of funds within a given sector. Under this approach, the return and percentage invested in each sector of the S&P 500 are compared to the sector return and percentage invested in each sector by the fund. The impact of investing within a particular sector can also provide valuable information to the evaluator. This approach is generally used when comparing the performance of a fund with an overall index. For example, using the S&P 500, securities may be classified according to the 10 following sectors: Consumer Discretionary, Consumer Staples, Energy, Financials, Health Care, Industrials, Information Technology, Materials, Telcom Services, and Utilities.

FIGURE 8.1   Equity Accounts Periods Ending June 30, 2006

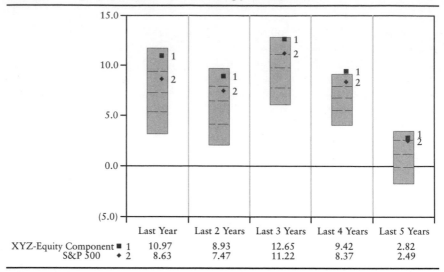

	Last Year	Last 2 Years	Last 3 Years	Last 4 Years	Last 5 Years
XYZ-Equity Component ■ 1	10.97	8.93	12.65	9.42	2.82
S&P 500 ♦ 2	8.63	7.47	11.22	8.37	2.49

TABLE 8.2   S&P 500 and Fund XYZ Summary Data, Second Quarter, 2006

(1)	(2)	(3)	(4)	(5)
	S&P 500		Fund XYZ	
Sector	Return	Weight	Return	Weight
Consumer Disc.	−0.45%	10.2%	−0.40%	10.5%
Consumer Staples	2.59%	9.6%	2.70%	10.2%
Energy	4.25%	10.2%	4.40%	13.0%
Financials	−0.11%	21.4%	−0.20%	19.5%
Health Care	−4.97%	12.3%	−4.50%	10.1%
Industrials	0.01%	11.7%	0.10%	12.1%
Information Tech.	−9.59%	14.9%	−9.50%	12.7%
Materials	−0.41%	3.1%	−0.30%	4.0%
Telecom Svcs.	−0.50%	3.3%	−0.40%	5.3%
Utilities	5.71%	3.3%	5.80%	2.6%
Total	−1.44%	100.0%	−0.90%	100.0%

Table 8.2 lists the returns and percentage weights of each sector comprising the S&P 500 and Fund XYZ. Column 1 lists the 10 sectors listed above. Columns 2 and 3 report the returns and weights of for each sector found in the S&P 500. Columns 4 and 5 report the returns and weights comprising Fund XYZ.

During the second quarter of 2006, Fund XYZ achieved a return on its equity component of –0.90 percent, while the S&P 500 registered a return of –1.44% (see Table 8.1). Thus, for the period measured, Fund XYZ's return although negative was better than the S&P 500 by 0.54 percent. Obviously, the professional manager's performance results relative to the S&P 500 Index can be attributed to better security selection within the sectors, and/or investing a greater percentage of the fund's assets in sectors that achieved higher returns.

Sector analysis can assist the investment committee in determining the sources of the 0.54% incremental return earned by the fund. The relative impact of security selection and sector weighting can be separated to identify the causes of this variance. Table 8.3 calculates the percent deviation caused by Fund's XYZ overweighting well performing sectors, while under weighting poorly performing sectors (i.e., relative to the S&P 500.)

Table 8.3 shows the methodology used to isolate the impact of security selection within each sector. Again, column 1 represents the individual sectors. Column 2 reports the sector weights of Fund XYZ. Columns 3 and 4 report the sector returns of Fund XYZ and the S&P 500, respectively. Finally, column 5 measures the relative securities contribution within each sector, and is computed by multiplying the column 2 by the difference between columns 3 and 4. The sum of column 5 represents the percentage difference in

TABLE 8.3 Contribution by Stock Selection, Second Quarter, 2006

(1) Sector	(2) Fund XYZ Weights (%)	(3) Fund XYZ Rates of Return (%)	(4) S&P 500 Rate of Return (%)	(5) Stock Selection[a] (%)
Consumer Disc.	10.5%	–0.40%	–0.45%	0.0053%
Consumer Staples	10.2%	2.70%	2.59%	0.0112%
Energy	13.0%	4.40%	4.25%	0.0195%
Financials	19.5%	–0.20%	–0.11%	–0.0176%
Health Care	10.1%	–4.50%	–4.97%	0.0475%
Industrials	12.1%	0.10%	0.01%	0.0109%
Information Tech.	12.7%	–9.50%	–9.59%	0.0114%
Materials	4.0%	–0.30%	–0.41%	0.0044%
Telecom Svcs.	5.3%	–0.40%	–0.50%	0.0053%
Utilities	2.6%	5.80%	5.71%	0.0023%
Security contributor				0.1003%

[a] Column 5 equals Col. 2 * (Col. 3 – Col. 4).

return due to security selection. As the table reveals, 0.1003% of the difference between the S&P 500 Index and Fund XYZ's return was due to security selection. The next step is to identify the difference between the index and fund return, which was the result of the manager's sector selection.

Table 8.4 shows the methodology used to isolate the impact of management's decision concerning sector investment. Column 1 represents the individual sectors. Columns 2 and 3 report the sector weights of Fund XYZ and the S&P 500 Index, respectively. Column 4 displays the S&P 500 rate of return for each sector. Finally, column 5 measures the individual sector's contribution to the return variance, and is computed by first subtracting Fund S &P 500 Indexes' weights from Fund XYZ's weights. Next, the S&P 500 Index (−1.44%) is subtracted from the S&P 500's individual sector returns. Finally, these two amounts are multiplied together. The sum of column five represents the percentage difference in return due to sector selection. Thus the manager's sector weighting decision resulted in an additional 0.04020% return above the S&P 500 Index.

The results of Tables 8.3 and 8.4 are summarized as follows:

Security Selection Contribution	0.1003%
Sector Allocation Difference	0.4020%
Deviation of Return	0.5023%

TABLE 8.4   Contribution by Sector Weighting, Second Quarter, 2006

(1) Sector	(2) Fund XYZ Weights (%)	(3) S&P 500 Weights (%)	(4) S&P 500 Rate of Return (%)	(5) Sector Difference[a] (%)
Consumer Disc.	10.5%	10.2%	−0.45%	0.0030%
Consumer Staples	10.2%	9.6%	2.59%	0.0242%
Energy	13.0%	10.2%	4.25%	0.1593%
Financials	19.5%	21.4%	−0.11%	−0.0253%
Health Care	10.1%	12.3%	−4.97%	0.0777%
Industrials	12.1%	11.7%	0.01%	0.0058%
Information Tech.	12.7%	14.9%	−9.59%	0.1793%
Materials	4.0%	3.1%	−0.41%	0.0093%
Telecom Svcs.	5.3%	3.3%	−0.50%	0.0188%
Utilities	2.6%	3.3%	5.71%	−0.0501%
Sector contributor	100.0%			0.4020%

[a] Column 5 equals (Col. 2 − Col. 3) * (Col. 4 − (−1.44%)).

RETURN-RISK COMPARISON

In the above analysis, Fund XYZ was evaluated on the basis of investment return. While this is indeed important, performance should not only be based on return, but also on the level of risk taken in achieving the return. Therefore, the performance of Fund XYZ will now be evaluated on the basis of return-risk characteristics. Figure 8.2 presents a scatter diagram containing the return and standard deviation for the equity component, the S&P 500, and representative portfolios, which comprise the investment universe. As the figure reveals, the equity portion of Fund XYZ (circle) lies in the northeast quadrant. This indicates that the fund has higher return and risk than the median portfolios. This is also true for the S&P 500 (represented by the diamond) which also has both a higher return and risk than the median portfolios. Thus, on a return-risk basis, both Fund XYZ's equity component and the S&P 500 is performing well.

Table 8.5 reports five-year annualized return and standard deviation for both the equity component of portfolio XYZ and the S&P 500. The portfolio return for this period was 2.82 with an annualized standard deviation of 17.90%. During this period, S&P 500 equity component had an annual-

FIGURE 8.2　Equity Accounts (US$) Five-Year Period Ending June 30, 2006

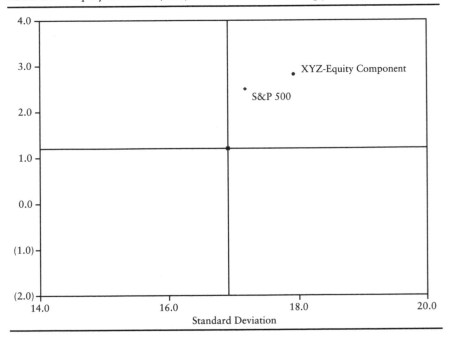

TABLE 8.5   Return-Risk Analysis, Equity Accounts (Five-year annualized measures)

	Return	Standard Deviation
Equity Component	2.82%	17.90%
S&P 500	2.49%	17.10%

FIGURE 8.3   Equity Accounts (US$)

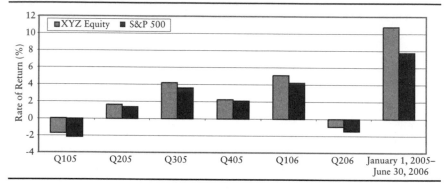

ized return of 2.49% and a standard deviation of 17.10%. Portfolio XYZ compares favorably to the S&P 500's in terms of return, but not in terms of standard deviation.

MARKET CHARACTERISTICS

Investment committee members should have a thorough understanding of the return-risk characteristics of equity portfolios. As discussed in Chapter 6, there are various measures that provide insight into the relationship between a fund and the overall market. Along these lines, the committee should play careful attention to the relationship between these returns. Figure 8.3 provides visual evidence of the relationship between Fund XYZ and the S&P 500 Index from January 1, 2005 through June 30, 2006. This figure depicts the quarterly returns of Fund XYZ and the S&P 500 over this period of time. It is noteworthy to view the apparent high correlation of their returns over this period of time.

This relationship can be quantified through the use of regression analysis. Here, the investment performance of Fund XYZ is compared to that of the market (S&P 500). These returns are then adjusted by subtracting from them the risk-free proxy (Salomon Brothers Treasury three-month bills.)

The resulting risk-adjusted return measures are used in the regression equation as follows:

$$Y_t = \alpha + \beta \bullet X + e_t$$

where:

Y_t = portfolio return in time period t
X = index return in time period t
α = regression intercept
β = regression slope
e = residual term

Table 8.6 provides summary statistics for the regression equation.

As the table reveals, Fund XYZ's alpha is estimated to be 0.40% (quarterly basis), which represents the return due to security selection. Recall from Chapter 6, that the alpha (or Jensen Index) is an indicator of the professional manager's contribution to investment performance. Thus, in this case, professional management was able to achieve a superior return relative to the S&P 500 Index.

TABLE 8.6 MPT Statistics for XYZ Equity Component, Five Years through June 30, 2006

Annualized Statistics	US$
Rate of return	2.82%
Standard deviation	17.91%
Quarterly Statistics	
Number of periods	20
Maximum return	16.00%
Minimum return	−19.00%
Average return	1.09%
Standard deviation	8.96%
Variance	0.80%
Regression Statistics	
Alpha	0.40
Beta	1.04
R^2	0.99
Correlation	0.99

FIGURE 8.4   Regression Equation Line

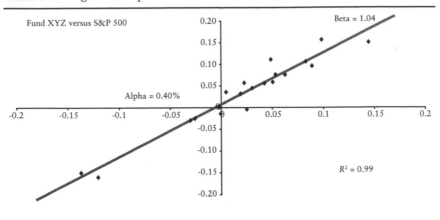

A portfolio's beta is a measure of systematic or market related risk. For the measurement period, Fund XYZ's beta was estimated to be 1.04. A 10% change in the return of the market, therefore, would be expected to produce a 10.4% change in the return for Fund XYZ. The fund possesses less systematic risk than the market as a whole.

Finally, the Fund XYZ's R^2 is 0.99. This correlation coefficient suggests that almost all (i.e., 99%) of the variability in the fund's return is explained by the market return. In this instance, Fund XYZ performed well on a risk-adjusted basis. This fund is characterized for being well diversified and having less volatility than the S&P 500. The market characteristic line for Fund XYZ using risk-adjusted rates of return and the S&P 500 as the market proxy is presented in Figure 8.4.

Additional Performance Measures

Several other measures of portfolio risk have developed. Among them are the Sharpe Index, Treynor's Measure, and the Appraisal Ratio. Each of these methods attempts to view return in the context of risk.

The Sharpe Index compares the excess return of a portfolio to its risk. Excess return is defined as the portfolio return in excess of the riskless rate of return. Recall that the numerator of the Sharpe Index (i.e., $R_j - R_f$) measures the so-called excess return of the portfolio, while the denominator measures the fund's overall risk or variability. In essence, the numerator provides the evaluator with a measure of the additional return or "premium" earned by taking on risk, while the denominator reports the level of risk taken during the measurement period. The higher the Sharpe Index, the greater return premium per unit of risk. Thus, this excess return to variability measure captures the trade-off between additional return and its associated risk. The Sharpe Index (*SI*) measure is defined as follows:

$$SI = \frac{(R_j - R_f)}{sd_j}$$

where:

R_j = the average return of portfolio j
R_f = the risk free rate of return using T-bills
sd_j = the standard deviation of excess returns of portfolio j

For the XYZ portfolio, the Sharpe Index (five years to June 30, 2006 using quarterly data) is as follows:

$$SI_{XYZ} = \frac{(0.0282 - 0.0216)}{0.1791} = \frac{0.0066}{0.1791} = 0.04$$

During the same measurement period, the Sharpe Index for the S&P 500 is as follows:

$$SI_{S\&P500} = \frac{(0.0249 - 0.0216)}{0.1717} = \frac{0.0033}{0.1717} = 0.02$$

A comparison of Portfolio XYZ and the S&P 500 Indexes' Sharpe Measure suggests that the Portfolio XYZ provides investors with a greater return premium per unit of risk. For every unit of risk, Fund XYZ investors receive 0.04 units of return, while holders of the S&P 500 receive only 0.02 units of return for every unit of risk. Thus, according to the Sharpe Index, investors are getting a higher return premium than had they invested in the S&P 500.

The Treynor Ratio (TR), is similar to the Sharpe Index except that it compares the fund's excess return to the fund's market risk as measured by its beta. The Treynor Ratio is used to compare the fund's excess return to the fund's market risk as defined by its beta. In essence, the Treynor Ratio measures the trade-off between the additional return earned (i.e., above the risk-free rate) and the portfolio's exposure to market risk. A higher ratio, therefore, would suggest the greater the reward. Thus the numerator in the equation is the same as the Sharpe Index. However, instead of using total variability, the Treynor measure divides excess return by the portfolio's beta. The formula is as follows:

$$TR = \frac{(R_j - R_f)}{\beta_j}$$

where:

R_j = the average return of portfolio j
R_f = the risk free rate of return using T-bills
β_j = portfolio j's beta

Earlier, Fund XYZ's beta was estimated to be 1.04. For Fund XYZ the Treynor Ratio would be

$$TR_{XYZ} = \frac{(0.0282 - 0.0216)}{1.04} = \frac{0.0066}{1.04} = 0.0064$$

Likewise, the Treynor measure for the S&P 500 over this same time period is found using the same formula. However, since the Beta of the S&P 500 is 1.00, the Treynor Ratio for this index would simply equal the numerator of the equation:

$$TR_{S\&P500} = \frac{(0.0249 - 0.0216)}{1.00} = \frac{0.0033}{1.00} = 0.0033$$

Again, the Fund XYZ offers greater reward for the risk taken (i.e., this time market risk), than the S&P 500. Therefore, it affords the investor a greater trade-off between the additional return earned and the portfolio's exposure to market risk than the market index.

Recall from Chapter 6 that the appraisal ratio divides the portfolio's alpha by the portfolio's unsystematic or diversifiable risk. Still, another performance measure is the Appraisal Ratio (AP). This measure is the ratio of the portfolio's alpha to the non-market or unique risk of the portfolio. The portfolio's alpha measures the average return over that predicted by the market return, given the portfolio's beta. The unsystematic risk is that risk which, in principle, can be eliminated via diversification. Hence the appraisal ratio indicates abnormal return per unit of diversifiable risk.

The Appraisal Ratio formula is

$$AP = \frac{\alpha_p}{\sigma_{(ep)}}$$

where:

AP = Appraisal Ratio
α_p = Alpha of the portfolio
$\sigma_{(ep)}$ = Diversifiable risk of the portfolio

For Fund XYZ the appraisal ratio is

$$AP_{XYZ} = \frac{0.4\%}{0.78\%} = 0.51\overline{.}$$

Table 8.7 displays the Sharpe Index, Treynor Measure, and the Appraisal Ratio for Fund XYZ and the S&P 500. As shown in the table, Fund XYZ

TABLE 8.7   Return/Risk Analysis, Selected Measures

Portfolio	Sharpe Index Coefficient	Treynor Measure	Appraisal Ratio
Fund XYZ	0.04	0.0064	0.51
S&P 500	0.02	0.0033	N/A

outperforms the S&P 500 using both the Sharpe Index and the Treynor Measure. Since the S&P 500 index does not contain unsystematic risk, the Appraisal Ratio cannot be computed.

ATTRIBUTION ANALYSIS

Investment managers employ different approaches to managing a portfolio. These include value, growth, income, as well as a number of other styles. Each of these approaches should be reflected in the choice of securities held within a given portfolio. Attribution analysis compares the investment characteristics of a fund with those in its investment universe. The fund profile provides a great deal of information concerning the makeup of the fund.

The usefulness of attribution analysis is that it provides the evaluator with a comparison of the characteristics of the portfolio developed by the investment manager to the characteristics of portfolios developed by other managers with supposedly similar styles. Suppose the investment committee has chosen an investment manager in order to generate current income for a portion of the fund's equity portfolio. The portfolios that the investment manager develops should have relative to all portfolios, a high market capitalization and dividend yield for these are general characteristics of income portfolios. Similarly, the portfolio should exhibit a relatively low price-earnings ratio and beta, and a moderate return on net worth and three-year earnings growth rate. A more useful comparison, however, is based on an examination of the above attribution of the investment manager's income portfolio to portfolios developed by a universe of income managers.

Figures 8.5 and 8.6 compare Fund XYZ's market data with a selected universe. Specifically, the fund's market capitalization, price-earnings ratio, dividend yields, beta, return on net worth and three-year earnings growth rates are compared to the investment universe via the use of bar charts.

A comparison of the information in Figure 8.5 versus Figure 8.6 reveals that Fund XYZ's investment manager assembled a portfolio whose market capitalization was high and rising, and at the end of June 2006 was in the top quartile of all portfolios managed by income managers.

This comparison reveals that the portfolio managers had selected stocks with an aggregate price-earnings ratio either below the median of the distri-

FIGURE 8.5   Equity Portfolio Statistics, Period Ending December 31, 2005

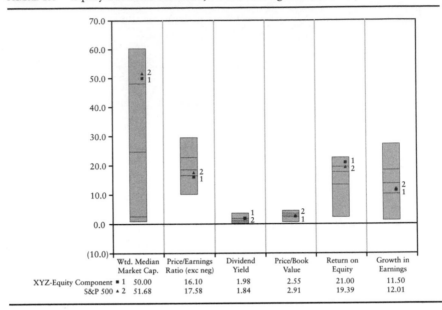

	Wtd. Median Market Cap.	Price/Earnings Ratio (exc neg)	Dividend Yield	Price/Book Value	Return on Equity	Growth in Earnings
XYZ-Equity Component ■ 1	50.00	16.10	1.98	2.55	21.00	11.50
S&P 500 ▲ 2	51.68	17.58	1.84	2.91	19.39	12.01

FIGURE 8.6   Equity Portfolio Statistics, Period Ending June 30, 2006

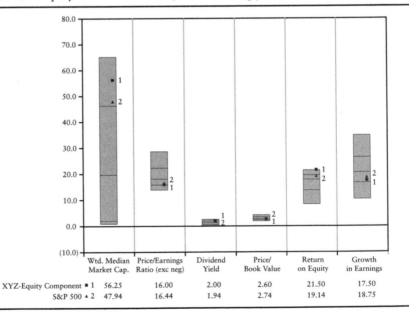

	Wtd. Median Market Cap.	Price/Earnings Ratio (exc neg)	Dividend Yield	Price/ Book Value	Return on Equity	Growth in Earnings
XYZ-Equity Component ■ 1	56.25	16.00	2.00	2.60	21.50	17.50
S&P 500 ▲ 2	47.94	16.44	1.94	2.74	19.14	18.75

distribution of P/E ratios among income managers. Related to this are the dividend yields on Fund XYZ which were on the high end of all comparable income portfolios. The portfolio also contained stocks whose price to book ratio was below the midpoint of all similar portfolios. Furthermore, Fund XYZ's had built a portfolio whose return on equity was above the median. Finally, the portfolio's earnings growth rate ranked in the lowest quartile of all portfolios compiled by investment managers.

Having compared the attributes of the income equity portfolio developed by the investment manager of Fund XYZ to those of his peers, we could conclude that the manager's actions, are in fact, designed to produce current income without high risk. However, as seen earlier in this Chapter, this manager has produced returns with higher risk as compared to the average peer group manager and benchmark. The investment manager of Fund XYZ is acting in accord with the objectives established by the investment sponsors with regard to style, but actual results appear to be in slight conflict with this conclusion.

SUMMARY

There are several approaches that the investment committee can undertake in the evaluation of equity performance. The starting point in such an analysis is to identify benchmarks by which to compare the investment results of the portfolio. It is important to select a benchmark that reflects the goals and objectives of the portfolio under evaluation. In addition to the selection of an appropriate index, investment universes are available for comparison purposes.

Using these benchmarks, portfolio performance can be examined on both a return basis and a risk-adjusted return basis. In addition to overall performance, portfolios can be evaluated using a sector approach, where the investment manager is judged not only on security selection, but also on sector selection. More sophisticated techniques such as modern portfolio theory uses tools such as regression analysis to measure investment performance against the market. The resulting data provides useful information such as market risk, the degree of diversification, and excess returns achieved through security selection.

Finally, financial and market characteristics of firms with similar goals and objectives can be compared through attribution analysis. Here such traits as capitalization, price/earnings ratio, dividend yield, earnings growth rate, return on net worth, and beta can be evaluated in order to gain a better understanding of the fund's financial and market attributes compared to peer group portfolios.

CHAPTER 9

Fixed Income Performance Evaluation

Institutional investors appear to allocate roughly 30% to 40% of their total portfolio holdings to fixed income securities. Moreover, the overwhelming majority of institutional fixed income funds are actively managed; that is, designed to achieve a risk-adjusted return in excess of a relevant benchmark. Frederick Dopfel, for example, reports that the average institutional fixed income portfolio has roughly 85% of its assets with active managers.[1] In contrast, individual investors appear to allocate about 20% of their total portfolio holdings to fixed income securities. A substantial portion of individual investor fixed income holdings are passively managed via index funds.[2]

Whether it is an institutional or individual investor there are several objectives in evaluating the performance of a fixed income fund. The first objective is to evaluate the characteristics of the fixed income fund, such as maturity, issuers, credit quality, and expected return and risk, to ensure they are consistent with the requirements established in the investment policy statement. A second goal is a decomposition of the fixed income portfolio's return and risk. The third objective is to evaluate the sources of the fixed income portfolio's return and risk to determine if the fixed income managers have enhanced value beyond that which could be obtained from a passive, indexed strategy and to identify the sources of any value creation.

As we discussed in Chapter 2, a well-designed investment policy statement should specify a range of desired characteristics for the overall portfolio. With regard to a fund's fixed income component, these characteristics should include asset allocation ranges, anticipated contributions to the total portfolio's return and risk, permissible issuers and sectors, performance benchmarks, credit quality, and expected returns, acceptable risks, and maturity distributions.

[1] Frederick E. Dopfel, "Fixed Income Style Analysis and Optimal Manager Structure," *Journal of Fixed Income* 14, no. 2 (September 2004), pp. 32–44.
[2] The data for individual investors are based on mutual fund holdings. See Chapter 10 for more detail.

ASSET ALLOCATION RANGES AND ANTICIPATED CONTRIBUTIONS

Determining ranges for a total fund's fixed income component and estimating the likely contribution of this component to the total fund's expected performance are derived from the overall portfolio optimization process. The elements of and steps in this process have been reviewed in previous chapters. Broadly speaking, fixed income securities are included in portfolios for two reasons. First, because their characteristics closely match the return requirements, risk tolerances, and constraints of investors. However, as there are relatively few portfolios invested exclusively in bonds, the diversification benefits are the second and over-riding reason for including fixed income securities in a portfolio. As we presented in Table 4.3, the returns on all three bond indexes were negatively correlated with the returns on all the equity market indexes. Fixed income securities provide potentially substantial diversification benefits when included in portfolios with equities. The targeted asset allocation ranges for the fixed income component will then depend on the investor's objectives, the fund manager's estimation of returns, risks and covariances among the selected asset classes, and the outcomes of the optimization process.

ISSUERS OF FIXED INCOME SECURITIES

Fixed income securities are originated and issued by the U.S. Treasury and agencies of the federal government, domestic nonfinancial and financial corporations, state and local governments (municipalities), and nondomestic corporations and foreign governments. Table 9.1 presents annual data from 1995 through mid-2006 on global outstanding bond market debt by issuer with an emphasis on U.S. bond market issuers. As shown in the table, global bond market debt outstanding as of mid-2006 totaled some $60.3 billion compared to about $27 billion in 1995. Global bond market debt has been expanding at a compound growth rate in excess of 7% per year in nominal terms and about 4% per year in inflation-adjusted terms.

Innovations in fixed income markets have occurred at a pace at least equal to those of the rest of the global financial sector. Each issuer of fixed income securities listed in Table 9.1 is providing securities with a seemingly ever growing and widening array of features, such as collateralized debt obligations (CDOs), and Treasury inflation-protected securities (TIPS) whose par values and coupon payments change in direct proportion to the consumer price index so that investors obtain a guaranteed real return. The number and variety of assets whose cash flows have been pooled into new

TABLE 9.1 Outstanding Global Bond Market Debt ($ billions)

Year	Municipal	Treasury	Mortgage Related	Corporate	Federal Agency	Money Markets	Asset Backed	International	Total
1995	1,293.5	3,307.2	2,352.1	1,937.5	844.6	1,177.3	316.3	15,900	27,129
1996	1,296.0	3,459.7	2,486.1	2,126.5	925.8	1,393.9	404.4	16,300	28,392
1997	1,318.7	3,456.8	2,680.2	2,359.0	1,022.6	1,692.8	535.8	15,300	28,366
1998	1,402.9	3,355.5	2,955.2	2,708.5	1,300.6	1,977.8	731.5	17,300	31,732
1999	1,457.2	3,281.0	3,334.2	3,046.5	1,620.0	2,338.8	900.8	18,400	34,379
2000	1,480.7	2,966.9	3,565.8	3,358.4	1,854.6	2,666.6	1,071.8	18,300	35,249
2001	1,603.5	2,967.5	4,127.6	3,836.4	2,149.6	2,587.3	1,281.1	18,200	36,753
2002	1,762.9	3,204.9	4,686.4	4,099.6	2,292.8	2,546.0	1,543.3	22,000	42,136
2003	1,900.5	3,574.9	5,238.6	4,459.4	2,636.7	2,526.3	1,693.7	28,000	50,030
2004	2,031.0	3,943.6	5,455.8	4,785.1	2,745.1	2,872.1	1,827.8	33,300	56,961
2005	2,225.8	4,165.8	5,915.6	4,959.8	2,613.8	3,420.2	1,955.2	33,000	58,256
2006	2,305.7	4,235.1	6,212.4	5,164.9	2,722.7	3,714.2	1,985.9	34,000	60,341

Source: Bond Market Association, *Securities Industry and Financial Markets Association Fact Book: Global Addendum 2006.*

securitized fixed income instruments continue to expand beyond mortgages and now include assets such as debt obligations, home equity loans, and recording royalties. The information in Table 9.1 reveals that asset-backed bonds including mortgage-related ones totaled about $7.9 trillion in 2005 and represented 31% of outstanding U.S. bond market debt versus only 24% in 1995.

Sustained growth in the size of the fixed income market and the ongoing evolution in the variety and complexity of fixed income instruments provide opportunities for investment committees and the fund managers they employ and oversee to enhance risk-adjusted portfolio returns. Taking advantage of these opportunities requires that investment committee members understand their basic properties and money manager(s) to comprehend their return and risk properties in sufficient detail. Taking advantage of the yield-enhancing opportunities associated with more complex fixed income instruments while mitigating their risk is no easy feat.

BOND INDEXES

As discussed in Chapter 2 bond indexes serve as the benchmarks for the performance evaluation of fixed income funds. Substantial increases in the number and variety of bond indexes, accompanying the expansion in the U.S. and global bond markets, have provided investment committees a wide range of choices with regard to benchmarks for fixed income performance measurement and evaluation.

The investment committee's strategy and objectives for the fixed income fund should be the primary determinants of the type of indexes they select. Committees adopting passive, 'meet the market' return strategies will select standardized benchmarks based on the specific market returns and risk they are attempting to mimic. Committees may choose broad "total U.S. market" and even "global markets" as the relevant framework, or define the appropriate market somewhat more narrowly, such as "Treasury and federal agencies" or "Investment Grade" based on issuer, maturity, and either historic or forecasted return and risk.

Standardized indexes should include a sufficient number of bonds, exclusive of U.S. Treasury and federal agency ones, such that nonsystematic or issuer specific risks are minimized. Bonds included in the index should be weighted by their market values and durations; the indexes total return should be reported daily; and the index should be investable and tradeable. Moreover, the indexes tracking error, that is, differences between the return and risk on the indexes and the portfolios designed to mimic them should be minimal.

Committees pursuing active "exceed the market" return strategies may also select standardized benchmarks, or have benchmarks customized by either modifying standardized indexes or developing ones unique to their investment objectives. Broad-based indexes can be modified by altering the weights given to issuers, sectors, maturities, and the like. In developing customized benchmarks, committees need be aware that bond market indexes are inherently more difficult to design, develop and implement than equity market indexes for several reasons. Reilly, Wenchi, and Wright discuss three reasons for this greater difficulty.[3] First, the scope of the bond market is much broader than that for stocks as it includes corporate, international, national, regional, state and local issuers whose bonds vary considerably along a host of dimensions including maturity, coupon rate, credit quality, and embedded options. Second, the composition of the bond market changes constantly as existing issues mature and new ones are issued. These changes in scope and composition change the interest sensitivity of bond markets and the indexes designed to track them. Third, bond markets are largely dealer driven, fragmented over-the-counter markets where not all issues may be frequently traded. As a result it may not be possible to accurately price all bonds included in a bond index.

Reilly, Kao, and Wright also report that return correlations among the large sample of bond indexes they researched are on the order of 90%.[4] These high correlations suggest that the indexes are reasonably close substitutes and their returns are largely influenced by one or more common, macroeconomic factors such as interest rates. In contrast, the three bond market indexes we examined in Chapter 4 (Lehman Treasury/Corporate; Merrill Lynch Corporate Master; JP Morgan Global Government) exhibited lower correlations. Correlations ranged from a high of 0.71 (Lehman and Morgan) to a low of 0.19 (Merrill Lynch and Morgan). Correlations averaged 0.69 between the Lehman index and the other two indexes; 0.43 between the Merrill Lynch index and the other two indexes; and 0.45 between the Morgan index and the other two indexes. Different factors may be at work in the bond markets we examined in Chapter 4.

BOND PRICES AND YIELDS

Bond Prices

Bonds are priced on a discounted cash flow basis. That is, the expected future cash flows on a bond are estimated, and the present or current value of

[3] Frank K. Reilly, Kao G. Wenchi, and David J. Wright, "Alternative Bond Market Indexes," *Financial Analysts Journal* 48, no. 3 (May/June 1992), pp. 44–58.
[4] Reilly, Wenchi, and. Wright. "Alternative Bond Market Indexes," p. 48.

these anticipated future cash flows are determined by choosing an appropriate required rate of return.

Equation (9.1) expresses mathematically the formula for the price of an option-free coupon bond:

$$P = \sum_{i=1}^{n} \frac{C_1}{(1+r)^1} + \frac{C_2}{(1+r)^2} + \cdots + \frac{C_n}{(1+r)^n} + \frac{M}{(1+r)^n} \qquad (9.1)$$

where:

P = market value of the bond

C = semiannual coupon interest payment

r = one-half the relevant required rate of return

n = number of semiannual payments

M = maturity value of the bond

As can be seen in equation (9.1), the cash flow stream on a bond is represented by the Cs and M, while r represents the required rate of return. Holding the cash flow stream constant, a higher (lower) value for r, that is, higher (lower) required rate of return, will result in a lower (higher) market value or price for the bond.

An alternative, more intuitive explanation for the inverse relationship between bond prices and interest rates can also be provided. Consider an investor who is purchasing a bond that will be first issued on day one. The coupon rate of interest the issuer must pay on the bond, for a given maturity, must be the current market rate of interest inclusive of the bond's risk characteristics. Otherwise, the bond would not be sold on day one for its par or maturity value.

Now, suppose that one day after purchasing the bond that is, on day two, our investor decides to sell it. How much can our investor receive for the one-day old bond? If interest rates have fallen from day one to day two, then newly issued bonds on day two will carry the lower coupon rate of interest reflecting the decline in market rates of interest. Our investor is trying to sell a bond that provides higher coupon payments than newly issued ones. As a consequence, there will be a greater demand for our investor's older bond as buyers of bonds prefer, other things equal, bonds with higher than lower coupon payments. The price of the "older" bond rises as a result. The opposite scenario would unfold in the event market rates of interest had risen.

The general expression for a bond's price given in equation (9.1) illustrates that a coupon bond's price has two cash flow components. The coupon payments are the first component. If they are fixed then the market price of the coupon payments can be viewed and valued as the present value of an ordinary annuity. The second cash flow component is the maturity or par value. This is a one-time cash flow expected to be received when the bond matures. It can be priced as the present value of a future lump-sum amount. Moreover, the general expression in equation (9.1) can also be modified to value consols, that is, bonds without maturity values as well as zero-coupon bonds, that is, bonds that do not make coupon payments.

Bond Yields

Bid and offer price quotes for bonds are observed almost continuously among bond dealers, and closing ask prices are widely reported. Investors can also establish the expected cash flows on a bond. Coupon rates of interest on bonds as well as maturities are also widely reported. Par or maturity values for most bonds are reasonably standardized. With this information one can readily compare quoted prices to anticipated cash flow streams. The only missing variable is the required rate of return.

A bond's yield to maturity is simply the single required rate of return that makes the present value of the expected cash flow stream equal to the current market price of the bond. In terms of equation (9.1), with known values for the P, Cs, M and n the yield to maturity is the r that makes the two sides equal. The yield to maturity measure of a bond's yield assumes that the investor will hold the bond until maturity, and that coupon interest payments received on the bond will be reinvested at this yield. In a similar manner, yields on bonds with embedded options as well as yields on amortizing bonds can be determined. However, the yield to maturity on a portfolio of bonds should not be measured by the yield on each bond in the portfolio. Instead, the current market value of the portfolio should be set equal to the anticipated stream of cash flows from the portfolio and the yield to maturity estimated as the required return that makes the present value of the cash flows equal to the market value of the portfolio.

The total return on a bond or portfolio of bonds can also be estimated. If the two assumptions above about yield to maturity are valid, then the total return will be the same as the yield to maturity. The total return on a bond is somewhat analogous to that on a stock in that cash flows—from coupon interest on bonds versus dividends from stock—and any capital gain or loss are two primary components of total return. Moreover, with coupon and amortizing bonds there is a third source of total return. This source is the incremental income produced by reinvesting either the coupon interest payments or principal repayments.

FIGURE 9.1   Treasury Yield Curve, 10-Year Treasury Bond Minus 3-Month Treasury Bill

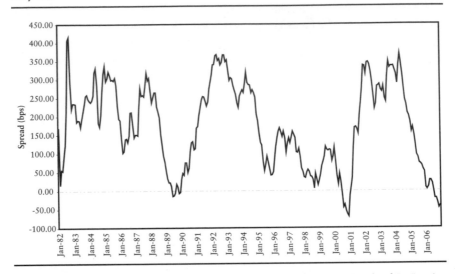

Source: Federal Reserve Economic Data (FRED), Federal Reserve Bank of St. Louis.

TERM STRUCTURE OF INTEREST RATES

A critical assumption in our discussion of pricing bonds and measuring yields is that a single required rate of return and yield to maturity is applied to each distinct cash flow, regardless of when it is scheduled to be received. This assumption is valid only when the yield curve, the relationship between yields to maturity and years to maturity on comparable bonds, is flat. As illustrated in Figure 9.1 flat yield curves are rarely observed. The appropriate interest rate for pricing bonds should be the yield on a default risk-free security, such as a Treasury bond, plus a risk premium whose maturity is the same as that of the bond being valued.

However, even bonds with the same maturities may have different cash flow properties if they have different coupon rates of interest. Pricing bonds on the basis of observed yield curves or yield curve spreads, even if maturities are identical, may result in mispriced bonds.

The proper way to measure required returns and, hence, to price bonds is via their cash flow properties. Each expected cash flow from the bond should be considered to be a cash flow from a zero-coupon instrument, and then valued using the yield on a zero-coupon Treasury security with the same maturity. A problem arises in this regard in that there are simply not a sufficient number of zero-coupon Treasury securities to permit a direct estimation of the "zero-coupon" yield curve. Several static and dynamic models have been proposed for estimating zero-coupon yield curves.[5]

Robert Ferguson and Steven Raymar analyze the empirical properties of six such models. They find "… the Vasiek-Fong model is the best of those we have examined. It provides a fast, reliable fit with OLS methods and, especially in the case of the six parameter specification, it is very accurate for the set of in-sample bonds and for the full simulated term structure."[6]

The sum of these cash flows is then compared to the bond's actual price and the implied yield difference reflects the default risk on the bond.

QUALITY OF FIXED INCOME SECURITIES

Specifying the acceptable risk characteristics for the fixed income portion of the fund is an important responsibility of the investment committee. Though an apparently straightforward task, this exercise can quickly become a complex one. Frank Fabozzi discusses 12 types of risks associated with investing in fixed income instruments.[7] Although a detailed discussion of these risks is beyond our scope, a brief description of each risk type is presented in Table 9.2. Then we turn to a more thorough description of the two most important types of risks associated with fixed income instruments, credit risk, and interest rate risk

CREDIT RISK

As mentioned above, credit risk refers to the likelihood or probability that a bond's issuer will not make interest payments and principal repayment according to the contractually scheduled time table. All bonds are subject to default risk, although in practice U.S. Treasury securities are priced so as to be devoid of such risk. Hence, credit or default risks are applicable to corporate, municipal, and international bonds.

There are several methods for measuring the credit risk of either a single bond or a bond portfolio. One widely-used method is to compare the yields on such bonds with U.S. Treasury bonds of similar maturities. Figure 9.2 presents weekly data on the yield differentials between bonds rated Baa by

[5] These models are discussed in Noel Amenc and Veronique Le Sourd, *Portfolio Theory and Performance Analysis* (Hoboken, NJ: John Wiley & Sons, 2003).
[6] Robert Ferguson and Steven Raymar, "A Comparative Analysis of Several Popular Term Structure Estimation Models," *Journal of Fixed Income* 8, no. 1 (March 1998), pp. 17–32.
[7] See Chapter 1 in Frank J. Fabozzi. *Bond Markets: Analysis and Strategies*, 6th ed. (Upper Saddle River, NJ: Prentice Hall, 2006).

TABLE 9.2   Risks Associated with Fixed Income Instruments

Risk Type	Description
Call risk	Risk that a bond issuer will retire a bond before maturity or the borrower whose loan is in an asset-backed or mortgage-backed security will repay principal before the scheduled due date thereby exposing investor to reinvestment risk and reduced price appreciation.
Default risk	Risk that the issuer will not make interest and/or principal payments at the contractually scheduled due dates.
Event risk	Risk that sudden, unexpected event (e.g., natural disaster or major industry strike) will impair the ability of an issuer to make interest and/or principal payments at the contractually scheduled due dates.
Exchange rate risk	Risk that bonds that have coupon and/or interest payments denominated in a foreign currency will realize a decline in the value of the cash flow in terms of the investor's home currency due to the depreciation of the foreign currency relative to the investor's home currency.
Inflation risk	Risk that expected purchasing power of the interest and principal payments will decline in value due to inflation.
Interest rate risk	Risk that increases in market interest rates will reduce the market value of bonds owned.
Liquidity risk	Risk that the costs of liquidating bonds will significantly reduce return.
Reinvestment risk	Risk that reinvestment of bond proceeds will produce lower returns because of a decline in market rates of interest.
Tax risk	Risk that tax rate reductions or repeal of tax-exempt status will lower returns on municipal bonds.
Volatility risk	Risk that the option value components of a bond with an embedded option will decline due to lower interest rate volatility.
Yield curve risk	Risk of nonparallel changes in the term structure of interest rates that produce lower returns on a bond portfolio.
Risk risk	Risk that outcome of a bond investment strategy cannot be determined in advance.

Source: Frank J. Fabozzi, *Bond Markets: Analysis and Strategies*, 6th ed. (Upper Saddle River, NJ: Prentice Hall, 2006).

FIGURE 9.2   Credit Quality Spreads, Moody's BAA Corporate Minus 10-Year Treasury Bond

Source: Federal Reserve Economic Data (FRED). Federal Reserve Bank of St. Louis.

Moody's and Standard and Poor's and the 10-year maturity Treasury bond. From the figure one can observe that yield spreads vary with the perception of systematic risk to the economy. Yield spreads decline during economic expansion and widen during economic downturns as well as during periods of heightened economic risk. Default risks generally recede in the midst of an economic expansion as corporate cash flows and earnings, and state and local government tax revenues increase. In contrast, default risk and associated spreads increase in periods of economic contraction as municipal tax receipts, corporate cash flows, and earnings diminish.

   Although an analysis of yield spreads can provide useful insights about bond credit risk, other factors may also influence these spreads. The majority of corporate bonds contain call provisions, for example, so that the yield spread between a corporate and similar maturity Treasury bond will be affected by call risk and volatility risk as well as credit risk. Consequently, yield spreads may not accurately reflect default risk. Furthermore, as we discussed above, a simple comparison of yield spreads may not accurately measure credit risk as it would fail to incorporate the term structure of interest rates. Once a zero-coupon Treasury yield curve has been constructed, however, we can more accurately measure default risk. The expected cash flows from the bond can be valued using the zero-coupon yields. The sum of these cash flows can then be compared with the bond's actual price. The implied yield differences should reflect the bond's default risk.

TABLE 9.3   Credit Ratings Used by the Credit Rating Agencies

Rating Agency			
S&P	Moody's	Fitch	Comment
Investment Grade			
AAA	Aaa	AAA	Highest quality
AA	Aa	AA	High quality
A	A	A	Upper quality
BBB	Baa	BBB	Medium upper quality
Noninvestment Grade			
BB	Ba	BB	Low quality
B	B1	B	Speculative
B–	B3	B–	Highly speculative
High Yield or in Default			
CCC	Caa	CCC	High risk
CC	Ca	CC	Extremely speculative
C	C	C	
D		DDD	In default

A second and more frequently employed method of evaluating bond credit risks is to rely on credit ratings. Standard and Poor's, Moody's, and FitchRatings assign credit ratings to corporate debt, municipal debt, and other fixed income securities based on a variety of analytical methods. Their credit rating grades are presented in Table 9.3. Bonds with a rating of AAA (Aaa in the case of Moody's) are the highest rated, indicating an extremely strong capacity to pay principal and interest. Bonds rated BBB (Baa for Moody's) and higher are considered investment grade, an important designation for many institutional investors whose investment policies limit their bond holdings to issues within this category. Ratings in many categories may also carry a + or – to further distinguish their credit risk.

INTEREST RATE RISK

The fundamental inverse relationship between changes in bond values and interest rate changes was established above. The critical issue is now to measure the sensitivity of individual bond prices and portfolio of bonds to changes in interest rates. Two properties of a bond, its maturity and its coupon rate of interest, affect its price sensitivity. With regard to maturity, the longer (the shorter) the term to maturity of a bond, other things equal, the greater (the lesser) its price sensitivity to interest rate changes. That is, the longer (the shorter) investors have to wait to receive the promised cash flows on a bond then the more (the less) sensitive will be the value of these cash flows to interest rate changes. In terms of coupon rate, the lower (the higher) the coupon rate of interest on a bond, other things being equal, the greater (the lesser) is its price sensitivity to interest rate changes. This second property reflects the fact that for lower (for higher) coupon bonds more (less) of the bond's total cash flows are accounted for by the repayment of principal.

To illustrate the first of these properties consider two bonds that are identical in all respects except their maturities. Suppose that both bonds are issued at a par value of $1,000, and possess coupon rates of interest of 5%. For simplicity, assume that coupon payments are made annually. The bonds differ only in that one bond matures in one year, while the second is an infinitely lived bond known as a consol.

Table 9.4 illustrates the dollar and percentage price change in the two bonds resulting from a 10% increase in interest rates. That is, interest rates rise by 50 basis points, or one-half percentage point, from 5.00% to 5.50%. The dollar value of the one year maturity bond declines by $4.74, or by less than one-half of one percent. In contrast, the market value of the much longer maturity consol falls by almost $91 or approximately 9.10%.

The second property of a bond affecting its price volatility, the coupon rate of interest, is depicted in the bottom panel of Table 9.4. The two bonds in this example have the same one year maturities, and are both priced to yield 5%. They differ only in that the first bond has a 5.00% coupon rate of interest while the coupon rate on the second bond is 10%.

Again, suppose interest rates rise by 10% so that the relevant discount rate is 5.50%. The market value of the 5.00% coupon bond declines by $4.74, while the market value of the bond with the 10.00% coupon drops by $4.97. In percentage terms, the lower coupon bond falls by slightly less than the higher coupon one.

TABLE 9.4   Dollar and Percentage Price Changes for Bonds

Coupon Rate	Maturity	Initial Price	New Price	$ Price Change	% Price Change
5.00%	1 year	$1,000	$995.26	–$4.74	–0.47%
5.00%	consol	$1,000	$909.09	–$90.10	–9.09%
5.00%	1 year	$1,000	$995.26	–$4.74	–0.47%
10.00%	1 year	$1,047.62	$1,042.65	–$4.97	–0.48%

DURATION

The price sensitivity of a bond to small changes in interest rates can be approximated by the bond's duration. Duration refers to the weighted average time to maturity of a bond, where the weights are the time periods before the present value of a respective cash flow is received. Cash flows whose present values are to be received sooner receive lower weights than those associated with more distant cash flows. The formula for a bond's duration is

$$
\text{Duration} = \frac{\sum_{i=1}^{t} \dfrac{T \times C}{(1+r)^t} + \dfrac{n \times M}{(1+r)^n}}{\sum_{i=1}^{n} \dfrac{C}{(1+r)^t} + \dfrac{M}{(1+r)^n}}
\tag{9.2}
$$

where:

C = semiannual coupon interest payment

r = one-half the relevant market interest rate of interest

n = number of years to maturity

t = number of semiannual coupon payments

M = principal value of the bond

T = period in which cash flow is received

The denominator in the duration formula is the market value of the bond. The numerator, which at first glance appears similar to the denominator, weights the present value of each cash flow, the C's$/(1 + r)^t$, by the time period in which it is to be received. Table 9.5 shows the calculation of the duration of a five-year maturity bond. Again for simplicity we assume annual coupon payments.

Using the data from Table 9.5, duration is calculated as follows:

$$
\text{Duration} = \frac{\$4,549.031}{\$1,000.00} = 4.549
$$

TABLE 9.5   Duration for Five-Year Maturity 5% Coupon Bond at Yield of 5.00%

Period	Cash Flow	Present Value at 5.00%	t * Present Value
1	$50.00	$47.619	$47.619
2	$50.00	$45.351	90.702
3	$50.00	$43.192	129.576
4	$50.00	$41.096	167.624
5	$1,050.00	$822.702	4,113.510
		$1,000.00	$4,549.031

The duration measure calculated above is known as the Macaulay duration, named for Frederick Macaulay who was among the first to use this measure in studying the returns on fixed income securities. A slight variant to the Macaulay duration is known as modified duration. The formula for it is given by

$$\text{Modified duration} = \frac{\text{Macaulay duration}}{1+r} \tag{9.3}$$

With regard to the above example, the modified duration of the bond would be:

$$\text{Modified duration} = \frac{\text{Macaulay duration}}{1+r} = \frac{4.549}{1.05} = 4.33$$

Bond durations have the desirable property of being additive. As a result, the duration of an entire bond portfolio can be computed as the weighted average duration of each bond, where the weights are the proportion of the fund in each bond. The formula for the duration of a portfolio of bonds is given by

$$\text{Bond Portfolio Duration} = \sum_{i=1}^{n} W_i \times D_i \tag{9.4}$$

where:

n = number of bonds
W_i = percent of the fund's value represented by each bond
D_i = duration of each bond

Once the duration of a bond (or a bond portfolio) has been calculated, then the approximate percentage price change in the bond can be determined from the following equation:

Percent price change
= (–Modified duration) × (Change in interest rate in basis points) $\qquad(9.5)$

With regard to the above example, suppose interest rates rose from 5.00% to 5.10%. The bond price change would be approximately:

$$0.00433 = (-4.33) \times (0.001), \text{ or } 0.433\%$$

The market value of the bond would be expected to decline by about $4.33. In reality, it would decline by $4.34.

Additional Duration Measures

Macaulay and modified duration provide accurate measures of interest rate risk when yield changes are small; when a bond's cash flows are not affected by interest rate changes; and when shifts in the yield curve are parallel. When any of these conditions are not met, then alternative duration measures should be employed.

One such alternative duration measure is designed for bonds with embedded options. Issuers of bonds frequently design them with call options that allow the issuer to redeem the bond before maturity. Put options, allowing investors to accelerate the maturities of bonds, are attached to bonds by isssuers to enhance their appeal to investors. Mortgage-backed bonds and many asset-backed bonds allow for prepayments of principal.

Changes in interest rates will affect the value of the options embedded in bonds. For example, when yields rise the value of the call options embedded in a bond will decline, the likelihood of the bond being called may diminish, and therefore the bond's expected cash flows may change.

Effective duration, also known as options-adjusted duration, is the appropriate duration measure for bonds with embedded options. To calculate effective duration we need to assume option adjusted interest rates rise and fall by small numbers of basis points. The value of the bond with the embedded option is then determined for the case of the rise in interest rates, P_-, and the case of declining rates, P_+. The new bond prices, P_- and P_+, should reflect the change in the value of the embedded option derived from standard option pricing models. The effective duration of the bond is given by

$$\text{Effective duration} = \frac{P_- - P_+}{2(P_0)(\Delta r)} \tag{9.6}$$

where:

P_- = the value of the bond's price owing to the rise in r
P_+ = the value of the bond's price owing to the fall in r
P_0 = the current price of the bond
Δr = the change in interest rate in basis points

Alternative measures of duration should also be used when yield curve changes are not parallel. Fortunately, parallel or level changes in interest rates appear to be the dominant factor in interest rate risk, explaining roughly 90% of the variation of the historical returns on U.S. Treasury STRIPS. However, changes in the slope of the yield curve, that is, either a flattening or steepening of the yields between shorter and longer term maturities, and changes in the curvature of the yield curve are also sources of interest rate risk.

Partial and key rate durations are two measures of a bond or portfolio of bonds interest rate risk to changes in the shape of the yield curve. Buetow, Fabozzi, and Hanke analyze these two additional duration measures.[8] Partial durations measure interest rate risk in terms of the par or on-the-run Treasury yield curve. Key rate durations are similar to partial durations except that the spot rate curve is the relevant reference curve. While the measures are similar the differences in estimated durations may be sizable, emphasizing the importance of understanding the differences between these two interest rate risk measures.

CONVEXITY

The duration measures presented above provide accurate measures of either a bond or portfolio of bonds price sensitivity as long as interest rate changes are relatively small. However, when interest rate changes become large, duration becomes less accurate in approximating a bond's price sensitivity because of a property bonds possess known as convexity. Convexity refers to the fact that the inverse price-yield relationship of a bond is not a linear but, instead, a curvilinear one. Hence, as interest rate changes become larger, relative to the initial yield, duration—a linear measure of price sensitivity—becomes less accurate.

In order to provide a more precise measure of a bond's or portfolio of bonds price sensitivity to sizeable interest rate changes, the convexity of the bond is calculated and used in conjunction with the bond's duration. Convexity can be thought of as the change in the change in the bond's price given a change in the rate of change of interest rates. The formula for a bond's convexity is given by:

$$\text{Convexity} = \frac{\displaystyle\sum_{i=1}^{t} \frac{T(t+1)C}{(1+r)^{t+2}} + \frac{N(N+1)M}{(1+r)^{n+2}}}{\displaystyle\sum_{i=1}^{n} \frac{C}{(1+r)^{t}} + \frac{M}{(1+r)^{n}}} \tag{9.7}$$

For the bond in Table 9.6, its convexity can be calculated as follows:

$$\text{Convexity} = \frac{\$23,936.53}{\$1,000.00} = 23.94$$

---

[8] Gerald W. Buetow, Jr., Frank J. Fabozzi, and Bernd Hanke, "A Note on Common Interest Rate Risk Measures," *Journal of Fixed Income* 13, no. 2 (September 2003), pp. 46–53.

TABLE 9.6   Calculation of a Bond's Convexity

Period	Cash Flows	$1/(1+r)^{t+2}$	$t(t+1)CF$	$\dfrac{t(t+1)CF}{1/(1+r)^{t+2}}$
1	$50.00	0.8638	100	$86.38
2	$50.00	0.8227	300	246.81
3	$50.00	0.7835	600	470.10
4	$50.00	0.7462	1,000	746.20
5	$1,050.00	0.7107	31,500	22,387.05
				$23,936.53

To illustrate how duration and convexity can be used to approximate a bond's price change, consider our five-year maturity, 5% coupon bond whose modified duration is 4.33 and whose convexity is 23.94. Suppose interest rates jump from 5.00% to 9.00%, a surge of 400 basis points. The approximate percentage change in the price of the bond is

Percent price change due to duration = (−Duration)(Change in interest rate)

−0.1732   = (−4.33)(0.04)

Percent price change due to convexity = 0.5(Convexity)
                                                               (Change in interest rates)^2

0.0192   = 0.5(23.94)(0.04)^2

Total percent price change = Percent price change due to duration
                                           + Percent price change due to convexity

−15.40% = −17.32% + 1.92%

Hence our bond would decline in value by roughly $154.00.

As was the case with Macaulay and modified duration, for bonds with embedded options an effective convexity measure is also required.

An important responsibility of the investment committee is to provide clear guidelines, if not outright limits, to the fund manager in terms of the amount of interest rate risk that should be associated with the fund's fixed income portfolio. This can be specified in terms of a portfolio's duration and convexity. Moreover, the investment committee, in the periodic reports it receives from the fixed income fund manager(s), should require that information on the portfolio's duration and convexity be included.

MATURITY CHARACTERISTICS

The investment committee also needs to either specify in the investment policy statement or communicate to the fund manager the desired maturity distribution of the fixed income portfolio. Generally, yields on bonds increase as bonds' maturities increase. Duration does as well. Hence, the investment committee confronts a trade-off between returns and risk. The investment committee must therefore determine a maturity distribution that is consistent with its return objectives and risk tolerance.

RETURN ANALYSIS

Performance attribution of fixed income portfolio returns is an especially challenging endeavor. The wide scope of the bond market in terms of such dimensions as issuers, investors, maturities, coupon rates, credit quality, and embedded options; the changing composition of the market as issues mature; and data requirements for benchmarks and individual bond prices all contribute to the challenge. Despite these challenges, an analysis of the return on a fixed income portfolio should address the following questions: (1) What factors contributed to the return on the portfolio? (2) How much of the return can be attributed to the actions of the portfolio manager? (3) How much of the return was associated with the fund's investment policy—including the investment strategy and tactics of the investment committee? (4) How much of the return can be attributed to expected and unanticipated changes in such things as the interest rate environment, shifts in the yield curve, movements in interest rate spreads among issuing segments, and so on.

An example of an innovative, state-of-the-art, commercially available system designed to provide accurate, detailed and insightful answers to the above questions is the BondEdge Performance Attribution (PART) system provided by Interactive Data Corporation.[9] The BondEdge system provides both factor-based and return-based models for fixed income performance attribution.

BondEdge Factor-Based Model

Factor-based models are designed to explain the causes of the benchmark and portfolio absolute returns by first identifying and then quantifying the key variables/factors that are the sources of the returns. The factors em-

[9] See Teri Geske, "The Performance Attribution Methodology in BondEdge: With a Discussion of Factor-Based and Returns-Based Approaches plus Transaction-Based Analysis," Research Publication, Interactive Data Fixed Income Analytics, 2007. The above discussion relies heavily on this research paper.

ployed by the BondEdge Part system (further discussed below) are intuitive and correspond to the primary sources of return and risk in the fixed income markets The factor-based approach, on a bond-by-bond basis, calculates what the returns on a portfolio and benchmark should have been in light of the actual changes in the sources of return and risk over the time period. It quantifies how decisions about the structure of the portfolio and the design of the benchmark led to their respective returns, and identifies precisely the portions of the return differences due to allocation choices about such variables as duration and sector.

Figure 9.3 presents a schematic layout of the factor-based PART return attribution categories. As can be seen, total return is decomposed into the following four categories of factors:

1. *Income return.* This is the coupon interest earned over the period for bullet maturity bonds and, depending on the type of bond, the effects of principal amortization may also be included.
2. *Paydown effect.* This category, for mortgage-backed securities, captures the change in bond values due to the return of principal over the period, regardless of whether or not it is scheduled amortization or prepayment.
3. *Price return.* This category attributes the percentage change in each bond's price over the period to one of three factors. The first is the *term structure effects* including amortization and roll, parallel shifts in the yield curve, which are further divided into effective duration and convexity effects, and nonparallel yield curve shifts. The second factor in this category is the *selection/quality effect,* which quantifies the return associated with either narrowing or tightening of the option adjusted spread observed for the bond's peer group over the period. The third factor in this category is the *security selection effect.* It is the portion of the bond's actual price return not attributable to the term structure and sector/quality effects, and essentially captures variations in spreads attributable to specific industries.
4. *Currency return.* For multicurrency portfolios with holdings in currencies other than the portfolio's designated base currency, the foreign currency return is translated to the base currency using spot foreign exchange rates decomposed into expected and active/unexpected currency returns.

BondEdge Returns-Based Model

Returns-based performance analysis focuses on the differences in the total returns between a bond portfolio and a relevant benchmark index. The em-

FIGURE 9.3 Visual Layout of Factor-Based PART's Return Attribution Categories

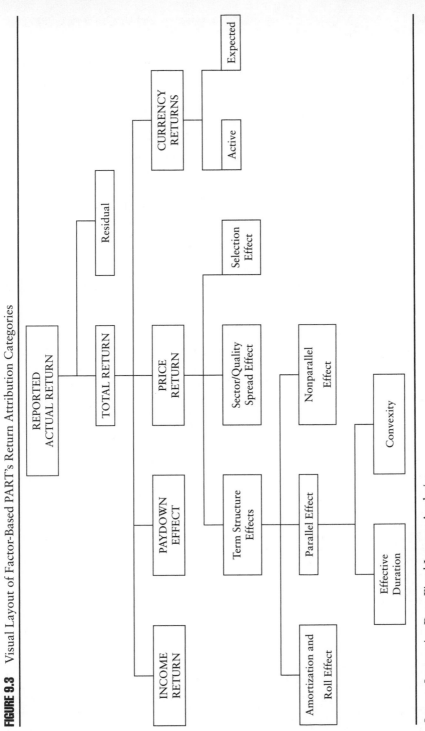

Source: Interactive Data Fixed Income Analytics.

phasis is on return differences owing to the portfolio manager's decisions, if any, about the weightings of bonds among categories compared to the benchmark, and the selection of bonds within a category relative to the benchmark index. Unlike factor-based models, performance compared to the benchmark is the defining feature of returns-based models.

BondEdge permits a choice of categories, such as sectors, industries, duration ranges, quality ratings, and the like to be used in the analysis as well as any hierarchy of decisions. The return for each bond is then assigned to the relevant category and any applicable subcategory for the benchmark and the portfolio. Return differences between the portfolio and benchmark owing to weighting decisions for each category explain why the portfolio performed better or worse than the benchmark index. Within a particular category of bonds, the security selection effect measures the portfolio's performance compared to the benchmark and allows an analysis of how much bond selection decisions either contributed to or diminished return versus the benchmark.

Table 9.7 depicts an illustration of the BondEdge returns-based attribution analysis. In this example, the benchmark index is comprised of four categories of bonds as shown in the far left column. The benchmark weighting for each category is the percent of market value (%MV) as seen in the far right column under the benchmark heading. The hypothetical portfolio manager's category weightings are given by the percent of market value (%MV) under the portfolio heading in the middle of the table. BondEdge measures the portfolio percent market value as the weighted average of the actual market weights at each point in time. As can be seen in the table, the hypothetical portfolio manager has over-weighted MBS by 10 percentage points, under-weighted Treasuries and corporate–industrial bonds by three and seven percentage points, respectively, and equally-weighted corporate-financial bonds.

TABLE 9.7   The BondEdge Performance Attribution Model

| Categories | Attribution | | Portfolio | | | Benchmark | | |
	Weighting	Selection	Return	Contr. to Ret.	% of MV	Return	Contr. to Ret.	% of MV
Treasuries	0.0012	0.0000	0.960	0.240	25.0	0.960	0.269	28.0
MBS	0.0053	0.0603	1.173	0.587	50.0	1.053	0.421	40.0
Corp-IND	0.0021	0.0240	1.130	0.170	15.0	0.970	0.213	22.0
Corp-FIN	0.0000	0.0070	1.040	0.104	10.0	0.970	0.097	10.0
TOTAL:	0.0090	0.0910		1.100	100.0		1.000	100.0

Source: Interactive Data Fixed Income Analytics, "The Performance Attribution Methodology in BondEdge."

In this example, the benchmark index generated a return of 1.00% over the period, while the hypothetical portfolio earned a return of 1.10%. These returns are the market value weighted totals of the returns in each category, given in the contributions to return (Contr. to Ret.) columns. The 10 percentage point/basis points superior performance can be decomposed into the portfolio manager's weighting decisions among sectors and bond selection choices within a sector.

The performance attribution associated with weighting decisions can be measured as the difference between the return on a specific category within the benchmark and the total return on the benchmark multiplied by any differential weight between the portfolio and benchmark for this category. As shown under the Weighting column in the table, the portfolio manager's overweighting to MBS and underweighting to Treasuries and corporate–industrial bond categories contributed to positive weighting effects as these sectors out-performed and underperformed, respectively, the benchmark's 1.00% return. However, the weighting decisions of the portfolio manager accounted for less than 1 of the 10 percentage points/basis points of portfolio's superior return. The portfolio manager's selection of bonds within the categories, notably the MBS but also the corporate–industrial and corporate–finance, explain more than 90% of the superior performance. The selection effect is measured as the difference in the return for a category within the portfolio compared to the return for that category within the benchmark multiplied by the weight for that category in the portfolio.

The BondEdge system also provides attribution analysis for portfolios where the manager's decisions extend beyond weightings among categories and bond selection within categories. Portfolio managers might further divide bond selection decisions based on expected term structure changes and use bond durations and convexity to guide these choices. The BondEdge attribution system would then measure the contribution of these decisions to the portfolio's return relative to the benchmark

CFA INSTITUTE STANDARDS

As in the case with equity portfolios, in recent years the CFA Institute (formerly the Association for Investment Management and Research, AIMR) has promoted standards in the fixed income arena for the presentation of information by money managers as well as requirements as to what must be disclosed. These requirements include the following:

- Calculate returns using time-weighted rates of return (as discussed in Chapter 6), calculations of returns on at least a quarterly basis; and geometric linking of returns.

- Include all actual fee-paying, discretionary portfolios in one composite or aggregate measure.
- Deduct all trading costs in calculating returns.
- Disclose whether the performance results are calculated gross or net of management fees.
- Disclose the tax rate assumptions if the results are reported net of taxes.
- Present at least a 10-year performance record. Present results since inception if the firm has been in business less than 10 years.
- Present annual returns for all years.

FIXED INCOME MANAGEMENT STYLES

Unlike the case with equity portfolio managers, at this time there is not an industry standard, widely agreed upon taxonomy of investment styles for portfolio management of fixed income securities. The absence of an industry standard complicates the evaluation of fixed income portfolio managers. Plan sponsor should therefore rely on the portfolio strategy they adopt for the fixed income portion of the fund, as well as the constraints they specify for the fixed income portfolio's issuer, credit quality, duration, and maturity in evaluating fixed income managers.

PASSIVE FIXED INCOME MANAGEMENT

Passive fixed income managers pursue either an indexing or an immunization strategy. An indexing strategy is one where the portfolio manager designs a fixed income portfolio so that its return and risk characteristics replicate those of an appropriately selected fixed income index. In contrast, an immunization strategy is one where the portfolio manager structures a fixed income portfolio so that it obtains a predetermined future value, regardless of movements in interest rates.

A fixed income indexing strategy, in concept, is similar to an equity indexing strategy. A benchmark index, either an existing one as discussed in Chapter 2, or a customized one as mentioned earlier in this chapter, is selected for its conformity to the plan's return and risk objectives, and then a fixed income portfolio is developed to mimic the characteristics of the index.

Problems in executing a fixed income indexing strategy that do not exist with an equity indexing strategy were addressed in our previous discussion of index design and construction. Notably these are that the broader-based, better known fixed income indexes contain in excess of 5,000 bonds. Some portion of these bonds may be highly illiquid as they are not frequently traded. As a result, it is very difficult to either include these securities in the fund's fixed income portfolio or to find substitute securities for them. The second practical problem in implementing a fixed income indexing strategy arises as bonds included in the index mature and are replaced by newly issued ones. The portfolio manager may be required to frequently rebalance the fixed income portfolio, adding to the transactions costs of implementing this strategy.

In response to the previously noted practical problems in implementing a fixed income indexing strategy, portfolio managers might seek to design a portfolio that closely tracks the targeted index. Stratified sampling approaches to bond indexing are frequently used in this regard.

Under this approach, the benchmark index is decomposed by its characteristics. These might include issuer, duration, credit risk, maturity, and the like. Then one or more bonds from each characteristic grouping or cell are chosen to be included in the fixed income portfolio so that its performance will closely match that of the index. Table 9.8 illustrates a simplified stratification. Bonds in the benchmark index are decomposed by issuer and credit quality. The percentages of the index represented by each cell are determined as illustrated in Table 9.8. The portfolio manager would then include in the portfolio bonds in each cell in proportion to their representation in the index.

Immunization strategies, in contrast to index ones, are a device for immunizing a fixed income portfolio from interest rate risk. They are often used when the objective is to provide sufficient funds to pay a future liability or liabilities. The strategy involves selecting assets for the fixed income portfolio so that the duration of the portfolio's assets is equal to the duration of the portfolio's liabilities. In this way, any decrease (increase) in the portfolio's asset value because of higher (lower) interest rates would be offset by equal decreases (increases) in the portfolio's liability value.

TABLE 9.8   A Hypothetical Stratification of a Fixed Income Index

Credit Quality	Issuer			
	Treasury	Agency	Corporate	Municipal
AAA to AA+	16.0%	13.0%		
AA to AA−			17.0%	
A+ to A−				11.4%
BBB+ to BBB−			9.6%	
BB+ to BB−				
B+ to B−				

ACTIVE FIXED INCOME MANAGEMENT

Fixed income portfolio managers who pursue so-called active styles are attempting to earn a return, adjusted for risk, in excess of that on a predetermined benchmark index. Essentially, managers with active styles operate upon the notion that the existing term structure of interest rates does not completely and accurately reflect what they consider to be mispriced bonds. In turn, they structure client's portfolios to take advantage of the perceived mispricing.

Active bond management styles vary along a number of dimensions including sector/issuer, maturity, duration, credit quality/spread, timing, security selection and international/foreign exchange rate. Across each dimension where mispricing is thought to occur the composition of the active manager's portfolio will differ from that of the relevant benchmark index. For example, if an active manager estimates interest rates are likely to fall by more than those contained in the structure of forward rates then her/his portfolio may have a higher duration than that of the benchmark index. Or, if an active manager expects corporate to Treasury spreads to widen then she/he may underweight the corporate sector relative to its benchmark index weighting.

Investors who employ active managers are seeking a consistent "alpha return," that is, actual returns in excess of those on the relevant benchmark index. They are necessarily willing to accept active risk, measured by the standard deviation of the active returns, in the process. Information ratios of active managers can help investors determine which active managers have provided pure alpha.

Information ratios measure the additional portfolio return from active management relative to the incremental diversifiable risk. The source of the additional return is based on the dimensions of the active strategy noted above and is represented in the portfolio by the differences in weightings compared to the benchmarks. The incremental nonsystematic risk arises because the benchmark portfolio presumably contains only systematic risk. Dopfel argues that active dimensions pertaining to duration, individual security selection, and market timing do not contribute as much to higher information ratios than active dimensions based on credit quality/spreads as the former are low frequency events compared to the latter. That is, active managers have fewer opportunities to bet on interest rate directions, for example, than they do on changes in credit quality spreads across large numbers of bonds.[10]

An illustration of a classification system for active fixed income managers is provided by Wilshire Associates, a prominent firm that provides investment information used in evaluating portfolio managers as well as

---

[10] Dopfel, "Fixed Income Style Analysis and Optimal Manager Structure," p. 34.

investment advisory services. The classification system Wilshire introduced is based on the concepts discussed throughout this book and is presented to further illustrate them.

The Wilshire TUCS (Trust Universe Comparison Service) Fixed Income Portfolio Groups starts by grouping fixed income portfolios according to the index they target. Grouping portfolios in this way means they all are subject to common interest rate changes during the performance period in question. As a result, "differences within the group are then due to the success of the sector and quality management, duration management relative to the index, selection of individual bonds, and other fixed income management techniques." Subsequent to this initial grouping, styles of fixed income managers are based on quantitative assessment of a portfolio relative to three widely used fixed income indexes—Lehman Brothers Intermediate, Government/Corporate, and Long-Term Bond Indexes.

The quantitative technique developed by Wilshire Associates employs the fixed income portfolio's average duration, the variability of its duration, the tracking error of its duration relative to the aforementioned indexes, and its average quality. A series of test, based on the above, is applied to each portfolio. The test results in each portfolio being classified into one of eight management styles: high-yield, short-term, intermediate, long-term, matched duration core, interest rate anticipation, and unclassified. The performance of portfolios in each of these styles can then be compared and evaluated to a universe of comparable portfolios.

PERFORMANCE ANALYSIS

The performance analysis methods we have been examining can be thought of as relative performance methods where we determine a fixed income manager's value-added by decomposing the differences between a portfolio's actual returns and those of a benchmark.[11] An additional element of this method is to compare and evaluate a fund's performance relative to a universe of similar portfolios.

Figure 9.4 presents the one-, two-, three-, four-, and five-year annualized return of hypothetical Fund XYZ fixed income component with that of the Lehman Brothers Government/Corporate Bond Index using bar charts. The universe selected ranges between 197 and 262 fixed income portfolios. The circles contained in the bar chart represent the annualized rate of return for the fund's fixed income component, while the square indicates the Lehman Brothers Government/Corporate Bond Index return over the same

---

[11] The BondEdge Factor-based approach does not require a benchmark. Portfolio returns may be compared to a benchmark or analyzed on a stand alone basis.

FIGURE 9.4   Fixed Income Accounts (USD), Monthly as of June 30, 2006 Quartile

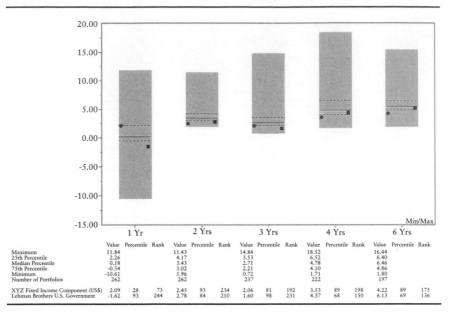

	1 Yr			2 Yrs			3 Yrs			4 Yrs			6 Yrs		
	Value	Percentile	Rank	Value	Percentile	Rank	Value	Percentile	Rank	Value	Percentile	Rank	Value	Percentile	Rank
Maximum	11.84			11.43			14.84			18.52			16.44		
25th Percentile	2.26			4.17			3.53			6.52			6.40		
Median Percentile	0.18			3.43			2.71			4.78			6.46		
75th Percentile	-0.54			3.02			2.21			4.10			4.86		
Minimum	-10.61			1.96			0.72			1.71			1.80		
Number of Portfolios	262			262			237			222			197		
XYZ Fixed Income Component (US$)	2.09	28	73	2.45	93	234	2.06	81	192	3.53	89	198	4.22	89	175
Lehman Brothers U.S. Government	-1.62	93	244	2.78	84	210	1.60	98	231	4.37	68	150	6.13	69	136

Source: Russell Investment Group.

period. The top of each bar represents the highest return for a given portfolio within the universe, while the bottom of the chart reflects the lowest return of a portfolio within the investment universe. Additionally, the horizontal lines contained in the bar chart represent the 25th percentile, median, and 75th percentile. The figure reveals that the fixed income component ranked below the 75th percentile for four out of five evaluation periods. The index also consistently ranked below or just slightly above the 75th percentile. It outperformed fund XYZ in three of the five valuation periods.

Figure 9.5 presents a profile of the return-risk characteristics of Fund XYZ fixed income component, Lehman Brothers Government/Corporate Bond Index, and the selected investment universe (Fixed Income Accounts). Viewing the scatter diagram reveals slightly different results than simply focusing on return. In terms of return-risk, the fixed income component resides in the southwest quadrant. This indicates that it achieves both a lower return and risk than the median portfolio. In contrast, the Lehman Brothers index achieved a slightly greater return than the median, while experiencing about the same risk. Thus, by all measures, the fixed income component performs well.

Factor models, such as the BondEdge factor-based system, are a complementary method of performance analysis. The factor model approach

FIGURE 9.5 Fixed Income Accounts (USD)—Monthly 2000 as of June 30, 2006 Scatter

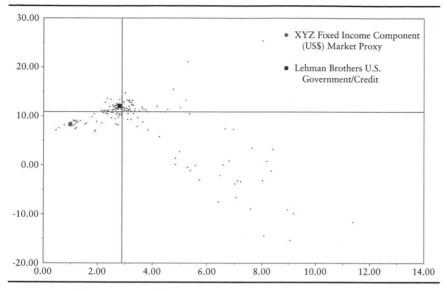

Source: Russell Investment Group.

consists of identifying factors that are thought to cause returns and risk and quantitatively estimating the sensitivities of a portfolio's returns to the identified factors. The contribution of each factor to the portfolio's return and risk can then be measured. Over a number of performance periods the contributions of each factor can be combined and used to evaluate a manager's sources of value added.

A typical factor model may take the form given by

$$R_{PT} = \Sigma_{i=1} \; \beta_{pi} F_{IT} + e_{pt} \tag{9.8}$$

where:

R_{PT} = portfolio return for time period T
β_{pi} = sensitivity of portfolio return to factor i
F_{IT} = return to factor I for time period T
E_{pT} = return to the portfolio not associated with returns to factors

Factor models provide a more absolute manner of analyzing portfolio performance. Their use has increased markedly in recent years as a professional consensus has emerged on some of the more common factors such as maturity, quality, level, shape and curvature of the yield curve. A reasonably widespread practice is to estimate a factor model for a benchmark index as well as a particular bond portfolio and to compare the factor sensitivities over time between the benchmark index and a specific portfolio. The differences over time in the sensitivities are then used to evaluate managers and their sources of value-added.

SUMMARY

Most investors include fixed income securities in their portfolios because of their potential diversification benefits. Relatively few investors have investment objectives that can be fully satisfied with portfolios totally allocated to fixed income securities. Institutional investors appear to allocate substantial portions of their fixed income holdings to active managers, who attempt to earn returns in excess of benchmark index returns, and accept risks that could otherwise be diversified away in the process. Sustained growth in the size of the global fixed income market and continuous innovations in the types and varieties of fixed income securities make bonds increasingly attractive to a broader array of investors. Fixed income securities are subject to a wide number of risks but credit risk and interest rate risk remain the most important ones for most investors. Credit risk or default risk deals the likelihood that the issuer will not be able to make timely interest payments and principal repayment. Interest rate risks arise from changes in the level, slope and curvature of the term structure of interest rates. Several measures of both a single bond or bond portfolio's duration and convexity can be used to quantify interest rate risk.

Fixed income portfolios can be evaluated based on either the fund manager's strategy or via factor models. The former method begins with a comparison of actual returns to those of an appropriate benchmark index. The index selected should represent the type of securities that are permitted according to the policy statement. Fixed income indexes, however, are more difficult to design, construct and maintain than are equity market indexes. The relative performance of a fixed income manager can then be decomposed and the manager's value added can be determined. Managers can also be compared to universes of other managers who follow similar styles. Factor models are quantitative models that seek to identify and estimate the factors that cause a portfolio's return and risk. A variety of models and factors have been developed.

CHAPTER 10

Investment Companies as Investment Vehicles

Investment company products—open-end and closed-end mutual funds, unit investment trusts, exchange traded funds—are the dominant investment vehicle for tens of millions of individual investors and sizable numbers of institutional investors. The use of investment company products as a primary investment vehicle reflects their several cost advantages, the wide scope of investment choices they offer, and—as in other segments of the financial sector—an ongoing array of innovations.

The information in Table 10.1 is indicative of the prominence of investment company products as investment vehicles. It presents basic data on the size, composition and growth of the U.S. market for investment company products for the two reasonably representative years of 1996 and 2005. Data are presented on assets and numbers of investment companies as well as ownership statistics. Roughly $9.5 trillion of assets were held by investment companies in 2005, an increase of some $5.8 trillion from 1996.[1] Moreover, the almost 10% compound annual growth rate in investment company assets appreciably outstripped both the growth in the economy and the inflation rate during this period.

Open-end (more commonly known as *mutual funds*) investment companies continue to represent the overwhelming bulk of investment company assets. As depicted in Table 10.1, their share of total assets stood at 94% in 2005, approximately the same as in 1996. In contrast, the shares of total assets held by closed-end funds and unit investment trusts have slipped since 1996. The decline has been concentrated in the share of total assets held by unit investment trusts. Exchange-traded funds (ETFs), first introduced in 1993, have largely captured the shares of total assets once accounted for by closed-end funds and unit investment trusts. From less than 1% in 1996, the proportion of total assets held by ETFs advanced to 3% by 2005.

[1] Global assets in investment company products at yearend 2005 stood at $17.8 trillion, according to the Investment Company Institute. See *Mutual Fund Factbook 2005*, Investment Company Institute, Washington, D.C.

TABLE 10.1   The Market for Investment Company Products: Size, Composition and Ownership

	2005	Percent of Total 2005	Percent of Total 1996	1996
Assets (billions)				
Total	$9,518	100.00%	100.00%	$3,747
Mutual funds	8,900	93.50%	94.01%	3,526
Closed-end funds	276	2.90%	3.92%	147
Unit investment trusts	41	0.04%	1.92%	72
Exchange-traded funds	296	3.11%	0.05%	19
Number of Investment Companies				
Total	15,308	100.00%	100.00%	18,574
Mutual funds	8,454	55.22%	33.88%	6,293
Closed-end funds	634	4.14%	2.68%	498
Unit investment trusts	6,019	39.32%	63.34%	11,764
Exchange-traded funds	201	1.31%	0.01%	19
Ownership				
Households				
Percent of total assets	88%		NA	
Number of households	53.7 million		36.8 million	
Institutions				
Percent of total assets	12%		NA	
Number of institutions	NA		NA	

Source: Investment Company Institute, *2005 Investment Company Fact Book.* Copyright 2005 by the Investment Company Institute (www.ici.org). Reprinted with permission.

The number of investment company products has narrowed by more than 3,000 since 1996. The data in Table 10.1 indicate that the decline has been most prominent in the numbers of unit investment trusts and, to a lesser extent, in closed-end funds. At the same time the numbers of mutual funds and ETFs have climbed briskly. About 54 million households representing some 91 million individual investors own an estimated 88% of all mutual fund assets. Another indication of the prominent role of investment company products is the shares they represent of outstanding financial securities. Roughly 25% of all equities; close to one-third of all municipal securities; 10% of all taxable bonds; and about 37% of all commercial paper are owned by investment companies.[2]

In light of the importance of investment company products as investment vehicles, we devote this entire chapter to examining their advantages and potential disadvantages. Investment committees can use this understanding in deciding whether such investment vehicles can assist them in achieving their investment goals and objectives.

INVESTMENT COMPANIES

Investment companies are financial intermediaries that create, sell, and redeem financial securities. These securities are claims on the investment company's assets and, as such, are liabilities of the investment company. In this regard investment companies are similar to other financial intermediaries like commercial banks, thrift institutions, defined benefit pension plans and insurance companies.

Independent investment advisers, that is, advisers not affiliated with other financial institution represent about 58% of all investment company sponsors. The remaining 42% are affiliated with banks, thrifts, insurance companies, security broker-dealers, and non-U.S. sponsors. These investment advisers are organized as corporations, trusts, or partnerships. In total, there were about 500 financial intermediaries that sponsored investment company products in 2005.[3]

Investment company sponsors appoint the initial board of directors of the investment company; determine the types of products, such as mutual funds, it will offer as well as the specific investment objectives of the products; shepherd the products through the regulatory and approval process; and organize the portfolio management, investment, operating and administrative aspects of the business. Quite often, the investment company will employ affiliated or independent third parties to carry out the investment management, operating and administrative parts of the business.

Once the investment company's products have been sold to the investing public, these shareholders then have voting rights (including the right to elect the fund's board of directors). By law, some directors must be independent ones. That is, they are not to have significant relations with fund sponsors and advisers. The directors are the investment company's govern-

---

[2] *Mutual Fund Factbook,* Investment Company Institute, 2005.
[3] *Mutual Fund Factbook,* Investment Company Institute, 2005.

ing body and, as such, they have oversight responsibilities for the fund's strategy, policies, officers, and regulatory compliance.

Pooling of investors monies is one of the distinctive features of investment companies, and an important source of their cost advantage compared to direct investments. When an investor purchases an investment company product, the monies are combined with those of all other investors and used by the investment company to purchase predetermined types of securities, such as equities, bonds and cash equivalents. The specific securities purchased are based on the investment objectives and policies set forth by the investment company and contained in the product's prospectus. The securities become an asset of the investment company. The investor receives claims on the investment company, for example, shares in a mutual fund, equi-proportional to the total amount invested. The cash flows (dividends, interest, proceeds from sales) received on the underlying securities that are the assets of the investment company are distributed on an equi-proportional basis to investors. Similarly, any change in the underlying market value of the investment company's assets is reflected on an equi-proportional basis to investors. Finally, expenses of operating the investment company are assigned to investors on an equi-proportional basis.

Economies of scale and scope in pooling investors' monies are the key to the cost advantages of mutual funds. In principle investors can on either their own or by employing professional investment managers do all of the things performed by mutual funds. Investors can design an asset allocation strategy, research markets and securities, execute security transactions, and maintain records to name just a few. However, for investment committees and investors whose funds are relatively small in dollar size and who transact with reasonably high frequency the costs of performing all of these functions effectively could be extremely high. By pooling the monies of a large number of smaller investors investment companies act like large investors and may obtain the cost advantages of doing so.

One important cost advantage arises from trading large blocks of securities. Substantial savings on brokerage fees and commissions may result. A second cost advantage emerges from investors being able to own fractional shares in a range of securities and portfolios, lowering the costs of achieving diversification and risk reduction. Additionally, the costs of professional investment management services including those for portfolio managers, security analysts, traders, and performance evaluators may be reduced by the pooling of funds. Likewise, the costs of recordkeeping and other administrative costs of managing a fund might be lowered via the pooling of funds. Finally, investment companies that offer a family or complex of products might experience economies of scope in the process of adding products and provide these additional products at lower costs to existing investors.

REGULATION OF INVESTMENT COMPANIES

The Investment Company Act of 1940 is the primary regulatory code for investment companies. The Act is administered by the Securities and Exchange Commission. In addition, investment companies come under the purview of the Securities Acts of 1933 and 1934, and the Investment Advisers Act of 1940 also pertains to investment companies. Finally, the behavior of investment companies is influenced by the U.S. tax code.

The focus of the Investment Company Act of 1940 is on the organization of investment companies and is designed to minimize conflicts of interest between investment company sponsors and their shareholders. The Act emphasizes disclosure to potential investors about the structure and operations of the investment company, and requires information to be revealed about the fund and its investment objectives. The Act further requires investment companies to submit semiannual reports to the SEC and fund shareholders.

In a similar vein to businesses planning to sell stocks and bonds to the general public, investment companies are required to register all public offerings of their securities, such as mutual fund shares, with the SEC and have the registration approved by the SEC before a prospectus may be offered to investors. The Investment Advisers Act of 1940 requires investment advisers who have at least $25 million of assets under management or who advise registered investment companies to register with the SEC and to conform to certain regulations designed to protect investors. This Act applies to the vast majority of advisers to investment companies.

The U.S. tax code provides "pass-through" tax status to registered investment companies. The pass-through status means the cash flows (dividends, interest, and realized capital gains) received by investment companies on their investment assets are not subject to federal income taxes at the investment company level—except for those retained—but are taxed at the shareholder level. Double taxation is avoided and taxable shareholders are subject to federal income taxes on the pro rata shares of dividends, interest and realized capital gains they receive from the investment company.

In order to qualify for pass-through tax status, investment companies must meet investment diversification standards and pass tests regarding their sources of income. In particular, at least 50% of the funds assets must be invested in securities but the securities of any one issuer can not represent more than 5% of the fund's assets nor more than 10% of the voting securities of the issuer. Additionally, not more than 25% of the fund's assets may be invested in the securities of any one issuer excluding government securities or the securities of other funds.

TYPES OF INVESTMENT COMPANIES

There are four basic types of investment companies: open-end, closed-end, unit investment trusts, and exchange-traded funds. The first two types are also known as "managed" investment companies because the underlying portfolios of securities that represent the assets of the investment company are managed by the investment company. Unit investment trusts, in contrast, are known as "unmanaged" portfolios because the underlying portfolios of securities are fixed for the life of the trust. Exchange-traded funds have features of both.

Open-End Funds

Open-end funds, better known as mutual funds, issue an unlimited number of shares.[4] As additional monies are invested with these funds new shares are issued and, in a related vein, as investors redeem shares they own in an open-end fund the investment company retires the shares. Shares are purchased and sold, before any fees, at their net asset value (NAV). NAV is computed as the market value of the securities owned by the mutual fund minus the fund's liabilities divided by the number of shares in the fund outstanding. Mathematically, NAV is computed from the following formula:

$$NAV = \frac{\text{Market value of fund assets} - \text{Liabilities}}{\text{Number of shares outstanding}} \qquad (10.1)$$

Mutual funds are required to use "forward pricing" for the purchase and redemption of shares. Forward pricing simply means that the fund is required to use the next computed NAV, rather than the previously computed NAV, in executing purchase and redemption orders. Since most mutual funds compute daily NAVs beginning at 4:00 P.M. Eastern Time when the New York Stock Exchange closes, orders received before 4:00 P.M. are executed at the day's NAV. Orders received after 4:00 P.M. are executed at the next day's NAV.

Types of Open-End Funds

The assets and numbers of mutual funds are concentrated in equity securities. As noted in Table 10.1 the $8.9 trillion of assets under management by mutual funds represents about 94% of all assets under management by

---

[4] There are cases where open-end funds have been closed at least temporarily to new investors.

investment companies, and the 8,454 separate mutual funds account for approximately 55% of the total number of investment company products.

In the first instance mutual funds may be classified by the broad types of securities in which they invest. These classifications are *stock funds, bond funds, hybrid or combination funds, and money market funds*. For 2005, 55% of mutual fund assets were invested in stock funds, 15% in bond funds, 6% in hybrid funds and 23% in money market funds. While the allocations to these broad classes of mutual funds do vary somewhat over time with changes in market conditions and interest rates, allocations to and the numbers of stock funds dominate individual investor holdings of mutual fund shares. We can confidently conclude that savings of individual investors are used primarily to purchase stock mutual funds.

On the other hand, institutional investors in general and businesses in particular allocate the majority of their mutual fund investments to money market funds. For 2005, some 56% of institutional ownership of mutual fund shares were invested in money market funds. Institutions appear to primarily use mutual funds as a low cost, convenient investment vehicle for their excess liquid assets.[5]

The four broad classes of mutual funds can be further subdivided by their particular *investment objectives*. The Investment Company Institute, for example, categorizes 33 types of mutual funds according to their general investment objectives. These 33 classes describe in more detail the specific types of securities in which the fund invests; whether the fund seeks to provide returns to investors via current income from dividends and interest, by way of capital appreciation, or a combination; and a sense of the fund's risk. Fund investment objectives are presented in Table 10.2. Additional classifications could be developed.

Fees and Share Classes

Open-end mutual funds may charge their shareholders a variety of fees related to the purchase and sale of shares and fund operating expenses. These fees and charges will affect the investor's net return on the fund and so investment committees should be aware of them. They primary fees and expenses are as follows:

- *Front-end load.* This is a fee paid, usually determined as a percentage of the monies invested, when the investor initially purchases shares in a mutual fund. Front-end loads vary widely but may not exceed 8.50%.
- *Back-end load.* This is a fee paid, again usually measured as a percentage, when the investor sells or redeems shares.

---

[5] *Mutual Fund Factbook,* Investment Company Institute, 2005.

TABLE 10.2   The Investment Company Institute's Classification of Mutual Funds

Stock Funds

Aggressive growth funds invest primarily in common stock of small, growth companies with potential for capital appreciation.

Emerging market equity funds invest primarily in equity securities of companies based in less-developed regions of the world.

Global equity funds invest primarily in worldwide equity securities, including those of U.S. companies.

Growth and income funds attempt to combine long-term capital growth with steady income dividends. These funds pursue this goal by investing primarily in common stocks of established companies with the potential for both growth and good dividends.

Growth funds invest primarily in common stocks of well-established companies with the potential for capital appreciation. These funds' primary aim is to increase the value *of* their investments (capital gain) rather than generate a flow of dividends.

Income equity funds seek income by investing primarily in equity securities of companies with good dividends. Capital appreciation is not an objective.

International equity funds invest at least 80% of their portfolios in equity securities of companies located outside the United States.

Regional equity funds invest in equity securities of companies based in specific world regions, such as Europe, Latin America, the Pacific Region, or individual countries.

Sector equity funds seek capital appreciation by investing in companies in related fields or specific industries, such as financial services, health care, natural resources, technology, or utilities.

Bond Funds

Corporate bond-general funds seek a high level of income by investing 80% or more of their portfolios in corporate bonds and have no explicit restrictions on average maturity.

Corporate bond-intermediate-term-funds seek a high level of income with 80% or more of their portfolios invested at all times in corporate bonds. Their average maturity is 5 to 10 years.

Corporate bond-short-term funds seek a high level of current income with 80% or more of their portfolios invested at all times in corporate bonds. Their average maturity is one to five years.

Global bond-general funds invest in worldwide debt securities and have no stated average maturity or an average maturity of more than five years. Up to 25% of their portfolios' securities (not including cash) may be invested in companies located in the United States.

Global bond-short-term funds invest in worldwide debt securities and have an average maturity of one to five years. Up to 25% of their portfolios' securities (not including cash) may be invested in companies located in the United States.

Government bond-general funds invest at least 80% of their portfolios in U.S. government securities and have no stated average maturity.

Government bond-intermediate-term funds invest at least 80% of their portfolios in U.S. government securities and have an average maturity of 5 to 10 years.

Government bond-short-term funds invest at least 80% of their portfolios in U.S. government securities and have an average maturity of one to five years.

High-yield funds seek a high level of current income by investing at least 80% of their portfolios in lower-rated corporate bonds (Baa or lower by Moody's and BBB or lower by Standard and Poor's rating services).

Mortgage-Backed funds invest at least 80% of their portfolios in pooled mortgage-backed securities.

TABLE 10.2 (Continued)

Bond Funds

National municipal bond-general funds invest predominantly in municipal bonds and have an average maturity of more than five years or no stated average maturity. The funds' bonds are usually exempt from federal income tax but may be taxed under state and local laws.

National municipal bond-short-term funds invest predominantly in municipal bonds and have an average maturity of one to five years. The funds' bonds are usually exempt from federal income tax but may be taxed under state and local laws.

Other world bond funds invest at least 80% of their portfolios in a combination of foreign government and corporate debt. Some funds in this category invest primarily in debt securities of emerging markets.

State municipal bond-general funds invest primarily in municipal bonds of a single state and have an average maturity of more than five years or no stated average maturity. The funds' bonds are exempt from federal and state income taxes for residents of that state.

State municipal bond-short-term funds invest predominantly in municipal bonds of a single state and have an average maturity of one to five years. The funds' bonds are exempt from federal and state income taxes for residents of that state.

Strategic income funds invest in a combination of domestic fixed income securities to provide high current income.

Hybrid Funds

Asset allocation funds seek high total return by investing in a mix of equities, fixed income securities and money market instruments. Unlike flexible portfolio funds (defined below), these funds are required to strictly maintain a precise weighting in asset classes.

Balanced funds invest in a specific mix of equity securities and bonds with the three-part objective of conserving principal, providing income, and achieving long-term growth of both principal and income.

Flexible portfolio funds seek high total return by investing in common stock, bonds and other debt securities, and money market securities. Portfolios may hold up to 100% of any one of these types of securities and may easily change, depending on market conditions.

Income-mixed funds seek a high level of current income by investing in a variety of income-producing securities, including equities and fixed income securities. Capital appreciation is not a primary objective.

Money Market Funds

National tax-exempt money market funds seek income not taxed by the federal government by investing in municipal securities with relatively short maturities.

State tax exempt money market funds invest predominantly in short-term municipal obligations of a single state, which are exempt from federal and state income taxes for residents of that state.

Taxable money market-government funds invest principally in short-term U.S. Treasury obligations and other short-term financial instruments issued or guaranteed by the U.S. government, its agencies or instrumentalities.

Taxable money market-nongovernment funds invest in a variety of money market instruments, including certificates of deposit of large banks, commercial paper, and banker's acceptances.

Source: Investment Company Institute, *A Guide to Mutual Funds.* Copyright 2006 by the Investment Company Institute (www.ici.org). Reprinted with permission.

- *Contingent-deferred sales charge*. This is a fee, a back-end load, imposed on the sale or redemption of shares before a specific date. It may be a sliding-scale back-end load where the back-end load declines the longer the investor owns the shares.
- *No-load*. Funds without a front-end load. In terms of assets, roughly one-half of all mutual funds are no-load.
- *12b-1 fees*. These are fees mutual funds are allowed to charge to shareholders for a variety of marketing and distribution costs as well as to compensate financial advisors. The fee takes it name from the Securities and Exchange Commission rule that permits it.
- *Operating expenses*. These are fees the mutual fund has incurred for the operating expenses of the fund, including portfolio management and fund administrative expenses. One important source of operating expenses for mutual funds is the cost involved in trading securities. The fund's *turnover rate,* the lesser of the fund's annual purchases or sales of securities as a percent of the fund's net assets, is often a nontrivial component of the fund's operating expenses.

Fees and expenses for mutual funds appear to be on a sharp downtrend. The Investment Company Institute reports that between 1995 and 2005 average fees and expenses for stock mutual funds dropped from 1.55% to 1.13%, while average bond mutual funds expenses fell from 1.45% to 0.90%.[6] More intense competition in the mutual fund marketplace; the continued growth of no-load funds; greater investments by pension plans who are often exempt from loads; and further realization of economies of scale are thought to be the primary causes of the recession in mutual fund fees and expenses.

Many, but not all open-end mutual funds have up to three classes of shares. These classes pertain to the identical underlying securities but differ according to their load and fee structures. Class A shares require a front-end load and shareholders are assessed 12b-1 fees. Class B shares impose a contingent deferred sales load and charge 12b-1 fees. Class B shares may also be converted to Class A shares. Class C shares are like Class B ones, but the contingent deferred sales load applies only to redemptions within the first year after purchase and Class C shares generally can not be converted to Class A shares.

Closed-End Funds

Closed-end funds are also managed portfolios but, unlike open-end funds, do not issue an unlimited number of shares and do not redeem shares. Instead, when a closed-end fund is established an offering of shares is made to

---

[6] *Mutual Fund Factbook*, Investment Company Institute, 2005.

the general public and the shares in the fund are then listed and traded on either organized or over-the-counter security markets. Shares in the closed-end fund may then be purchased and sold in much the same way as shares of common stocks.

As indicated in Table 10.1 closed-end funds represent relatively small shares, roughly 3% and 4%, respectively, of total investment company assets and products. These shares have not appreciably changed in the last ten years. In an absolute sense the assets held by closed-end funds as well as the numbers of such funds have continued to expand over the last 10 years, though their rates of increase have lagged those of open-end funds and exchange traded funds.

Closed-end funds are primarily bond funds. Sixty-two percent of closed-end fund assets of $276 billion were in bond funds in 2005. Almost 70% of the 634 closed-end funds in 2005 were bond funds. Research at the Investment Company Institute suggests that more affluent individual investors are the primary purchasers of closed-end funds.

Market conditions should determine the share prices of closed-end funds, as they trade on organized and over-the-counter securities markets. Nonetheless, the market determined share prices for closed-end funds should not diverge too much, too often, or for too long from the fund's underlying NAV as this would otherwise seem to present an opportunity for riskless profit. Yet, situations of closed-end funds prices diverging from NAVs, especially discounts to NAV, appear all too frequently. Research on this anomaly has yet to completely resolve the puzzle.[7]

Unit Investment Trusts

Unit Investment Trusts are known as unmanaged portfolios. A unit investment trust is formed when an investment company buys a fixed portfolio of securities and holds this fixed portfolio for fixed length of time. The trust then sells shares in this fixed portfolio to investors. All cash flows from the securities are passed through to the trust's shareholders. When the trust expires then the proceeds from the sale of the securities are paid to shareholders.

Shares in unit investment trusts trade at the trust's NAV. When shares are either bought or sold prior to the trust's expiration they are purchased from existing shareholders or sold to either the trust's sponsor or to existing or new shareholders. If they are sold to the trust's sponsor then the sponsor must liquidate securities from the underlying portfolio.

---

[7] The puzzle is examined in more depth by several researchers. See, for example, Zvi Bodie, Alex Kane, and Alan Marcus, *Investments*, 7th ed. (New York: McGraw-Hill Irwin, 2007).

Table 10.1 shows that the assets and numbers of Unit Investment Trusts have declined noticeably in the 10-year period from 1996 to 2005. Many trusts have expired and not been reestablished. The surge in exchange traded funds may be largely responsible for the falloff in unit investment trusts.

Exchange-Traded Funds

Exchange-traded funds (ETFs) have features of open-end and closed-end funds as well as unit investment trusts. Like open-end funds, they issue unlimited numbers of shares. Like closed-end funds they are listed and traded on organized and over-the-counter securities markets. Some of the original ETFs were organized as unit investment trusts, but most are now mutual funds. Of the 201 ETFs available in 2005, 193 were organized as mutual funds and just eight as unit investment trusts. However, it is their differences from other investment company products that explain their soaring popularity.

ETFs are baskets of securities established by investment companies. Once established, the fund is listed and traded on either an organized or over-the-counter securities market. Like common stock, ETF shares are traded continuously at current market prices instead of once per day at the end-of-the-day's NAV as is the case with mutual fund shares. They may therefore provide investors with incremental liquidity. Moreover, like common stock shares but unlike open and closed-end fund shares, ETF shares can be traded via market, limit and stop orders as well as short sales. Derivative contracts such as options and futures may also be available on some ETFs, allowing investors to either hedge or speculate on their returns. These features provide flexibility to investors. Additionally, as exchange-traded investment vehicles investors may purchase ETFs directly through security brokers and pay commissions rather than loads. Operating expenses for investment companies who sponsor ETFs may also be lower than for some open-end funds.

ETFs were first introduced in 1993 and, as indicated in Table 10.1, while their assets and numbers are still relatively small compared to mutual funds, their growth rates have been striking. The majority of currently available ETFs are equity index funds—mimicking the performance of widely followed stock market indexes. In 2005, 95% of ETFs assets were in equities with only 5% in bonds. Ninety-seven percent of the 201 ETFs were equity funds. More recently, the variety of ETFs has expanded to sector, country, region, and commodity funds. The flexibility of ETFs has made them especially appealing to institutional investors.

ETFs also may possess a tax advantage over equity mutual funds. While ETFs are mutual funds and subject to the same tax rules as other mutual funds discussed above, they have used a method called "redemption in kind" to provide a potential tax advantages to investors.

When investors redeem shares in a typical equity mutual fund the fund may be required to sell shares of the underlying securities. If the sale results in a capital gain then the capital gain is distributed to all shareholders in the fund on a pro rata basis. Fund shareholders are then subject to a capital gains tax even if they did not want to sell their shares.

ETFs have circumvented this potential tax liability by satisfying redemptions with shares of stock in the underlying portfolio of securities, or finding new buyers for investors wishing to redeem their shares. In both "redemption in kind" situations, the underlying shares are not sold and a tax liability does not exist.[8]

SELECTING MUTUAL FUNDS

With more than 15,000 investment company products to choose from, including almost 8,500 mutual funds, investment committees can likely find either a fund or portfolio of funds that closely meet their investment objectives. At the same time the sheer number of investment company products makes the task of finding the most suitable ones a considerable challenge. In this regard researching the characteristics of investment company products has replaced the researching of individual securities.

A mutual fund's investment objective(s) is a useful and important starting point. Consistency between a mutual fund's investment objectives and the investment committee's goals is an obvious initial screen in selecting a fund. Sponsors seeking the return and diversification benefits of real estate investments, for example, might focus on REITs. Tax-exempt sponsors might exclude from their research municipal bond funds.

Information on a fund's particular investment objectives and investment policies as well as much additional valuable information are contained in the fund's *prospectus, part B of the prospectus* also known as *the statement of additional information,* and the *annual report* and the *semiannual report.* In addition to information on the fund's investment objectives information is provided on the fund's investment strategy; its portfolio composition and security holdings; its investment performance; its investment manager(s) and applicable load, fee structure and expense ratios. These filings are required by the Investment Company Act of 1940, and are available to all existing and prospective shareholders.

---

[8] James M. Poterba and John B. Shoven, "Exchange Traded Funds: A New Investment Option for Taxable Investors," *American Economic Review* 92, no. 2 (May 2004), pp. 422–427.

Subsequent to identifying funds whose broad investment objectives are consistent with the investment committee's the next step is to collect and analyze information on specific funds within the chosen class. There are a sizable number of such information sources. For example, the Investment Company Institute publishes a voluminous, alphabetic quarterly listing of all mutual fund, closed-end fund and unit investment trust sponsors who are Institute members. Links to fund web sites and telephone numbers are included. The financial media are a second source of mutual fund information. Print and online versions of publications such as the *Financial Times, Barron's, Investor's Business Daily,* and the *Wall St. Journal* report daily and weekly information on fund performance measures, NAVs and year-to-date total returns. More comprehensive and detailed quarterly and annual performance measures are reported in many of these publications.

Nonsubscription online sites are a third source of mutual fund information. Sites such as *Yahoo Finance* and *Bloomberg*, to name just two, provide data on fund performance, pricing, and expenses among other things.[9]

A third source of mutual information is provided by research organizations that specialize in the analysis and evaluation of mutual funds. Four highly respected organizations are *Lipper Analytical, Wiesenberger's Investment Companies, Value Line,* and *Morningstar's Mutual Fund Sourcebook.*

PERFORMANCE EVALUATION

Practitioners and researchers have invested considerable resources over the years addressing the issue of whether or not active mutual fund managers add value and, if so, then how much. That is, in addition to the costs advantages of mutual funds, do managers of active mutual funds possess superior knowledge and information such that they consistently add value via such skills as the selection of the securities for a fund's portfolio; the timing of when to buy and sell securities; or the design of the overall portfolio?

Research on this issue has been carried out from a number of perspectives using a variety of empirical techniques.[10] A consensus has yet to emerge from

---

[9] www.finance.yahoo.com/funds and www.bloomberg.com are the respective web addresses.

[10] Three representative articles are: S.P. Kothari and Jerold B. Warner, "Evaluating Mutual Fund Performance," *Journal of Finance* 56 (October, 2001), pp. 1985–2010; Jarl G. Kallberg, Crocker L. Liu, and Charles Trzcinka, "The Value Added from Investment Managers: An Examination of Funds of REITs," *Journal of Financial and Quantitative Analysis* 35 (September 2000), pp. 387–408; Russ Wermers, "Mutual Fund Performance: An Empirical Decomposition into Stock Picking Talent, Style, Transactions Costs and Expenses," *Journal of Finance* 55, no. 4 (2000), pp. 1655–1695; and Tobias J. Moskowitz, "Discussion," *Journal of Finance* 55, no. 4 (2000), pp. 1695–1703.

the research. One strand of research indicates that the returns obtained by active mutual fund managers are often less than those of passive benchmark portfolios of equities and passive stock market indexes even before expenses. Related findings are that poorly performing funds tend to be consistently poor performers; those active managers who provide superior returns do so for relatively short periods of time, generally for a few quarters; that active fund managers tend to mimic the performance of successful managers; that active managers may add the most value when shareholders may most need them— that is during periods of market declines; and that incentive or performance based fees for active fund managers are generally a worthwhile device.

A second strand of research suggests that active managers may, in fact, add consistent value. Added value has been found for active managers of REIT funds, and may be attributed to their specialized knowledge and superior information of real estate market conditions. Recent research also suggests that active managers do provide higher *gross* returns on average compared to relevant benchmarks owing to their security selection skills, but that the additional trading costs and expenses of doing so result in *net* returns that are less than the benchmarks.

There is also some evidence of "window dressing" and tax-motivated behaviors on the part of active fund managers. Window dressing refers to the practice of selling poor performing securities and purchasing good performing ones, or changing sector allocations of securities, just prior to the end of quarter, semiannual and annual portfolio reporting requirements in order to make portfolio holdings look better to shareholders. Tax-motivated behaviors include year end selling of securities that have performed poorly during the year. Such practices would bias upward performance evaluation. However, it is not clear how wide-spread and significant these practices are.

SUMMARY

The potentially sizable cost advantages, tax treatment, wide range of choices, and product innovations make investment company products an attractive investment vehicle in the implementation of investment committees and individuals investment strategies. Cost advantages arise from economies of scale and economies of scope associated with the pooling of investors monies. The pass-through tax treatment of mutual funds cash flows avoids the double taxation of corporate income. More than 15,000 investment company products exist in the U.S. alone. Innovations, such as sector funds and ETFs, occur on an ongoing basis. These features may be especially appealing to investors who act as their own investment managers and those whose funds are relatively small.

Selecting the most appropriate among the large number of investment company products has been considerably facilitated by classifying them according to investment objectives and by the many publicly available print and online sources of information. Highly reputable research organizations provide detailed and comprehensive information, analysis and evaluation of most investment company products.

Active mutual fund managers may add consistent value owing to their specific knowledge and information about characteristics of particular securities and ability to time market cycles. However, in many cases it appears the incremental value is offset by higher trading costs and expenses. Undoubtedly, researchers will continue to investigate this issue.

Investment Manager Search Process

The investment committee will be called upon periodically to conduct a portfolio manager search. For a newly created portfolio, this process usually begins shortly after the committee drafts the investment policy statement. For funds already in existence, a periodic review of the portfolio's investment performance may trigger discussions among committee members with regard to changing professional managers. Usually, a series of disappointing investment performance results provide the impetus for discussions concerning the wisdom of continuing with the same investment manager. In either event, it is likely that committee members will at some time be called upon to engage in a search for a new money manager.

To be sure, the selection of a portfolio manager is one of the most important responsibilities of those charged with serving on investment committees. The search process itself is a major undertaking and requires a significant commitment of time and energy for those involved. The process involves the design and development of criteria for choosing a new manager; the identification of prospective fund managers; the solicitation of proposals; and the evaluation of submitted proposals. Moreover, after the initial review of proposals, the committee must decide which fund manager(s) it wishes to evaluate further. Finally, the committee must select a fund manager(s). This is the single most important decision made by the committee.

SEARCH COMMITTEE

The composition of the search committee can vary. The search process can be conducted by either the entire investment committee or a by subcommittee. For larger investment committees, it may be advisable to appoint a subcommittee to conduct the search for an investment manager. Once the search committee completes its charge, it should then make recommendations to the full committee.

The composition of the search committee should be representative of the investment committee. Individuals with prior experience in conducting investment management searches should be included in this committee. The committee's activities will be such that having members with administrative and technical skills is essential. Therefore, personnel possessing these skills should be actively involved in the process.

The role of the chair is critical to the effectiveness of the committee. The chair is required to assign various responsibilities associated with conducting the search. These responsibilities include overseeing the solicitation of proposals, maintaining and condensing the data and other materials provided by candidates, communicating with candidates, scheduling meetings, arranging for reference checking, and presenting the committee's recommendations to the investment committee.

ESTABLISHING GOALS

The process of identifying candidates should begin with the establishment of the investment manager criteria. The manager is to operate the fund in a manner consistent with the goals of the fund. The manager is charged with achieving a set of predetermined performance objectives, while operating within the constraints specified in the fund's investment policy statement. Therefore, it is necessary that the candidate's compatibility with the sponsoring organization's philosophy as well as with the portfolio's goals and objectives be explicitly considered.

The starting point, then, is to define the type of investment manager whose management philosophy and approach are consistent with the goals of the fund. If the investment goals require a growth-oriented approach to investing, then only those candidates whose expertise is in successfully managing growth portfolios should be considered. Likewise, a portfolio with an income-oriented or value-oriented goal should be matched with those candidates within these investment approaches. For this reason, the search committee must evaluate the compatibility of its goals with the candidates' investment management styles. In short, before the search process is started, the investment committee must carefully identify its needs.

NUMBER OF MANAGERS

One of the first decisions that should be made by the search committee is whether to consider more than one investment professional to manage the fund's assets. There are several reasons why a committee might consider multiple managers. For example, multiple managers may permit an incremental higher level of diversification for the fund. In addition to enhanced securities diversification, multiple managers may provide for additional diversification in style or investment approaches. Along these lines, the committee could choose to hire a value manager, growth manager, and perhaps a high-tech manager. Regardless of investment approaches, the successful managers should be well disciplined enough to stick to their own techniques. If the objectives of the portfolio change so that new investment approaches are required, the committee should immediately reevaluate the suitability of their current investment manager(s).

Multiple managers may be attractive if the sponsor wants a balanced portfolio. In this instance, the committee selects a manager for its equity portfolio and a one for its fixed income portfolio. Each manager would be responsible for achieving goals suitable for the type of assets it controls. The committee could also choose to employ the services of multiple managers for each component of the balanced fund. Many investment professionals recognize that different skills are required to manage equities and fixed income securities.

Also, there are costs associated with employing multiple fund managers. Extra time and efforts will likely be required to monitor and evaluate the performance of the additional managers. That is, the cost of evaluating one manager who is responsible for investing the entire fund is likely less than that of evaluating several managers, each of whom is responsible for one portion of the fund. Moreover, there is a large and growing body of research literature that is consistent with the view that it is extremely difficult for fund managers to consistently outperform the relevant market index benchmarks, especially on a risk-adjusted basis. Perhaps as a consequence many fund managers in reality have very similar portfolios in terms of asset allocation and securities held. Recognizing this, the investment committee should take care that, if it intends to use multiple managers, they actually obtain the benefits in terms of incremental diversification and enhanced performance rather than duplication of efforts.

The choice of how many managers to employ may be influenced by the size of the portfolio. Smaller funds may not be suitable for a multimanager approach. The fee structure of money managers may prohibit multiple managers. Furthermore, asset reallocation between money managers would be more difficult to coordinate with multiple managers.

When the size of the investment portfolio is small, an attractive alternative may be to adopt a mutual fund strategy. This choice provides even the smallest investment portfolios with maximum diversification and expert management. In these instances, a two-step approach may be appropriate. First, the investment committee must decide on the asset allocation range, given the requirements of the portfolio. Here, the committee can seek professional assistance. Second, the committee would choose among various mutual funds whose goals and objectives mirror that of the portfolio.

CANDIDATE IDENTIFICATION

After the committee determines the proper investment management style, it must identify a list of potential candidates for proposal solicitation. This requires the committee to identify successful investment managers whose philosophy and management styles match the requirements of the fund. Typically, this will involve the identification of investment managers who have achieved attractive performance results based on their stated objectives on a consistent basis.

At this point, the investment committee should focus on several factors in aiding it in identifying prospective candidates. Attention should be paid to more easily identifiable quantitative criteria as well as more subjective ones. As we discuss here, the past investment results and fee structures of potential managers should be thoroughly scrutinized. But in a world where performance and fees tend to converge over time, the choice of one or more managers may ultimately be based on such issues as quality of service, compatibility of investment philosophies, trust, and communications.

Remember, that the choice of an investment manager involves, in essence, establishing a business relationship with an entire organization. Engaging the services of a stellar investment strategist yields only frustration and disappointment if, for example, phone calls to the organization are not returned, or if operational inadequacies prevent account statements from being transmitted in a timely, accurate, and an informative manner.

While variations in the performance of operating units exist in all organizations, we are of the view that such variations are relatively smaller in good than in poor investment management organizations. Simply put, consistently achieving investment objectives required by clients requires consistently strong performance by all operating units of an investment organization. However, in an industry where vestiges of heavy regulation still remain, this is not always found.

The growth of the investment management industry has been largely based on strengths in the marketing of investment services and on achieving solid gross returns for clients. Total Quality Management approaches in the investment services industry, as has been the situation in much of the broader services sector, are still relatively new. The investment committee should recognize these features of the industry and, in our view, base its recommendations on a number of quantitative factors as well as critical qualitative factors.

A variety of organizations provide investment management services. These include registered investment advisors (RIAs), asset management divisions within security broker-dealers, and insurance companies, banks trust departments, and some mutual funds. The range of services and the size of such organizations is enormous. The larger investment management organizations obviously provide a full range of investment services and products, encompassing most—if not all—of the components of a well-developed investment process as well as the complete range of investment styles and products. Smaller investment companies, in contrast, may specialize in particular niches of the investment process. Trade-offs might exist between the choice of either a larger or smaller investment company along such dimensions as depth of professional staff, fees, personal attention, service quality, and the like.

One trend in the investment industry that is gaining popularity among both large and small organizations is the use of outside managers to actually invest fund monies. The investment committee should be aware of whether or not the organization they employ is actually investing their funds or, instead, directing them to others to do so. Proponents of this "managing the managers" approach contend that it allows for greater specialization with attendant gains. Critics, however, argue that it merely adds an additional layer to the investment management process with attendant higher costs.

Various investment services track the investment performance of money managers. These include Pension Investment Performance Evaluation Report (PIPER) and SEI. Also, names of investment managers can be found in publications such as the *Money Market Directory*, and the listing of RIA. In addition to these sources, several organizations maintain proprietary lists of investment managers along with performance figures. In fact, the committee may employ the services of pension fund consultants to identify suitable money managers and to assist it in the selection process. Finally, names of professional investment managers can be obtained by way of referrals.

MANAGEMENT AND RELATED FEES

In addition to performance results, the search committee should carefully consider fees and other expenses charged by professional investment managers. Investment expertise is essential to the success of the fund. However, excessive fees and other related expenses can reduce the overall investment return.

Therefore, the compensation issue should be clearly understood. Usually, investment managers provide a fee schedule detailing the cost of managing a portfolio, which is based on the size of the assets under management. To be sure, the fees charged by professional managers may vary significantly from one to another. Typically, investment managers charge a fee based on the amount of money under management, as well as the amount of income (i.e., interest and dividends) the portfolio receives. These fees may not cover all of the services that the fund may require. For example, additional fees such as the costs of trading securities, and any upfront fees may be required. Therefore, it is important to determine exactly what services that the basic fee covers. The investment manager should also be required to disclose the costs of all additional services. Finally, the fee schedule should also specify the timing of payment (quarterly, semiannual, annual, etc.) and whether or not these fees cover custody and safekeeping services.

Table 11.1 presents a hypothetical fee schedule. This schedule provides information on a hypothetical fund's market value and the corresponding fee charged. For example, a fund with a market value of $24,000,000 would be charged an annual fee of $96,000 (i.e., $24,000,000 times 0.40%). Some fund managers will provide eleemosynary funds with discounts. Finally, these fee schedules may be negotiable.

Investment committees often overlook additional fees and expenses which are not as obvious as the ones discussed so far. There can be significant additional fees if the investment manager invests in mutual funds. In addition to the management fees, the fund could incur expenses, such as front-end and back-end loads. Furthermore, 12b-1 fees charged by mutual funds for advertising and commissions paid to brokers can greatly increase the overall management cost. Unfortunately, the impact of these expenses on overall investment performance may not be apparent until after a new manager is in place.

The search committee has a responsibility to examine other costs as well. For example, the candidates should be required to furnish the committee with a commission schedule. It is heard of, for funds to be charged 25 to 50 cents or more for each security share traded, even though the actual costs are a few pennies per share. For example, an investment manager may have an agreement whereby it directs trades to a brokerage house in return for research services. In essence, the fund ends up paying for the investment manager's outside research without ever being aware of these arrangements.

TABLE 11.1   ABC Manager Sample Fee Schedule

Fund Market Value	Annual Fees
$500,000–$1,000,000	0.75%
$1,000,000–$10,000,000	0.65%
$10,000,000–$20,000,000	0.50%
Above $20,000,000	0.40%

FIRM SIZE AND OWNERSHIP

Another factor that the search committee should be aware of when developing a candidate list is the size of the management firm. Almost all investment managers specify the minimum size assets that they will manage. The investment committee should determine whether the size of their fund falls within this minimum.

There are other size issues which should be addressed as well. Investment committee members of smaller funds are often concerned that large money managers will not devote the time and individual attention that their portfolio requires. This is certainly a valid concern and should be addressed. Likewise, a small management firm may also present some valid concerns. For example, these firms may be deficient in terms of management professionals. The committee should carefully consider the risk if the "star performer" is no longer associated with the firm. It is always important to determine beforehand, who will manage the fund, if the designated professional manager is no longer available. Finally, the aspect of employee ownership should not be overlooked. Investment professionals, who have a stake in the firm can be expected to have a deeper commitment to their firm's overall success. The search committee should carefully consider these issues when the final selection is made.

REQUEST FOR PROPOSALS (RFP)

Once the list of investment managers has been obtained, the committee contacts these firms seeking proposals. Figure 11.1 contains a sample request for proposal (RFP). The RFP should contain all necessary information to allow the candidates to respond. The RFP should state the size of the fund, and its goals and objectives, as well as any distribution requirements. Finally, the RFP should specify a deadline for the requested materials to be received.

The RFP should explicitly identify areas that it wishes the candidates to address. Candidates should be asked to provide performance information of monies under management with objectives similar to those of the fund. The candidates should provide a statement concerning their investment philosophy and style. This should include its risk management and diversification strategies, methods of security selection, use of market timing, asset allocation method, and average size of its portfolio both in terms of dollars and securities held. The candidates should also indicate the framework in which purchase and/or sale of securities decisions are made. Additionally, other information such as the total funds under management, average fund bal-

FIGURE 11.1   Request for Proposals

Dear Investment Manager:

The Pension Investment Committee of XYZ Corporation is presently seeking proposals from investment firms to manage its pension fund. The current market value of the fund is approximately $24,000,000. A copy of the fund's Investment Policy Statement is enclosed to assist you in responding to the RFP.

In order to evaluate your proposal we request that it address the following issues:

- Your firm's investment philosophy and approach to managing XYZ Corporation's pension fund. This should include your management style, risk management techniques, diversification strategy, asset allocation methodology, degree of securities concentration, and turnover rates.
- Total funds managed on a discretionary basis. This should be categorized with regard to asset type as well as taxable and nontaxable basis.
- Performance results including risk adjusted measures (calendar year basis) on a one-, three-, five-, ten-, and twenty-year basis. These data should be presented with dividends reinvested and without dividends reinvested. The performance figures should be provided on a gross and net of fees basis. (The return presentation should conform with the Global Investment Performance Standards.)
- Performance measures during advancing and declining markets.
- Biographical information on the investment professionals in your firm. Please indicate who will have primary responsibility for the management of the fund as well as this (these) person's (s) prior investment performance record. This should include assets under management, average asset allocation, and annualized return statistics.
- Complete fee structure, including a separation of management fees, trading commission costs, custodial and safekeeping fees, and other relevant expenses.
- List of references.
- Three to five years' audited financial statements.

Please feel free to provide any additional material that you believe will assist the committee in its decision making process. The deadline for proposal submission is September 1, 200X.

Thank you for your efforts on behalf of the XYZ Corporation's pension fund.

Sincerely yours,
Chair,
Pension Fund Search Committee

---

ance, number of professionals employed, turnover rates, and minimum-size fund accepted should be reported.

One of the most important areas which the RFP should address concerns the historic performance of the investment managers. In providing information on its historic performance, the investment managers can develop composites based on a number of accounts under management.

The resume of the individuals responsible for managing the account should be provided. Audited financial statements should also be provided. The proposals should include the SEC's Corporate Review and Disclosure Form ADV, Part II. The RFP should inquire as to the use of outside research services and the candidates' fee schedules. Finally, the candidates should provide references from current and former clients. This information is extremely valuable in choosing the investment manager. The committee has a responsibility to check these references very carefully, prior to making their decision. The committee chair may delegate this task to one or more members of the search committee.

The performance time periods should be explicitly stated. For example, the candidates might be asked to provide annualized rates of return on a one-, three-, five-, ten-, and twenty-year basis. In order to avoid comparison problems, it is recommended that all performance results be measured over common periods. For example, the RFP might require candidates to use the calendar year (i.e., January to December) when reporting results. Additionally, the candidates may also be asked to provide performance results over varying market climates (i.e., bull and bear markets). The committee may also specify whether the performance figures should be with or without reinvestment of dividends.

These performance composites should be based on the Global Investment Performance Standards (GIPS). Figure 11.2 presents the Construction of Composite guidelines contained in Section II of the Global Investment Performance Standards. As the exhibit reveals, GIPS sets forth explicit guidelines as to how fund managers are to construct their presentation composites. The adherence to these guidelines by investment manager candidates enhances the ability of the investment committee to evaluate the relative performance fairly.

Figure 11.3 reports GIPS's guidelines for the Presentation of Composites that are contained in Section II (Provisions of the Global Investment Performance Standards) of the Global Investment Performance Standards. The section provides additional guidelines for managers to follow when presenting composite data to potential clients.

Adhering to the Performance Presentation Standards set forth in the Global Investment Standards publication is an important step in ensuring that investment performance is fully disclosed. The adoption of uniform standards of comparison is essential to the evaluation of investment performance. Therefore, the investment committee should strive to use comparable investment results when evaluating performance. The adoption of the GIPS performance standards or other industry accepted standards is an important step in reaching this goal.

FIGURE 11.2   GIPS Composite Construction

- All actual, fee-paying, discretionary PORTFOLIOS MUST be included in at least one COMPOSITE. Although nonfee-paying discretionary PORTFOLIOS may be included in a COMPOSITE (with appropriate disclosures), nondiscretionary PORTFOLIOS are not permitted to be included in a FIRM'S COMPOSITES.

- COMPOSITES MUST be defined according to similar investment objectives and/or strategies. The full COMPOSITE DEFINITION MUST be made available on request.

- COMPOSITES MUST include new PORTFOLIOS on a timely and consistent basis after the PORTFOLIO comes under management unless specifically mandated by the client.

- Terminated PORTFOLIOS MUST be included in the historical returns of the appropriate COMPOSITES up to the last full measurement period that the PORTFOLIO was under management.

- PORTFOLIOS are not permitted to be switched from one COMPOSITE to another unless documented changes in client guidelines or the redefinition of the COMPOSITE make it appropriate. The historical record of the PORTFOLIO MUST remain with the appropriate COMPOSITE.

- Convertible and other hybrid securities MUST be treated consistently across time and within COMPOSITES.

- CARVE-OUT segments excluding cash are not permitted to be used to represent a discretionary PORTFOLIO and, as such, are not permitted to be included in COMPOSITE returns. When a single asset class is carved out of a multiple asset class PORTFOLIO and the returns are presented as part of a single asset COMPOSITE, cash MUST be allocated to the CARVE-OUT returns in a timely and consistent manner. Beginning 1 January 2010, CARVE-OUT returns are not permitted to be included in single asset class COMPOSITE returns unless the CARVE-OUT is actually managed separately with its own cash balance.

- COMPOSITES MUST include only assets under management within the defined FIRM. FIRMS are not permitted to link simulated or model PORTFOLIOS with actual performance.

- If a FIRM sets a minimum asset level for PORTFOLIOS to be included in a COMPOSITE, no PORTFOLIOS below that asset level can be included in that COMPOSITE. Any changes to a COMPOSITE-specific minimum asset level are not permitted to be applied retroactively.

Recommendations

- CARVE-OUT returns SHOULD not be included in single asset class COMPOSITE returns unless the CARVE-OUTS are actually managed separately with their own cash balance.

- To remove the effect of a significant EXTERNAL CASH FLOW, the use of a TEMPORARY NEW ACCOUNT is RECOMMENDED (as opposed to adjusting the COMPOSITE composition to remove PORTFOLIOS with significant EXTERNAL CASH FLOWS).

- FIRMS SHOULD not market a COMPOSITE to a prospective client who has assets less than the COMPOSITE'S minimum asset level.

Source: Section II of the Global Investment Performance Standards. CFA Institute. February 2005, pp. 11–12. CFA® and GIPS® are trademarks owned by CFA Institute.

FIGURE 11.3 Presentation and Reporting

The following items MUST be reported for each COMPOSITE presented:

- At least 5 years of performance (or a record for the period since FIRM or COMPOSITE inception if the FIRM or COMPOSITE has been in existence less than 5 years) that meets the REQUIREMENTS of the GIPS standards; after presenting 5 years of performance, the FIRM MUST present additional annual performance up to 10 years. (For example, after a FIRM presents 5 years of compliant history, the FIRM MUST add an additional year of performance each year so that after 5 years of claiming compliance, the FIRM presents a 10-year performance record.)
- Annual returns for all years.
- The number of PORTFOLIOS and amount of assets in the COMPOSITE, and either the percentage of the TOTAL FIRM ASSETS represented by the COMPOSITE or the amount of TOTAL FIRM ASSETS at the end of each annual period. If the COMPOSITE contains 5 PORTFOLIOS or less, the number of PORTFOLIOS is not REQUIRED [corrected September 2005].
- A measure of DISPERSION of individual PORTFOLIO returns for each annual period. If the COMPOSITE contains 5 PORTFOLIOS or less for the full year, a measure of DISPERSION is not REQUIRED [corrected September 2005].
- FIRMS may link non-GIPS-compliant returns to their compliant history so long as the FIRMS meet the disclosure REQUIREMENTS for noncompliant performance and only compliant returns are presented for periods after 1 January 2000. (For example, a FIRM that has been in existence since 1995 and that wants to present *its* entire performance history and claim compliance beginning 1 January 2005 MUST present returns that meet the REQUIREMENTS of the GIPS standards at least from 1 January 2000 and MUST meet the disclosure REQUIREMENTS for any noncompliant history prior to 1 January 2000.)
- Returns of PORTFOLIOS and COMPOSITES for periods of less than 1 year are not permitted to be annualized.
  1. Performance track records of a past FIRM or affiliation MUST be linked to or used to represent the historical record of a new FIRM or new affiliation if:
     i. Substantially all the investment decision makers are employed by the new FIRM (e.g., research department, PORTFOLIO managers, and other relevant staff),
     ii. The staff and decision-making process remain intact and independent within the new FIRM, and
        - The new FIRM has records that document and support the reported performance.
  2. The new FIRM MUST disclose that the performance results from the past FIRM are linked to the performance record of the new FIRM.
  3. In addition to 5.A.4.a and 5.A.4.b, when one FIRM joins an existing FIRM, performance of COMPOSITES from both FIRMS MUST be linked to the ongoing returns if substantially all the assets from the past FIRM'S COMPOSITE transfer to the new FIRM.
  4. If a compliant FIRM acquires or is acquired by a noncompliant FIRM, the FIRMS have 1 year to bring the noncompliant assets into compliance.
- Beginning 1 January 2006, if a COMPOSITE includes or is formed using single asset class CARVE-OUTS from multiple asset class PORTFOLIOS, the presentation MUST include the percentage of the COMPOSITE that is composed of CARVE-OUTS prospectively for each period.

FIGURE 11.3   (Continued)

- The total return for the BENCHMARK (or BENCHMARKS) that reflects the investment strategy or mandate represented by the COMPOSITE MUST be presented for each annual period. If no BENCHMARK is presented, the presentation MUST explain why no BENCHMARK is disclosed. If the FIRM changes the BENCHMARK that is used for a given COMPOSITE in the performance presentation, the FIRM MUST disclose both the date and the reasons for the change. If a custom BENCHMARK or combination of multiple BENCHMARKS is used, the FIRM MUST describe the BENCHMARK creation and re-balancing process [corrected January 2006].
- If a COMPOSITE contains any nonfee-paying PORTFOLIOS, the FIRM MUST present, as of the end of each annual period, the percentage of the COMPOSITE assets represented by the nonfee-paying PORTFOLIOS.

Presentation and Reporting—Recommendations
It is RECOMMENDED that FIRMS present the following items:
   a. COMPOSITE returns gross of INVESTMENT MANAGEMENT FEES and ADMINISTRATIVE FEES and before taxes (except for nonreclaimable withholding taxes),
   b. Cumulative returns for COMPOSITE and BENCHMARKS for all periods,
   c. Equal-weighted mean and median returns for each COMPOSITE,
   d. Graphs and charts presenting specific information REQUIRED or RECOMMENDED under the GIPS standards,
   e. Returns for quarterly and/or shorter time periods,
   f. Annualized COMPOSITE and BENCHMARK returns for periods greater than 12 months,
   g. COMPOSITE-level country and sector weightings.
   - It is RECOMMENDED that FIRMS present relevant COMPOSITE-level risk measures, such as beta, tracking error, modified duration, information ratio, Sharpe ratio, Treynor ratio, credit ratings, value at risk (VAR), and volatility, over time of the COMPOSITE and BENCHMARK [corrected September 2005].

Source: Section II of the Global Investment Performance Standards. CFA Institute. February 2005, pp. 14–16. CFA® and GIPS® are trademarks owned by CFA Institute.

In short, the RFP will provide the investment committee with information critical to the search process. The committee may want to have prospective investment managers complete a questionnaire to capture much of the information in a uniform manner. Figure 11.4 contains a sample Portfolio Manager Inquiry. This document solicits information pertaining to the company's background as well as its operational characteristics. This standardized document can be used to compare the responses of the candidates.

SCREENING OF CANDIDATES

The next step in the process is to evaluate the proposals submitted by the candidates. Each proposal should be screened to determine whether all requested information has been provided. In most instances, this will not be a problem. Usually, the candidates will provide additional materials, and

FIGURE 11.4   Portfolio Manager Inquiry

I. Company Information
  A. Company Name
     Headquarters Address
     Year Founded
     Branch Office Address(es)
     Year(s) Opened

  B. Company Ownership
     Name(s) and Ownership share (%) of Principals
     1.
     2.
     3.
     4.
     5.

Has Company Ownership by Principals changed in the last (circle) three or five years? ___No ___Yes   If yes, briefly explain.

If the company is a subsidiary, please name parent.

What percentage of the company is owned by employees other than those named above? _____percent.

  C. Company Organization
     The company is a: Registered Investment Advisor _____; Securities Broker/Dealer _____; Mutual Fund _____; Commercial Bank _____; Insurance Company _____; Other (specify) _____.

What are the minimum _____ and maximum _____ account sizes accepted?

What is the average size account?
What is the number of accounts and dollar amounts under management per portfolio manager?

Number of Employees _____

Staff	Number	Average Years of Professional Experience
Equity Portfolio Managers		
Fixed Income Managers		
Investment Strategists		
Research Analysts		
Equity Traders		
Fixed Income Traders		
Economists		
Operational Personnel		
Compliance Personnel		
Marketing Personnel		
Management Personnel		
Other		

FIGURE 11.4   (Continued)

II. Company Operations

Does your company use (circle one) top-down or bottom-up approach to the investment process?

What percentages of the monies managed by your company are actively (_____%) versus passively (_____%) managed?

What importance does your company place on each of the following in the investment process?

	Most Important		Somewhat Important		Least Important
	5	4	3	2	1
Asset Allocation					
Market Timing					
Security Selection					

How are the following issues decided by your company?

	Committee	Portfolio Manager
Asset Allocation Mix		
Equity Selection		
Fixed Income Selection		
Mutual Funds Selection		

Does your company use outside managers to invest some of the assets your firm manages? If yes, please explain.

Does your company use derivative instruments to manage risk? If yes, please explain.

often, the packages are quite large. Thus, the problem becomes condensing the volumes of materials submitted into a workable package.

The use of a summary sheet can greatly facilitate this process. The summary sheet should identify each candidate along with information concerning his/her proposal. Table 11.2 presents a sample summary sheet. Typically, this sheet would include the size of funds under management, the performance results over several periods, asset allocations, and the fee schedule. Additional information, such as the account turnover, employee turnover, and staff size may also be included in the summary sheet. This exhibit should be used as a supplement to the investment packages.

TABLE 11.2 Sample Summary Sheet

Investment Company	ABC	DEF	GHI
Discretionary Accounts ($000,000)			
Balanced	$642,987	$521,984	$451,876
Equities	195,983	103,847	232,762
Fixed Income	78,964	59,725	102,863
Total	$917,934	$685,556	$787,501
Balanced Account Asset Allocation Ranges			
Equities	45–65%	40–60%	40–65%
Fixed Income	35–55%	40–60%	35–60%
Equities—Total Return Percent (net of fees) Dividends Reinvested			
1 year	12.54	11.97	10.39
3 years	10.83	11.45	12.23
5 years	11.10	11.76	11.98
10 years	12.07	11.86	12.06
Fixed Income—Total Return Percent (net of fees) Interest Reinvested			
1 year	7.83	7.76	7.39
3 years	8.43	8.32	8.18
5 years	8.88	8.67	8.41
10 years	9.02	8.49	8.54
Annual Fees (Based XYZ's MV)	$96,000	$82,000	$87,000

Next, the summary sheets and supporting proposals should be evaluated by each search committee member in light of the fund's goals and objectives. During this review, each member should identify the strengths and weaknesses of the candidates. After the members have had sufficient time to study the individual packages, the entire search committee should meet to discuss the relative merits of each investment manager. The committee should then narrow the list of candidates to those that it wishes to interview. Along these lines, it would be useful to agree upon the number of candidates to be interviewed. Once an agreement has been reached, the actual selection can be accomplished through developing a consensus among search committee members. If a consensus emerges, then individual committee members may be asked to rank each candidate. If there is a disagreement regarding who is to be interviewed, then the committee may expand the list of candidates.

While this increases the time requirements, it also fosters greater communication among committee members.

CANDIDATES PRESENTATIONS

Once the finalists have been identified, the committee must develop an interview schedule. The time allotted each candidate as well as the period over which the interviews will take place must be decided. The amount of time given should generally be sufficient to allow for the candidates to make their presentations and for the committee members to ask questions. If properly prepared, a two-hour limit should be a sufficient amount of time. It is also important that all interviews be conducted over a reasonably short period of time. This will allow the committee to make comparisons while the information is fresh. A sample candidate notification letter is presented in Figure 11.5.

FIGURE 11.5   Interview Announcement

October 30, 200X

Mr. Investment Manager
ABC Advisors
1 Park Place
Investment City, USA

Re: Investment Presentation

Dear Mr. Manager:

This letter is confirming the scheduled time for your presentation before the XYZ Corporation Pension Search Committee on the following date:

> December 1, 200X—8:00–10:00 A.M.
> Board Room
> XYZ Corporation

It is our understanding that Mr. Wellsworth and Mr. Smith will be making the presentation to the committee. Your presentation will be scheduled for the first hour of the meeting. The remaining time will be reserved for questions and answers.

Please telephone me at the above number if there are any changes.

Sincerely yours,

Chair,
Pension Fund Search Committee

The presentations can be viewed in two parts. Typically, the presentation begins with the candidates describing their investment philosophy and management style. The presentation also touches upon their historic investment results, their procedures and policies, and the fee structure for their services.

After the candidates finish the formal presentation, the search committee will begin their questioning. It is important that search committee members decide on the type of issues to be addressed by each candidate before the meetings take place. The questions should cover both investment management and administration issues. This leads to a more effective and organized interview process.

The committee might start off by asking the managers the following question, What accounts have you lost in the last 24 months, and why? Several issues need to be raised during this time. The committee should determine who will ultimately be responsible for managing the fund. Sometimes, the actual individual charged with managing the fund is not one of the individuals involved in conducting the presentation. The presenters often disappear after the account has been awarded. Furthermore, it is not unusual for individuals responsible for prior performance results to no longer be affiliated with the firm. The committee has the right as well as the responsibility to insist that the person who will be managing the fund be in attendance at the interview. Finally, the committee must verify that the presentation results reflect the performance record of those who will be managing the fund.

Additional questions should be asked relating to the management of the fund:

- Given the fund's goals and objectives, what changes if any does the candidate envision in regard to asset allocation and/or securities holdings?
- What performance information will be provided by the candidate, and over what period of time?
- How often will the candidate meet with the committee to review investment performance?
- What return does the candidate believe is attainable given the fund's objectives?

After this portion of the interview is completed, the committee chair should ask the candidate if there are any questions that he would like to ask. This will give the candidate an opportunity to raise questions concerning issues that may have surfaced earlier. It is very important that all issues relating to the management of the portfolio be identified and openly discussed prior to the committee making its final decision.

VERIFICATION AND REFERENCE CHECKING

Proper verification of performance results is critical to the money manager selection process. It is essential that the verifier be familiar with the policies and practices of the target firm as well as the standards to be applied to the subject firm. It is strongly recommended that investment managers subject themselves to an independent review of their performance results. Figure 11.6 reproduces the preverification guidelines contained in Section III of the GIPS.

In order to be in compliance with the GIPS standards, the investment results must be subjected to verification. The search committee should contact several references for each candidate to ascertain whether there are any issues that need to be considered prior to awarding the account. These references should be asked questions regarding their satisfaction with the candidate's performance results and their overall level of service. For example, "would you hire them again?" and, "specifically, what negatives have you observed?" It is also very important to contact previous accounts to see why these accounts were terminated.

FIGURE 11.6   Preverification Procedures

The following are the minimum procedures that verifiers must follow when verifying an investment FIRM'S compliance with the GIPS standards. Verifiers must follow these procedures prior to issuing a verification report to the FIRM:

1. Preverification Procedures
    a. Knowledge of the FIRM: Verifiers must obtain selected samples of the FIRM'S investment performance reports and other available information regarding the FIRM to ensure appropriate knowledge of the FIRM.
    b. Knowledge of GIPS Standards: Verifiers must understand all the RE-QUIREMENTS and RECOMMENDATIONS of the GIPS standards, including any updates, reports, guidance statements, interpretations, and clarifications published by CFA Institute and the Investment Performance Council, which will be made available via the CFA Institute website (www.cfainstitute.org) as well as the *GIPS Handbook*. All clarification and update information must be considered when determining a FIRM's claim of compliance.
    c. Knowledge of the Performance Standards: Verifiers must be knowledgeable of country-specific laws and regulations applicable to the FIRM and must determine any differences between the GIPS standards and the country-specific laws and regulations.
    d. Knowledge of FIRM Policies: Verifiers must determine the FIRM's assumptions and policies for establishing and maintaining compliance with all applicable REQUIREMENTS of the GIPS standards. At a minimum, verifiers must determine the following policies and procedures of the FIRM:

FIGURE 11.6 (Continued)

  i. Policy with regard to investment discretion. The verifier must receive from the FIRM, in writing, the FIRM's definition of investment discretion and the FIRM's guidelines for determining whether accounts are fully discretionary;

  ii. Policy with regard to the definition of COMPOSITES according to investment strategy. The verifier must obtain the FIRM's list of COMPOSITE DEFINITIONS with written criteria for including accounts in each COMPOSITE;

  iii. Policy with regard to the timing of inclusion of new accounts in the COMPOSITES;

  iv. Policy with regard to timing of exclusion of closed accounts in the COMPOSITES;

  v. Policy with regard to the accrual of interest and dividend income;

  vi. Policy with regard to the market valuation of investment securities;

  vii. Method for computing the TIME-WEIGHTED-RATE OF RETURN for the portfolio;

  viii. Assumptions on the timing of capital inflows/outflows;

  ix. Method for computing COMPOSITE returns;

  x. Policy with regard to the presentation of COMPOSITE returns;

  xi. Policies regarding timing of implied taxes due on income and realized capital gains for reporting performance on an aftertax basis;

  xii. Policies regarding use of securities/ countries not included in a COMPOSITE's BENCHMARK;

  xiii. Use of leverage and other derivatives; and

  xiv. Any other policies and procedures relevant to performance presentation.

 e. Knowledge of Valuation Basis for Performance Calculations: Verifiers must ensure that they understand the methods and policies used to record valuation information for performance calculation purposes. In particular, verifiers must determine that:

  i. The FIRM's policy on classifying fund flows (e.g., injections, disbursements, dividends, interest, fees, and taxes) is consistent with the desired results and will give rise to accurate returns;

  ii. The FIRM's accounting treatment of income, interest, and dividend receipts is consistent with cash account and cash accruals definitions;

  iii. The FIRM's treatment of taxes, tax reclaims, and tax accruals is correct and the manner used is consistent with the desired method (i.e., gross- or net-of-tax return);

  iv. The FIRM's policies on recognizing purchases, sales, and the opening and closing of other positions are internally consistent and will produce accurate results; and

  v. The FIRM's accounting for investments and derivatives is consistent with the GIPS standards.

Source: Section III of the Global Investment Performance Standards. CFA Institute. February 2005. p. 22. CFA® and GIPS® are trademarks owned by CFA Institute.

Once the preverification process is completed, the reviewer must examine the methodology used to construct the performance results and composites. Figure 11.7 reports the verification procedures required by GIPS.

FIGURE 11.7 Verification Procedures

---

a. Definition of the FIRM: Verifiers must determine that the FIRM is, and has been, appropriately defined.
b. COMPOSITE Construction. Verifiers must be satisfied that:
  i. The FIRM has defined and maintained COMPOSITES according to reasonable guidelines in compliance with the GIPS standards;
  ii. All the FIRM's actual discretionary fee-paying PORTFOLIOS are included in a COMPOSITE;
  iii. The FIRM'S definition of discretion has been consistently applied over time;
  iv. At all times, all accounts are included in their respective COMPOSITES and no accounts that belong in a particular COMPOSITE have been excluded;
  v. COMPOSITE BENCHMARKS are consistent with COMPOSITE DEFINITIONS and have been consistently applied over time;
  vi. The FIRM's guidelines for creating and maintaining COMPOSITES have been consistently applied; and
  vii. The FIRM's list of COMPOSITES is complete.
c. Nondiscretionary Accounts. Verifiers must obtain a listing of all FIRM PORTFOLIOS and determine on a sampling basis whether the manager's classification of the account as discretionary or nondiscretionary is appropriate by referring to the account's agreement and the FIRM's written guidelines for determining investment discretion.
d. Sample Account Selection: Verifiers must obtain a listing of open and closed accounts for all COMPOSITES for the years under examination. Verifiers may check compliance with the GIPS standards using a selected sample of a FIRM'S accounts. Verifiers SHOULD consider the following criteria when selecting the sample accounts for examination:
  i. Number of COMPOSITES at the FIRM;
  ii. Number of PORTFOLIOS in each COMPOSITE;
  iii. Nature of the COMPOSITE;
  iv. Total assets under management;
  v. Internal control structure at the FIRM (system of checks and balances in place);
  vi. Number of years under examination; and
  vii. Computer applications, software used in the construction and maintenance of COMPOSITES, the use of external performance measurers, and the calculation of performance results.

FIGURE 11.7   (Continued)

This list is not all-inclusive and contains only the minimum criteria that SHOULD be used in the selection and evaluation of a sample for testing. For example, one potentially useful approach would be to choose a PORTFOLIO for the study sample that has the largest impact on COMPOSITE performance because of its size or because of extremely good or bad performance. The lack of explicit record keeping or the presence of errors may warrant selecting a larger sample or applying additional verification procedures.

e. Account Review: For selected accounts, verifiers must determine:

i.   Whether the timing of the initial inclusion in the COMPOSITE is in accordance with policies of the FIRM;

ii. Whether the timing of exclusion from the COMPOSITE is in accordance with policies of the FIRM for closed accounts;

iii. Whether the objectives set forth in the account agreement are consistent with the manager's COMPOSITE DEFINITION as indicated by the account agreement, PORTFOLIO summary, and COMPOSITE DEFINITION;

iv. The existence of the accounts by tracing selected accounts from account agreements to the COMPOSITES;

v.   That all PORTFOLIOS sharing the same guidelines are included in the same COMPOSITE; and

vi. That shifts from one COMPOSITE to another are consistent with the guidelines set forth by the specific account agreement or with documented guidelines of the FIRM's clients.

Source: Section III of the Global Investment Performance Standards. CFA Institute. February 2005. pp. 23–24. CFA® and GIPS® are trademarks owned by CFA Institute.

Final Selection

Once the verification process is completed, the committee should meet again and discuss the various merits of each candidate. Often the review of the presentations and supporting documents by the entire committee leads to a consensus as to the choice of money managers. At least this process will result in the narrowing of choices. The committee can then proceed with a vote on the preferred candidate. If the search committee is a subcommittee, then it can recommend a candidate to the full investment committee for its approval.

COST OF SWITCHING

Once the decision has been made to switch fund managers, the fund enters into a transition period. During this time, the new managers evaluate the current holdings of the portfolio to ascertain what changes are needed. These changes will not only involve the allocation of funds between the various investment categories (i.e., equities, fixed income, and cash and equivalents) but also the actual securities within each category.

Changing the portfolio's composition involves some expenses. Transaction fees such as commissions are higher than under normal circumstances. The manager will attempt to time the purchases and sales as to minimize costs; nonetheless there will most likely be significant changes. Certainly, if the new management is to be evaluated properly, an evaluation of fund performance should be based solely upon their decisions.

The evaluators of fund performance should recognize that there will be a transition period. During this period, it is difficult to evaluate the performance of new managers. The committee should establish a grace period so that the new investment managers can restructure the portfolio in an orderly fashion. The new management must carefully consider the timing of sales and purchases in relation to the market fundamentals. The investment committee should recognize this important aspect of changing investment managers.

ADMINISTRATION OF CHANGE

The actual movement of the account requires substantial paperwork. Notifying the current money manager is required to ensure a smooth transition. The committee may want to "freeze" the investment activities of the incumbent manager so that the new manager does not have to reverse transactions when the account is transferred. However, the committee must make sure that during this process there is constant communication between itself and the incumbent manager. The committee must have a plan dealing with investment actions that must be taken quickly during the transition period. In the final analysis, the investment committee must supervise all of the administrative aspects the management change requires.

SUMMARY

The selection of portfolio managers is the single most important decision that a committee must make. The results of this decision are ultimately reflected in the fund's performance results. The search process for investment managers is conducted by the full investment committee or a subcommittee. The committee can employ the services of investment professionals or conduct the search itself.

The process begins with the establishment of the selection criteria. Next, the committee identifies individual firms whose investment philosophies and approaches match their fund's needs. Then RFPs from these investment professionals are solicited. Upon receipt of the proposals, the committee members begin the screening process. Acceptable candidates are invited to make formal presentations. The committee will then make a selection from the candidates.

After the selection of a new investment manager is made, there is a period of transition. The committee can expect the new manager to restructure the portfolio. The new manager needs time to make the necessary purchases and sales. The committee members should be mindful of this period. The switching of managers also requires administrative coordination as well.

CHAPTER 12

Conducting Investment Committee Meetings

Effective communication creates an atmosphere where all stakeholders are on the same page. Committee meetings are an excellent forum to ensure that there is proper alignment between all parties. Properly structured committee meetings provide a framework for information exchange and decision making. Committee meetings are intended to provide a formalized discussion of the issues concerning all aspects of the investment management process. The meetings provide the setting for a wide range of discussion ranging from investment policy issues to actual fund performance. These meetings can ensure that the fund's investment goals and objectives are being carried out in a prudent and responsible manner.

Investment committee meetings should promote better communication among the committee members and the money managers. While it is important to have a set agenda, it is also important to allow time for frank and open discussion. The agenda must be well thought out and should allow for committee members to introduce subject areas as needed. This, however, does not happen by accident. It requires careful planning by the committee chair to conduct a successful meeting.

MEETING PREPARATIONS

Typically, the investment committee is charged with monitoring and evaluating the performance of the investment portfolio and to handle administrative issues as they arise. It is the committee's responsibility to communicate with the professional managers any changes or anticipated events that may affect investment policy, strategies and/or tactics. This communication should include factors that may affect the overall organization and by extension have an impact on the future management of the portfolio. For example, events such as layoffs, relocation, and bankruptcy may place a burden on the fund's cash flows. Clearly, these and other types of events may have a profound impact on the fund's future and the professional managers should be notified as soon as possible.

These meetings can take place on a monthly, quarterly, or annual basis, and should at least be scheduled shortly after the measurement period's investment performance results are available. For example, if the policy statement calls for a quarterly review of performance, quarterly meetings should be scheduled during the month following the end of the quarter. The timing of these meetings should be such that they closely follow the measurement period so that corrective actions, if necessary, can be implemented, yet long enough to allow for the compiling of materials dealing with the portfolio performance and market comparisons. The time and place of these meetings should be such to ensure maximum participation by all interested parties. Figure 12.1 provides a sample meeting announcement letter.

Other housekeeping items in preparation of the meeting should also be remembered. The meeting room should be secured. Computer hookups, for power point presentations, overhead projectors, screens, papers, pencils, and other equipment and supplies needed during the meeting should be obtained and inspected to ensure they are in good working order. In the event that one or more parties participate through teleconferencing, the phones lines should be tested prior to the start of the meeting. Refreshments should be provided for all attendees. The meeting environment sets the tone for a productive meeting.

FIGURE 12.1   XYZ Corporation Meeting Announcement Letter

March 20, 200X

Dear Ms. Jones:

The next meeting of the XYZ Pension Committee is scheduled as follows:

> Thursday, April 12, 200X
> 8:00 a.m.–10:00 a.m.
> XYZ Board Room
> XYZ Corporation

The agenda along with the 1st quarter of 200X investment performance results will be mailed separately. Please feel free to contact me if you have any questions.

Sincerely yours,

Chair, Pension Investment Committee

AGENDA AND MEETING MATERIALS

The meeting's agenda as well as other reference material should be distributed to the committee members well in advance of the scheduled meeting date. Providing such information at the time of the meeting itself leads to confusion and fosters disorganization. Specifically, committee members would be required to survey the material while simultaneously listening to the proceedings. This prevents the member from devoting his or her full attention to the issues currently being discussed by the committee.

SETTING THE AGENDA

The agenda specifies the sequence of the activities to be discussed at the meeting. The agenda covers administrative issues, as well as performance issues to be considered during the meeting. In planning the agenda, the chair should ask the following questions: What needs to be accomplished? In what order should these items be addressed?

The committee should consider the time requirements necessary to deal with the administrative issues to be discussed when setting the agenda. Some issues can be dealt with quickly within the present committee structure. Other issues may require the formation of subcommittees to handle them. In these latter instances, the chair should carefully assign subcommittee members so that the proper balance of expertise and perspective is achieved. The reports from various subcommittees should be incorporated into the agenda.

Figure 12.2 presents a sample of a hypothetical agenda. As shown in the exhibit, these meetings begin with a motion to approve the minutes of the prior meeting. Keeping proper minutes provides a record of the items discussed by the committee. The next item on the agenda concerns administrative issues. These issues may involve items related to investment policy, plan administration (i.e., selecting a trustee), or they may involve the fund's investment performance.

If these administrative issues can be dealt with by a committee of the whole, then discussion time should be allocated prior to or after the money managers are scheduled to meet with the committee. If, for example, administrative discussions are expected to consume one hour of time, the investment managers should be invited to make their presentations at the beginning of the second hour of the meeting. If, on the other hand, the actual time devoted to these issues is unknown, it might be advisable to proceed first with the report of the money managers. Attendance of the money managers during these discussions is normally not encouraged. The committee may want to keep specific items that are under discussion private. Therefore,

FIGURE 12.2   XYZ Fund Meeting Agenda January 21, 200X

Item:	Responsibility
Approval of Minutes of the October 23 meeting	Chair
Approval of the Agenda	Chair
Administrative Issues	Chair
Report of Search Committee	Chair, Subcommittee
Investment Performance	Ms./Mr. Manager
Ratification of Purchases	Chair
Ratification of Sales	Chair
Old Business	Open
New Business	Open
Adjournment	

investment managers should be invited into the meeting at the conclusion of the administrative portion of the agenda.

RESPONSIBILITIES OF THE CHAIRPERSON

Conducting the investment meeting requires a special combination of knowledge and skill. Clearly, the chair needs to be familiar with the details of investment performance evaluation. However, he or she also needs the personal skills to foster an environment which promotes an open exchange of ideas and encourages communication. The chair needs to steer the committee away from the unproductive use of their time, and needs to be diplomatic when seeking closure. Thus, an autocratic approach to chairing a committee is seldom successful. In contrast, a chair with a participatory philosophy who solicits advice and opinions from all participants is generally viewed as the most effective.

INVESTMENT CONSULTING SERVICES

In order to properly conduct the investment committee meeting, it is important that all committee members are properly prepared. Sometimes, individuals are invited to serve on investment committees because of their involvement in the community and/or positions held within the organization, and are often unfamiliar with the technical aspects of investments. For these individuals, the entire process can be overwhelming. It is essential that support is provided for these individuals.

Investment consultants may be helpful in these situations. The investment consultants often provide market comparison data as part of their service. The investment consultant can construct a performance index, which matches the goals and objectives of your fund. Investment consultants can lead the committee through the evaluation process in an organized and highly effective manner. Members can draw on the expertise of consultants to explain the interpretation of the performance results. The more knowledgeable the committee members, the more successful will be the investment committee. Having well-prepared committee members is the key to conducting a successful meeting.

Committees often retain the services of professional portfolio consultants to evaluate the money managers. The consultant conducts an in-depth analysis using proprietary models and market indexes. Such an analysis provides the committee with an independent means of evaluating the performance of the fund's managers. While the cost of a consultant's service varies, the benefit can be significant when the board consists of members who are not skilled in the investment process.

Most often, the portfolio manager will review and discuss performance results from a "top-down" perspective; that is, the discussion will start with a review of the broadest aspects of the investment environment and proceed sequentially to narrower issues. An outline of such top-down review might be as follows:

INVESTMENT PERFORMANCE REVIEW AND OUTLOOK

The investment review and outlook process includes:

1. *Economic Review and Outlooks.* Economic review and outlooks involve an assessment of the economy's performance in the most recent period, including an analysis of growth in real GDP; the growth in the economy's primary sectors; information on inflation and employment; an evaluation of the economy's actual performance relative to that forecasted. Also, a forecast of economic activity for the forthcoming period including an assessment of the stage of the business cycle and newsworthy domestic and international economic trends should be presented.

2. *Economic Policy and Review.* Economic policy and review involves an assessment of, and outlook for, Federal Reserve monetary policy, especially as it affects interest rates and nominal economic activity, as well as any significant developments regarding federal government spending, tax policy, regulatory policy, and international trade and exchange rate issues.

3. *Market Review and Outlooks.* For the fixed income markets, market review and outlooks involves an assessment of, and outlook for, interest rates including changes in the shape of the Treasury yield curve and spreads between Treasury securities and relevant corporate bonds, as well as a review of relevant fixed income indexes. For the equity market, this an assessment of, and outlook for corporate earnings and a review of relevant domestic and international equity market indexes. For other markets an assessment of, and outlooks for, short-term interest rates, and a review of relevant indexes for such investments as real estate, collectibles, and commodities are required.

4. *Fund Performance Review.* Fund performance review begins with an overall performance of the universes and relative indexes.

   Peer Group comparisons can be a very useful tool in evaluating managers. There have been studies showing that the percentage of managers outperforming their assigned benchmarks is small, therefore lending to the argument to compare results to an additional standard such as peer groups. However, there is an even more important argument for utilizing peer group comparisons. If the unfortunate decision is ever made to discharge a current manager, basing that decision on how your current manager has performed relative to a group of his or her peers from which you may select that manager's replacement is prudent. The typical types of peer groups are endowments/foundations, pension funds, balanced funds, equity funds, fixed income funds, other asset classes (such as real estate, hedge funds, etc.).

   As mentioned in the earlier chapters, indexes may be used as a benchmark for evaluation purposes. Often the use of such benchmarks raises the bar for the investment manager and thus should be used in conjunction with peer group universes. Unlike universes, indexes will not reflect financial costs such as commissions, transfer taxes, and rebalancing expenses. It is for these reasons that outperforming indexes such as the S&P 500 is a daunting task.

   After a review of the universes and relative indexes, there is an evaluation of the performance of equity, fixed income, and the like components relative to the relevant benchmark. Then the impact of asset allocation and security selection on overall and component performance is assessed.

5. *Individual Security Review.* Review of individual security holdings includes an understanding of the rationale for additions to or deletions from the fund.

At the end of the process, the committee should evaluate whether the portfolio achieved the desired results, and if not, why. Was the fund's shortfall (or success) due to the investments held, or was it due to asset selection? Finally, the committee must evaluate whether the manager's investment performance meets the requirements outlined in the policy statement. If the manager is not properly following the investment guidelines, corrective action needs to be taken.

The money manager's investment outlook usually follows the review of the portfolio performance. He or she will address the overall direction of the economy as well as the expected direction of the financial markets. Does the manager expect interest rates to rise or fall? Will there be a tightening or easing of monetary conditions? What is expected in terms of inflation? How will the stock market perform? The manager will address the investment risks and other assumptions underlying his or her forecast.

The money manager should be asked what changes, if any, are planned during the next measurement period. Are there plans to dispose of any holdings? What acquisitions are planned? Will the existing asset allocation mix be altered? The committee must evaluate the planned investment strategy in light of the economic forecast. Are they consistent? The committee should reevaluate the asset allocation in light of changing market and economic conditions.

The committee may want to set time aside after the manager's presentation to review among themselves the investment performance results. It may be helpful to gain the perspective of the committee members concerning performance while the report is fresh in everyone's mind. This is especially true when the committee is considering the termination of a manager or is working with a newly hired one.

Review of Investment Policy Statement

The Investment Policy Statement (IPS) should be reviewed on a periodic basis, but no less than annually to address the fiduciary responsibilities of the Board. The investment policy statement should outline the objectives of the portfolio and the control procedures that will govern the management of the assets.

The issues that should be addressed in a properly drafted investment policy statement are:

- Investment objectives
- Investment guidelines
  Risk tolerance
  Time horizon
  Spending policy (if appropriate)
  Asset class preference
  Expected return

- Procedures for selecting money managers or mutual funds
- Securities guidelines
- Procedures for monitoring money managers or mutual funds

Over the years, policy documents have evolved far beyond simply stating that a fund should operate to comply with the diversification requirements of the "prudent man" doctrine. Today, policy statements are detailed documents that articulate a fund's broad objectives. They include asset allocation and risk/return expectations, and, for each manager, specific objectives and guidelines for managing fund assets. They also include how to hire, monitor and, most importantly, when and why to replace a manager.

A strong investment policy that will clearly delineate the monitoring and review of managers:

1. Provide ongoing supervision of investment program.
2. Prepare a detailed monthly appraisal of consolidated holdings and portfolio transactions.
3. Prepare quarterly performance attribution reports comparing the performance of the portfolio against market indexes, stated investment objectives, and managers of similar style.

Also contained in the investment policy statement should be clear language as to when a manager moves from being reviewed to consideration for termination (i.e., 75th percentile performance over a rolling three and/or five-year period, performance lower than 90% of the approved benchmark over a rolling three- and/or five-year period etc.). Once approved by the investment committee, all language relating to the expectations, monitoring and termination of managers must be clearly communicated to managers. This ensures that no confusion or tension exists in the relationship between managers and the client.

In addition to the risk versus return considerations, the IPS should take into consideration costs of investment, diversification and experience of the Board responsible for the management of the portfolios in question. This includes the use of multiple managers in specific asset styles—versus—the use of core or balanced managers.

OLD BUSINESS

Often discussions of investment issues raised during a meeting are not resolved at that time. Either the lack of committee time or the need for additional information leads to postponement of issues. The *old business* portion of the meeting is reserved to revisit unresolved items from the previous meeting. The agenda should identify the issues to be discussed under this heading.

NEW BUSINESS

The *new business* portion of the meeting is designed to allow participants to discuss a wide range of issues concerning the fund. This part of the meeting can be used to solicit discussion from committee members regarding a host of topics. These may range from revisiting the goals and objectives of the fund, adequacy of the policy document, risk acceptance level, as well as investment specific issues.

SUMMARY

The purpose of the investment policy meeting is to carry out the committee's administrative responsibilities and to evaluate the portfolio's performance. The key to conducting a successful meeting is proper planning. The chair has the ultimate responsibility for the direction of the meeting. He must strive to create an open environment where a free exchange of ideas can take place.

The agenda should lay out how the sequence of events is to occur during the meeting. The meeting itself should deal with administrative issues of concern as well as the investment performance of the fund. During the earlier portion of the meeting, the committee's deliberations may be held apart from the money managers.

The main agenda item of most meetings is likely the investment review and outlook portion. Here investment managers present an overview of the economy and market environment and review the performance. During this time, committee members may ask questions concerning the investment results and future prospects. Finally, the agenda provides for discussions on a variety of issues under the headings of old and new business items.

Index